At a Dream Workshop

Betsy Caprio
and
Thomas M. Hedberg, S.D.B.

Paulist Press
New York/Mahwah

On the cover: Photograph of a capital on the church of Saint-Lazare, Autun, France (attributed to Gislebertus, early 12th century). Depicted are the Magi, with the heavenly messenger coming to them with a warning dream.

Symbolically, they picture the awakening of the personality from its deep sleep that is not aware of a connection to God, to a half-awake or "something's happening" state, to consciousness of the link to the divine possible for all.

Copyright © 1987 by
Betsy Caprio and Thomas M. Hedberg

Library of Congress Cataloging-in-Publication Data

Caprio, Betsy.
    At a dream workshop.

    1. Dreams—Religious aspects—Christianity.
I. Hedberg, Thomas M. II. Title.
BF1031.C245 1987   201'.9   87-20201
ISBN 0-8091-2925-6 (pbk.)

Published by Paulist Press
997 Macarthur Boulevard
Mahwah, New Jersey 07430

Printed and bound in the
United States of America

Contents

DEDICATION

*To three very special people
who have shared our
dreams:
Neil Bezaire
Kathleen Conway
John Hedberg*

Acknowledgements

We're most grateful to the people who, over the years, have attended dream workshops; many have come at the nudging of their dreams, some from distances of hundreds and even thousands of miles. We thought of identifying the participants in these pages by name, rather than by occupation—which has the drawback of describing people via their roles in life. However, names give so little information about participants, and would also detract from our desire to maintain confidentiality about the dreamers you'll meet. From beginner to very experienced dreamer, each has been a sign to us of God's goodness to those on the spiritual quest.

A special thanks to Strephon Williams of Berkeley, California for permission to print our adapted version of his "Night Sea Journey" meditation. The original may be found in his *Jungian-Senoi Dreamwork* manual (Berkeley: Journey Press, 1979 ed.). We have tried other such reflections over the years but keep returning to Strephon's because of its poetic flavor and on-the-mark images. He is the author, along with Louis Savary and Patricia Berne, of another book on dreams which we highly recommend, *Dreams and Spiritual Growth* (New York: Paulist Press, 1984). Thanks also to Dr. Meredith Mitchell, Jungian analyst and friend, and to Oxford University Press of London for permission to reprint "The Angel Gabriel" from *The Oxford Book of Carols*.

We would like to honor here the late Rita Jean Riley, who was led by her dreams, and whose devotion to their message has been an inspiration to many. James Michael Lee of Religious Education Press in Birmingham was very much a catalyst person in the writing of this work, and we deeply appreciate his vision of the dream in the church, as well as the shared vision in poetry by Michele Clark of Manhattan Beach, California, which appears at the close of this book (and was inspired by Jacob's dream in Genesis). Al and Mary Alvarado of Sand Sierra Business Machines in Ridgecrest, California were of great help with our production needs, as was the support of time and prayer given by Jeannie Pinel, and Fred and Asela Garcia from Youth Encounter Spirit. We must not forget our thanks also to the staff of the Max and Lore Zeller Library at the C. G. Jung Institute of Los Angeles for their ever-helpful assistance in research.

Finally, we would like to state most appreciatively our debt to the thought and written work of Dr. Edward F. Edinger of Los Angeles. Our readers will see, as they go through these pages, how we have quoted him at length and urged them on to study his books. In particular, we have referred to Dr. Edinger's work on the mysteries of the Christian faith and the events in the life of the people of Israel (which anticipated the story of Jesus in a collective way). Both have been explored now for centuries—and some fifty years ago C. G. Jung gave us further rich insight into how these external religious events are also intrapsychic events or internal religious experiences. Many fine minds have developed Jung's thought in this area, but none more clearly than Edinger. Their work helps each of us continue to move from the traditional standpoint of merely following the example of the Israelites and/or Jesus, to the age-old mystical ideal of living out the mysteries within our own souls. This was certainly not a new idea with analytical psychology—the religious visionaries of all the world faiths have sung of interiority for millennia; it is the clarity and inclusiveness with which Edinger writes that makes his work of particular value.

In addition, this psychological understanding of the paschal mystery (which need not deny its theological reality) reaches those for whom institutional religion is dead—or may never have existed; for such persons, understanding and experiencing the individuation process may indeed be their salvation. We would add that such insight may also be the salvation of the institutional religions at this time of great upheaval in their lives. Dr. Edinger carries out with great distinction—and with the thanks of many—the task set before us by his mentor, C. G. Jung:

> . . . it is the prime task of all education [of adults] to convey the archetype of the God-image, or its emanations and effects, to the conscious mind."
>
> —*Psychology and Alchemy,* 1944[1]

Introduction

The year 2000 A.D. is in the air, just over the horizon. Talk of "the millennium" is creeping into our consciousnesses as we write this book; we hear references to this watershed time in human history on television, in the press, all around us. People have begun to make plans for New Year's Eve, 1999, wanting to be able to say, "This is what I was doing when the year 2000 came in; this is how I welcomed the next millennium."

Those familiar with the history of western civilization are reminded of the preparations of the hearts and minds of earlier millennialists: the people of the tenth century. The world had not come to an end, as many had expected, with the first century A.D. No, perhaps the wrap-up would come with the year 1000, it was thought. Medieval life slowed down—what need was there to plan, to give form to earthly visions when there might not be a tomorrow? And so, December 31, 999 arrived, and passed.

"Did we miscalculate?" the wise ones asked. "Perhaps our original dating was off, and the year 1000 A.D. hasn't really yet come. We'll wait a few more years." Each New Year's Eve brought the same sort of foreboding; each subsequent year in the eleventh century was lived as, just possibly, the last year of the planet Earth and her peoples. Then came 1010 A.D., and 1020 A.D. "Look what's happened," people began to say. "The world hasn't come to an end. We're still here. We have life. We have a future. There is hope." And with that the beautiful pointed cathedrals began to be built, their spires piercing the horizons as a sign of this new aspiration. No longer were people to worship in dimly lit, womb-like or tomb-like buildings, but in these spacious and light-filled churches, with the rainbow's hues pouring down on them through stained glass windows.

The earth began to be appreciated once again, as it had not been since classical and Gospel times. No longer were the saints and angels confined to solemn panels of mosaic and gold-plated wood, but they began to be pictured out in the everyday world, the flowers and

1

trees and animals of native villages around them. Life was not just a preparation for death; a New Age had come. So it was, in the western world in the eleventh century.

There are those among us today, at the end of the twentieth century, who truly prepare themselves for an Armageddon. Holed up in valleys and on hillsides throughout the northern hemisphere, armed with survival supplies and weapons to fend off those who would poach on them, they wait—as did their ancestors one thousand years before—for the last days of the age. For them, the coming of the millennium holds dread and the smell of doom. They are, however, a minority.

For many of the rest of us, this calendar event has a deep positive feel to it. We know the history of the tenth century and the eleventh, and have heard now, for years, the language about a New Age, an Age of Aquarius, just around the corner. The coming of the millennium has, for many, a promise attached to it, a promise of a richer way of living in the world. There is a *spiritual* unfolding that has been in the air in force for over a hundred years that, somehow, has woven itself into this point in time when we shall leave the 1900's and move into the 2000's. Most of us living now will see that day.

In the mid-1800's, America's transcendentalists already were speaking the language of renewal and of a more deeply spiritual life. Walt Whitman sang the body electric over a hundred years ago, and thought of turning to live with the pious animals, " . . . so placid and self-contain'd."[1] His European counterparts were exploring the religions of the east, then Sigmund Freud was bringing to our attention once again the soul, even though his language was that of the physician, not the spiritual teacher.

We might trace the seeds of a possible New Age down through our century, the twentieth, pausing at Zurich with C. G. Jung and his deeply religious view of the psyche, looking at our own 1960's flower children in retrospect and reading between the faded denim lines to find again their longing for a life that is spiritually attuned.

None of us has been unaffected by the women's movement. It— and even Americans' excitement over their own national lady, the Statue of Liberty in New York Harbor—points today, toward a rebirth of appreciation of the feminine, and perhaps even a return of the goddess/the feminine side of God to balance out (not replace) the patriarchy.[2] The exploration of outer space, once thought to be just around the corner, has stumbled and been slowed down to a pedestrian pace—leaving its fans asking if their fascination with outer space is not possibly a metaphor for some fascinating inner space even more available to them.

And we hear rumblings in the institutional religions in our day, rumblings and mumblings and grumblings that also echo this hunger of the human heart for a life with meaning and profundity ("metagrumbles," Abraham Maslow called them).[3] Our other institutions—educational, political, all of them—may most often seem to be ensnared in materialism and extraversion, yet even there can be found the visionaries excited about a better way, a deeper life.

One of the *most* remarkable spiritual (re)discoveries in the end of this twentieth century has been the dream. People have always dreamt. For centuries, in the east and the west, the dream was honored universally as our primary connection to the mysterious, but very real, world of spirit. And then, somewhere in the middle of our present millennium, this precious gift slowly became devalued and shoved off into the realm of the soothsayer, the primitive, the magical. (It had plenty of company; much else that was precious—but not "scientific"—went into that fringe world also.)

But now the dream is being reclaimed by us, the dreamers. The good books on using our dreams to inform our conscious waking life began to appear in the late 1960's and early 1970's, not very long ago. Ann Faraday's books changed the lives of thousands, as she courageously spoke for taking the dream out of the exclusive hands of the experts and putting it back in the hands and lives of the everyday dreamers.[4] Morton Kelsey and John Sanford and others dug into the lore of the Judaeo-Christian tradition for us, reclaiming the dreams of Scripture and our own religious enlivening that comes through the dream.[5] Courses and workshops on listening to one's dreams began to be offered by schools and by religious institutions, in striking contrast to a time not much earlier when such instruction would have been thought "unscientific" or "heretical," respectively.

Caught up with so many others in the wonder of the inner cosmos, we too have dreamt and shared our experiences with others who cared about the dream. This book is a transcription of the dreaming workshop developed by the authors during the mid-1980's. You will meet us as you join in on paper with a group of very real dream workshop participants, and will find that we approach the dream in a religious context. Sometimes we title the workshop a "dream retreat."

Whether you, our reader, are a beginner in the exciting exploration of the dream, or whether you join in to fine-tune your skills in dreaming, we welcome you and invite you to consider setting apart two and a half days for this workshop, just as did the original participants you'll be meeting. If your framework for the soul is not the same as our committedly religious one, you will be able to make your translations into your own language as you move along through the workshop. All the comments and contributions are accurate quotes from real people, synthesized so that a facsimile experience can be put down on paper for the reader.

Will you join with us then, as *we* prepare in one way for the New Age? Our weary planet is burdened with many ills, and many abuse her and her children. Yet still, the vision of a better way grows and grows. The coming of the year 2000 elegantly symbolizes the coming of age that is possible for each of us—this is a *spiritual* maturing, a life linked to the energies of God which envelop and permeate us all. The more of us in tune with these energies, the more likely it is that the next millennium may be one of growth and deeply satisfying soul-evolution rather than one of destruction. It is the dreams from the world within that can help outfit us for an outer "dream world." We invite you to be with us

At a Dream Workshop

The Center for Sacred Psychology
Box 643
Gateway Station
Culver City, CA 90232
February 1987

Thomas M. Hedberg
Betsy Caprio

Getting Ready for the Dream Workshop

We suggest that you gather together the materials you will need just as if you were going to be making this three-day workshop with the group. The ideal would be to set aside as much time as you can, so that you can enjoy and profit from the dream workshop experience as fully as possible—it will then be an at-home retreat time for you, the reader.

Materials for the Dream Workshop

- dream log or notebook
- journal (may be the same as the dream log)
- pen; colored felt-tip markers, crayons, colored pencils (whatever you prefer)
- bible
- any pictures you can find of Luke 1:26-38 (the annunciation or salutation of the angel to Mary)

Here is the schedule for the dream workshop which will be followed:

First Evening

	Arrive and settle in
7:30 p.m.	SESSION ONE: Introductions and leaving the world behind
	Setting the scene for the night
8:45	Break to prepare for sleep

9:15 SESSION TWO: Dream Invocation Ceremony
10:00 The end of the day
       Silence until breakfast.

Second Day

8:00 a.m. Gather for morning prayer
8:30   Breakfast
9:30   SESSION THREE: Debriefing the nighttime and the
          ceremony
10:30   Break
10:40   SESSION FOUR: Basics of dream work (beginners and
          advanced groups)
Noon   Break before lunch
12:30 p.m. Lunch
1:30   Quiet time (to sleep? . . . perchance to dream?)
3:30   SESSION FIVE: Finding our dream guide (part one)
4:20   Break
4:30   SESSION SIX: Finding our dream guide (part two)
5:30   Break before dinner
6:00   Dinner
7:30   SESSION SEVEN: Inviting the dream guide
8:15   Break to prepare for sleep
8:45   SESSION EIGHT: Dream Invocation Ceremony
9:30   The end of the day
       Silence until breakfast.

Third Day

8:00 a.m. Gather for morning prayer
8:30   Breakfast
9:30   SESSION NINE: Debriefing the nighttime and the
          ceremony
10:30   Break
10:40   SESSION TEN: A theoretical framework
Noon   Break before dinner
12:30 p.m. Dinner
1:30   SESSION ELEVEN: What lies ahead?
2:30   Closing gathering

And here is a list of the almost fifty participants you'll be meeting at this dream workshop:

- Rev. Tom Hedberg and Betsy Caprio, from the Center for Sacred Psychology in Los Angeles
- Several homemakers, including one young mother of a new baby, away from her child for the first time
- Teachers, including two retired women, one university professor and one graduate instructor (both male), one high school teacher (male), and the following people involved in religious education:
  —a Lutheran minister of Christian education (a woman)
  —a director of a Reformed temple religious school (a man)
  —a Protestant seminary professor, specializing in Christian education (a man)
  —the laywoman director of religious education in a Roman Catholic parish
  —an Episcopal deacon, director of Christian education (a woman)
  —two Roman Catholic sisters, working in a parochial school (one is principal)
- Several married couples: a retired candy-shop owner and his wife
  two psychotherapists who run an outpatient clinic
  a private investigator and his wife
  a stockbroker and her husband
  an aerobics instructor and her husband
  an Anglican priest and his wife
  a nurse and his wife
- Others from an assortment of backgrounds, involved in a wide variety of types of work: two graduate students, several businessmen, a mailwoman, two secretaries, a waitress, a telephone line repairwoman, a temple counseling center director, the choir director of a Methodist church, a youth minister for an ecumenical cluster of Christian churches, a Roman Catholic parish priest, the deacon of a Melkite rite parish, and a retired pastor of a Baptist congregation.

When you are ready, let your imagination take you to a beautiful location in southern California. Your dream workshop experience begins.

The Dream Workshop

The First Evening

(You drive up a winding road in a suburban area, past large homes hidden behind hedges and cypress trees. Your destination is the Holy Spirit Center in Encino, California, a conference and retreat center in Los Angeles' San Fernando Valley. The center comes into view, a Spanish hacienda in the style of the old southwest. Turning into the driveway on the left, you can smell the orange trees in bloom even before you see them.

It is April, Easter season, and as you pull onto the road which winds behind the main building you see the grove of orange trees with their coverings of white star-shaped blossoms. How surprising it is to find such a place of peacefulness just ten minutes from the metropolis. You begin to anticipate the "sabbath time" you have given yourself as a gift, a time for honoring dreams and their special place in your own spiritual life.

After parking, you find the registration desk. You are expected, given a conference schedule, and are shown your way to your own quiet and private room. This will be your home for the next two and a half days. After settling in, you see that it's time for the first session to begin, so you follow the sound of voices to the large conference room. It is a relaxed place, with overstuffed chairs for sixty or more, a window wall opening onto the orange grove and a large stone fireplace at one end of the room. Two other walls are filled with books.

You find yourself a chair and settle in for the dream conference opening.)

Tom:
Hello, everyone. It's just after seven-thirty, and we'd like to get started. Would you all please find your spot and join us? *(Another few minutes pass as the large group gets itself settled. From down the hall, you can hear a bell rung to summon those who may still be in their rooms.)*

Tom:
Well, welcome! I've been looking forward to being here with you ever since we scheduled this conference—which was, oh, almost a year ago. What we've got planned is a time apart that will help all of us reverence the dream in our lives as a precious gift, a way of listening to God. And we hope this will be a restful time of personal renewal

11

and quiet for you, as well as a time for learning. I'm Tom Hedberg, and this is my dream companion, Betsy Caprio. Most of you know something about who we are from the brochure, so we won't go into long introductions now—as the time we're spending together goes by, you'll get to know us.

Betsy:
I want to welcome everyone too, and we know that for most of you it's probably been sort of a rush to get here, and that you've had a busy day already. This first evening we just want to unwind and sink into our theme. Tomorrow and the next day we'll get a little more active and start talking theory as well as practice. For tonight, though, let's just let ourselves *be* here, and relax, and let ourselves be open to whatever God wants to send us. How does that sound? *(General murmurs of appreciation. This group is tired! You become aware of soft music playing in the background.)*

Tom:
The music you're hearing is our dreaming theme, and you'll become familiar with it over the next few days. Whenever you hear it, you'll know that a session is about to begin. Now, let's start our time together with prayer.

Betsy:
Will you join me? I'd like to read from the Book of Job:

> God is greater than humans.
> God speaks first in one way, and then in another. . . .
>   God speaks by dreams, and visions of the night
>   as we slumber in our beds. Then it is that
>   God whispers in our ears.
> All this God does again and yet again,
>   letting the light of life shine bright on us.[1]

Tom:
Lord, we give you thanks this evening for the dream, and for the dreams that have led the people of God from the earliest times—the people of Israel: Joseph, Daniel, Mary and the second Joseph, and those who have followed them: Ambrose, Francis, Thérèse, Don Bosco, Emmanuel Swedenborg, so many others. We thank you for this precious gift, the dream—a form of revelation.

Betsy:
And we pray for us, their descendants: that our ears may be opened, and our hearts and minds and spirits readied for the messages you would have us receive in this time we spend together. Amen. *(The group responds in kind.)*

Tom:
Now, we need to just take a quick survey of who's here, so we'll know where you are—or, at least, have an idea of where you are. We know from your registrations that this is very much an interfaith group, with Jews and Christians represented, and several denominations of Christians included. Also, we learned from what you sent in that many of you are involved in some sort of helping profession, either full time, or as volunteers—and that pleases us, especially, because it means the work we do together here in this short time will have a ripple effect and reach others, if only indirectly.

Betsy:
Let's just have a quick show of hands to give us an idea of where you are as dreamers. For instance, how many of you would say this is a very new topic for you? *(About a third of the group raises its hands.)* And, how many would say they are more than beginners, but not exactly experts either?—perhaps you've read a couple of the good books, and logged your dreams for a while, and maybe worked with some of them—but you're not quite at the point of saying that dreams are an essential ingredient in your own spiritual life. *(This time about half the group raises its hands.)*

Tom:
And then, that would leave how many? Just a few, who have been involved with their dream life for a length of time in this way. . . . *(A half-dozen people or so raise their hands.)*

Tom:
Fine—that gives us a good cross-section. Maybe we should give you a little of our own background as dreamers, so you'll know something of what the dream has meant to each of us. Betsy?

Betsy:
Well, my memories of the dream in my own life go way back to my childhood in New York City. I remember my mother talking about her dreams when I was very young—she had some very vivid ones,

but (this would have been in the mid-1930's and the 1940's) no one to talk to about them. Every so often, she would share one with me, and the one I especially remember was her nightmare of a giant zeppelin bursting into flames. It was before the Hindenburg explosion, but that familiar image will give you the picture.

She woke up in the middle of the night with a great start and real terror, and couldn't get back to sleep. And, the next day, after having told my father and me about it at breakfast, my mother took me on the bus into Manhattan—I remember they were still double deckers then, and I always liked to go upstairs. After we sat down, she glanced over the shoulder of the man sitting in front of us and saw in his paper the very picture she had dreamed the night before— the dirigible in flames! She was so shaken up by this that we got off the bus and got another one home, and my mother picked up a paper on the way home and found the story. My recollection is fuzzy, but I believe it was about a blimp over the west coast—and it had exploded the night before at just the time of my mother's dream picture.

Now, of course, this is a most unusual sort of dream—you could call it telepathic or even precognitive—but my point is that from the time I was very young, it was impressed upon me that dreams exist and have a reality of their own, even though in those days laypersons didn't have much understanding of just how that reality functioned.

Melkite rite deacon:
When you don't have any sort of framework, cognitively, for that kind of experience, it just sort of sits there in limbo—and you often can't find anyone to talk to about it.

Betsy:
Yes—that's it exactly. And just to finish up the specifics on my background in dreams, I'll say that in the late 1960's I discovered the work of Morton Kelsey and John Sanford, who were just beginning to translate C. G. Jung's psychology into churchy language—actually, Jung had been writing in that vein for many, many years, but his works were still comparatively inaccessible.

I knew I'd come home when I read their books, and I'm sure many of you here have had the same experience. About ten years down the road I found myself weaving the dream, especially, into my work in religious education and giving workshops on the subject, but always very cautiously, because I knew what a strange topic it was in church circles. And, besides that, we lived not too far from Salem,

Massachusetts . . . *(laughter)* . . . and I knew better than to move too fast on new things in the world of organized religion!

Tom:
What's the old saw?—that when something new comes along, at first it's heresy, then after twenty-five years it's allowed in as a fringe movement, then after a hundred years we discover that Augustine or Thomas Aquinas had talked about it all along. That's certainly true with the dream!

Betsy:
Just for the record, how many of you are familiar with Kelsey's and Sanford's books on dreams?[2] *(Almost two-thirds of the group responds.)* Good. Tomorrow we'll have a bunch of books out for you to look at—all on dreams—and their books will be here so those of you who aren't fans of theirs yet can get a look at their work. And how about your dream history, Tom?

Tom:
O.K. Let me just ask, first, how many of the people here have in any way woven the dream into their work with others? *(No more than four or five raise their hands.)* By the time we leave, day after tomorrow, we hope you'll all have some ideas on how that could happen for you and your students or your congregation or your clients, if you'd like to take this material to that next step, but first, we have to make it our own.

Now, my own first memory of the value of the dream comes from my school days in Bellflower, not far from here, when I studied under the Salesian priests—their religious family was founded by John Bosco in the last century in Italy. Maybe you know him as "Don Bosco"—that's not his brother, they're the same person. (You remember "Don" as in *The Godfather,* no? Don Corleone—but he wasn't a priest!) "Don" is a title of respect in the Latin-speaking countries.

Anyway, little Johnny Bosco had a vivid dream life, and we learned a lot about it in that school—particularly his dream in which he saw both the questions and answers of a test that was going to be given to him as a boy. Now, here I was flunking math, and then learning of the power of the dream which had given John Bosco so much help in *his* test—in fact, he reported he was able to write down questions and their answers to his teacher's test that the teacher hadn't even gotten around to dictating to the class. So I said, "This is for me," but it doesn't quite work that way, does it?

At any rate, what did happen was that, like Betsy, I was impressed at an early age with the power of the dream, even though I didn't have any personal experience that would verify that for me. During my college years, I became fascinated with Freud's theory of dream interpretation when I first studied psychology—and this was very safe for the shy, self-conscious me. I could learn about others' dreams, and in sort of a sneaky way get some insight into my own life—yet, I still failed to ponder my own dreams or see real value in them, or even honor them enough to write them down.

It was only the real influence of the feminine in my life that encouraged me to pursue dreams, and that came through my sister Kath. She introduced me to the Jung Institute in Los Angeles in 1971. Now, I'd gotten some background in Jung in school, but it was all very heady and intellectual. And I knew that Jung was somewhat unacceptable in the academic and scientific worlds because he was considered a "mystic" (a nasty word, you know)—someone who spoke of the spiritual world and was considered a little out of touch with reality, to put it mildly. Freud's thought fit better the purely scientific and medical model that was preferred.

Yet, I found Jung compatible with Christian theology on *almost* all counts—plus, he gave me the keys I needed to understand and begin to interpret my own dreams and see them as part of the spiritual reality of my life. And, I'll just give you one example of a dream from that time that profoundly influenced my life—it came about the time I was graduating from college, and I had been going through tremendous fears about what I was going to do with my life. I had a recurring dream, over and over again. In the dream I see myself in what looks like a large town square. There are four horses attached to me, pulling me in four different directions. I didn't have a clue as to the dream's meaning, and it was only with the help of a wise Jesuit spiritual director that I really began to understand its symbolism.

At that time, there were four major directions in my life: one was my father's invitation to come and join him in the construction business—he had built churches and schools all around this area as the Hedberg Construction Company (thought I'd get in a little plug for you, Dad). Another pull was to become a psychiatrist, another to stay in the work I was doing in Santa Clara, and the fourth (and it really seemed like the fourth in a race of three) was the priesthood. The dream was saying I couldn't stay in such a state of tension, that I would have to make a choice.

So, this just gives you a little overview of how dreams have been important to me, starting when I was still in grade school. And, as you can see, my approach to the dream is definitely a theistic one—like Betsy, I believe the dream comes from God, the God dwelling within us. Not everyone involved with dreaming comes from that place, of course.

Sister:
Getting back to Don Bosco, I wondered when you were talking about him whether or not he was able to share his dreams with the people of his day.

Tom:
Well, no—not really. His mother listened to them when he was a boy and encouraged him, but later on he swore all of the members of his community to secrecy whenever he told them of a dream. All his life he was sent dreams that guided his work with the young people—especially boys—of northern Italy. He was born near Turin.

Sister:
So Turin—of, what, the early nineteenth century?—wasn't much different from Salem, as far as being open to the dream, that is.

Tom:
Right—except that by that time they had finished burning people who didn't fit into the expected mold, you just got excommunicated! Just remember—and we'll talk more about this tomorrow—that for the first thousand and more years of Christianity, and for centuries earlier in the Jewish tradition, the *acceptance* of the dream as a message from God was the norm.

Betsy:
So, we're recalling something old that got lost when we weave the dream into our own spiritual lives today—definitely not coming up with something new.

Tom:
Let's move on now. You should all have a copy of the schedule for our time here together. Just hang on to it. It doesn't seem that we need to go over it tonight unless someone has any special question right now.

Salesman:
Just one: will you wake us up in the morning? I'm wondering if I'll be so busy dreaming that I could miss the morning prayer and breakfast!

Tom:
Oh, don't worry about that; we'll ring a bell at 7:30 to let you know there's a half hour before things get started. Anything else? . . . O.K. Now, Betsy is passing around to you slips of paper and also blank paper for those who don't have some of their own—just raise your hand if you need the latter. How about pencils? *(You get a small strip of paper from Betsy, and also get out your own writing materials.)*

Tom:
When we come to a conference like this, we bring all sorts of mental stuff with us. Maybe today you had a long business meeting you thought would never end, or if you're the one who takes care of a family you had to do all sorts of things to get them and yourself ready for your departure. Or maybe you had classes, or crises in the parish, or—well, whatever.

Now, on the little slip of paper just write a line or a few words that have to do with whatever it is you've brought with you that might be your chief distraction, or worry, or roadblock over the next three days. What is it that might keep you from being fully present at this conference? *(You have a few minutes to think this over, then to write your thoughts on a separate piece of paper.)*

Betsy:
You can see I've got the fire lit in the fireplace. When you've put down whatever it is that might get in the way of your being here completely, just sit quietly, holding the paper in your hands. Think about whatever you've written as long as you need to. Then, go to the fireplace and give your concerns to the fire—just throw them in and let them be burned. They'll still be there when you get home again, but you'll have done something that says "I'm letting you go for a while while I take time for my own inner life." *(Some low music is playing in the background and, one-by-one, people are casting their most pressing concerns to the flames. You perform a similar ritual that will help you to be fully present to the conference events.)*

Betsy:
And, there are snacks on the table in the next room, and some drinks without caffeine (because we want you to sleep tonight). Maybe you'd

like to get something while you're up and bring it back with you. Let's do it in silence, though. *(About five minutes pass while people quietly finish the burning ritual and many stretch and/or get a snack.)*

Betsy:
For the next half hour, here's what we're going to do. As you see on your schedule, our evening ends with a dream invocation ceremony. We're going to ask God to send us the gift of the dream, just as people in ancient times used to go to dream temples and go through dream incubation rites. But, just as they did, we have to prepare for such a ceremony—and for this you'll need some blank paper and something with which to write. Our preparation will be in three stages.

Tom:
Will you just relax quietly in your chairs now? Just let the music *(which has gotten slower and more audible)* relax you even more. You might want to slow down your breathing so it's in rhythm with the music, or use some other way of relaxing that works for you, like clenching different sets of muscles and then letting them go. *(A few minutes pass in which you unwind even more. It's dark outside now, and the room has grown dimmer too.)* This is a time to let your soul speak to you, and I'll ask you to let the answer to this question surface from deep inside: "On what matter would I *most* like some guidance from God?"

Now, several things may present themselves, in which case you need to ask this: "Which of these matters seems to be asking for attention most strongly?" *(Take as long as you need to allow this listening to happen.)*

Sometimes when we are asked to do something like this, we can just go blank. I'm going to put a few ideas on the board in case anyone needs a suggestion or two. And, one last word from me: I want to encourage you to be sure that whatever subject you pick, it's something on which you really want honest information. Be sure that if you use this subject as your dream topic—for that's what we're getting ready to do—you'll be ready for an answer, no matter what it is.

(On the board, Tom writes the following list:
—a current problem (inner or outer)
—some way in which I need direction
—a decision that needs to be made
—a question about a relationship
—an event whose meaning I want to explore more deeply

—a fear whose cause is hazy
—the meaning of a previous dream.
You can hear some of the people around you respond to his written
suggestions. The music has grown even more relaxing.
After another few minutes, Betsy lowers the music.)

Betsy:
And now, step two. In your journals or on the paper you have, we'd
like you to write about the matter you've chosen *in detail*. We'll give
you enough time for this—about fifteen minutes. Describe as fully as
you can the history of the issue or question you've chosen, its major
aspects and causes, your feelings—hopes, fears, and so forth—about
it, why the matter is important to you, various alternatives in connection with it (perhaps ways you have gone with it or things you
have tried) and their results, and even your feelings as you write all
of this. (I'll put all these points on the board too.)

The reason for doing this is to help us unclutter our minds, our
souls, our channels about the subject. It's a way of getting the static
out. And, as you write, let the words flow naturally into prayer—it
can be written, or just in your heart.

THE TOPIC I HAVE CHOSEN IS_____

_____

Tom:
And now, the third step in our preparation. Let all that you've written rest in your lap, and—again—be as relaxed as you can. You've
gotten out all your thoughts (or many of them) that have to do with
whatever topic you've selected. And from all this, you're now going
to allow the matter to crystallize itself into *one* phrase, or word, or
question, or, even, just one image that has to do with the topic of your
dream quest tonight.

Quietly wait until something comes up from within you: a word
that says it all, or a question, or a phrase that distills everything, or
an image that puts your matter into a nutshell. It will come. Just
wait for it.

And when it does come, write the word or words, or draw the picture—keeping it very simple—as large as you can. Take a whole
page. Betsy has more paper if anyone needs it.

Tom:
(over the music, several minutes later) And just focus on what you've written or drawn quietly, meditatively, prayerfully. *(The room is very quiet; the lights have been dimmed even more, and the fire has burned down. You find yourself able to focus intently on what you have put on the paper—the summary of this preparation for the dream ceremony.)*

Betsy:
We're going to send you back to your rooms in a minute, to get ready for bed and prepare your room for the night. Then we'll reassemble here for our ceremony.

Tom:
And we'll ask you from now until we gather for morning prayer to observe the silence, just as if we were in a monastery.

Betsy:
Please go to your rooms when we finish these instructions. Get as ready for bed as you feel you will be comfortable doing, for you're going to return to this room. Robes and slippers and curlers are fine. Do whatever else you need to do before bedtime: brush your teeth, put out clothes for the morning—whatever.

Then, quietly place your last piece of paper—with your summary word or picture (or your journal, if that's what you've used)—under your pillow. And put some paper and a pen or pencil by your bed so you'll have dream-recording materials at hand in the morning.

Finally, stand or kneel beside your bed and—in whatever way you like—bless it. Make it a holy place for the night's sleep. There are several things you might do: make the sign of the cross on it or all around it, if that's part of your tradition; take a little of the holy water we have here with you when you leave the room, and bless the bed with that, or picture angels all around your bed—remember the *Hansel and Gretel* prayer: "When at night I go to sleep, fourteen angels watch will keep"?[3] Or perhaps you'll want to imagine yourself to be like one of the famous dreamers of scripture: Jacob, lying out on the ground instead of on a bed, with a rock for a pillow—or, Samuel, who slept in the temple in front of the ark. You can picture your own small room to be such a place, or some other.

In half an hour, our dream induction ceremony for this evening will begin, so you'll have plenty of time to get ready for bed and then to put your last page under your pillow and set up your dream logging materials for the morning, and then to bless your place of rest in any way you like. We'll ring a soft bell as the half hour is just about up, and just remind you once more to please keep the silence that will help prepare our souls for the night. *(With the others, you collect your belongings and move toward your room. There, you follow the instructions without rushing, and move back toward the large gathering place before the bell has been rung.*

The chairs have been separated so there is room for people to pass between them easily. Candles in the wall sconces and candelabra light the room; they are placed all around at different heights and are of many colors. There is the scent of incense in the air, or perhaps it is the candles that are scented. The soft and strange music plays on, and—gradually—the others return to the room. Some are in pajamas and robes, others still fully dressed. The woman who sits in front of you has her hair in many curlers that stick out at angles, and a very young woman has even brought her teddy bear!

Tom and Betsy have both put Japanese-style kimonos over their clothes, and are padding around in soft slippers too.)

Tom:
Welcome to our dream invocation ceremony. In the fifth century, Bishop Synesius of Cyrene said:

> The time that nature has ordained for us to consecrate to repose brings us, with sleep, an accessory more precious than sleep itself; that natural necessity becomes a source of enjoyment, and we do not sleep merely to live, but to learn to live well. . . . We should pray for a dream. . . . We are at the same time priest and initiate. . . . God will come to our aid.[4]

Tonight, when our ceremony is finished, each of us will leave in silence, holding within us the word or the picture that's now under our pillows. As quickly as possible, we'll go to bed, placing ourselves in the presence of God and holding our words or our image in our heart, focusing upon whatever it is that is already waiting in our place of rest. And we'll ask for a dream about the matter we've chosen—or, the matter that's chosen us. We'll ask for a dream *if* the Author of dreams wishes to send us one. It's important to be without expectations.

Betsy:
And in the morning, when you awaken—with no alarms, please— just lie still to see if something has come during the night. Take note

of anything that's in your mind, or perhaps the first thing you see or hear on waking. Continue to lie quietly. See what else comes.

If there's something—anything—record it in your dream log. And perhaps your writing will move you to something else: a prayer, or a poem, or a picture. You may be able to rest quietly for as much as a half hour, or even longer—remember, this set-apart time is your gift to yourself. Then, at 7:30, you'll hear the bell ringing, and at 8:00 we'll meet outside by the lake for morning prayer. We really want to encourage everyone to have the deepest reverence for this process in each of us.

Tom:

Join with us now as we take a trip down through the ages, and we see the great dreamers of the world's religious traditions that have come before us. They are our ancestors. We are links in a great chain of dreamers who knew the dream came from their God. *(One by one, beautiful colored slides are projected onto the wall in front of you, very large—men and women dreamers, rich and poor, famous and humble; you follow along as their names are read off.)*

Betsy:

Jacob, and his ladder of angels joining earth to heaven;[5] Joseph, his son;[6] Samuel, hearing God calling him. Let's stay with his story for a bit, since it gives us such a good model of the perfect attitude toward our dreams, and also helps us root our ceremony in the Word of God. You'll remember that Samuel was apprenticed to Eli in the temple:

> One day Eli was lying down in his room. His eyes had lately grown so weak that he could not see. The lamp of God had not yet gone out, and Samuel was sleeping in the temple of the Lord, where the ark of God was. The Lord called to Samuel, and he answered, "Here I am." He ran to Eli and said, "Here I am, you called me." And Eli replied, "I did not call you, my son; go back to sleep." So Samuel went back to sleep.
>
> Once again the Lord called Samuel, who rose and went to Eli. "Here I am," he said, "you called me." And Eli replied, "I did not call you, my son; go back to sleep." And Samuel went back to sleep again.
>
> The Lord called Samuel again, for the third time. Getting up and going to Eli Samuel said, "Here I am, you called me." Then Eli understood that it was the Lord calling Samuel and he said to him,

"Go to sleep, and if you are called, reply 'Speak, Lord, your servant is listening.' " So Samuel went and lay down in his place.

Then the Lord came and stood by, calling as before, "Samuel! Samuel!" Samuel answered, "Speak, Lord, your servant is listening."[7]

Samuel probably lived about three thousand years ago—but we could not find a better teacher about the correct attitude toward the dream. And one last example from the Hebrew scriptures: Daniel, interpreting the Babylonian king's dream.[8]

Tom:
From two apocryphal stories of the New Testament, here's Joachim,[9] and Mary, dreaming that she'll be the mother of the Messiah.[10] Joseph, her spouse, learning in a dream that he can marry Mary,[11] and later that he must take Mary and the Child and flee to Egypt.[12] The magi, being warned about Herod in a dream,[13] and Peter, from Acts 11, dreaming about the unclean animals.[14] John the Evangelist—or the author of Revelation—who (we are told) was sent the symbolic images "in a vision" (in Greek and Hebrew, the word "vision" and "dream" are used as one).[15]

Betsy:
In the infant Christian church St. Helena dreams of the true cross,[16] and her son, Constantine, dreams of how to win his great victory in the year 312, a victory that led to the end of the persecutions of the Christians.[17] Here is Ambrose of Milan,[18] and Jerome, who translated the scriptures into the vernacular because of a dream,[19] and Gregory Nazianzen,[20] and Ursula, all saints of the early church who gave witness to their dreams,[21] as did Basil the Great and Augustine and Athanasius, and so many others. In those days, the dream lived.

Tom:
And it lived on through the Middle Ages, for people like Jane of Aza, Dominic's mother, who dreams of a black and white dog racing through Europe with a torch in its mouth—a precursor of what her yet-to-be-born son would do.[22] Dominic appears in a dream to Pope Innocent III, who then gives him permission to begin the Order of Preachers, the Dominicans.[23] And here's Francis of Assisi, in a similar scene[24] and Francis again, dreaming of the Christ;[25] Joseph of Arimathea, appearing in the Middle Ages in connection with the Grail legend—he is supposed to have received the chalice of the Last Supper in a dream.[26]

Betsy:
Times changed. The world became more rational, more sensible; there was less room for the ephemeral dream in the western world, but it had always been alive in the east, from the earliest pictures in the Hindu world of Vishnu, dreaming the world into being,[27] and the dream of Maya, mother of the Buddha, that she will have a marvelous son,[28] and Mohammed, whose mission was revealed by the archangel Gabriel in a series of dreams.[29]

Tom:
Then we're at the door to the twentieth century, our time, with only an occasional dreamer—but they stand out: Emmanuel Swedenborg, recorder of a famous journal of dreams,[30] and Thérèse of Lisieux, brought peace before her early death through a dream,[31] and Don Bosco, of whom I spoke earlier,[32] and Isaac Hecker, founder of the Paulist Fathers. . . . [33]

Betsy:
And so many more, but most of all, we here tonight, descendants of all these dreamers throughout the history of religion.

We are like those to whom Jesus said, "Let down your nets." *(The famous Duccio painting of Jesus and the fishermen hauling in nets filled with catch is shown.)*[34] Each night we have a chance to let our dream nets down into the depths within ourselves, Or, perhaps, some of us are more like deep-sea divers. *(Undersea divers against a blue-green ocean are shown; sunken treasure lies beneath them.)* Divers searching for the riches in the deep sea, those elusive—yet plentiful and nourishing—contents of the waters within. Like them, we want to go more deeply within . . .

and

down . . .

That is our mission during these three days together. *(The slide showing the divers is made somewhat blurry by being put out of focus. There are a few minutes of quiet—time for the panorama of dreamers which have been shown to be digested.)*

Tom:
Now, we want to bless each of you before bedtime, just as you blessed your sleeping place. We'll walk among you, and will be using holy water. If anyone would rather we didn't do this, just hold up your hand as we get to you, and instead we'll stand at your side and pray

silently. We're very used to people needing different kinds of blessings, so don't hesitate.

Betsy:
And as we're blessing you, we'll ask you to focus again on the image or the word or words you've left under your pillow, back in your room. Close your eyes, and try to picture whatever it is you've put there— just as you wrote it or drew it. If you've used words, you might let them run over and over in your mind, even while picturing the letters. *(A different sort of music is now playing, and to it you call to mind the special dream seed waiting under your pillow. Tom comes down your side of the room, standing silently beside person after person. Some raise their hands to signify that he not use the holy water for them; you follow your own lights on this when he arrives at your chair. His words are: "May the God of Jacob and Joseph, of Mary and Helena, and of so many of our spiritual ancestors be with you this night—and may you wake in the morning with new insight from the Lord.")*

Tom:
(slowly and quietly, over the dream music) And now, it's time for our final invocation of the dream this night. Be with me in spirit, please, and, when I finish, just go off to your rooms in silence. *(Upon opening your eyes, you see the deep-sea divers' picture has been replaced by one of an old sailing ship on the waters. It lists slightly to one side. No one is visible in the picture; there is only the ship with its full sails, against a night sky and the dark sea. In the sky is a crescent moon.)*

It is time. I have come to the end of my day, but my life is not finished at this point. Only the outer tasks are laid aside to be taken up again tomorrow. Now, as I let the cares and the joys of the day's experiences drain from me in a last remembrance and a letting go, I prepare myself for the gift of new life.

As I enter sleep, my new day begins. As my eyes close, my awareness of God's time—eternal time—awakens. I am a journeyer, a traveler in a direction unknown. I move forward knowing that I do not control my future, but only my choices. And the gift I bring as I approach this other realm is my choice for openness, nothing more.

The ship awaits me at the dock. Is it masted with many sails— or only a slim and sleek few? My ship stands before me as I see her now with my inward eyes. I take only the essentials: the journeyer's staff, sandals, pouch and cloak. How do I look as I prepare to embark? What gifts and simple substances for my needs do I take with me in my pouch on this night sea journey?

And now, I meet my captain. Is it a man? A woman? And how dressed? How strong and capable of reaching our destination?

And what will be my part in this voyage? What is it that only I can do? What is it that only the captain can accomplish?

Somewhere, somehow, now we are embarking, and the mists of the night flow in to meet us as we set sail into the wind. My own thoughts are like flurries, occurring almost at random. But wait! What do I bring with me in my heart as our boat leaves shore on this journey of ours?

Is there not a question—or a special thought—or a special picture that I wish to fling across the tides of the waters this night? May I ask only that question for which I am willing and ready to receive the answer. May I bring with me only that phrase or that image with which I can continue to live after the voyage is done and the ship back in harbor.

The mists enclose me now. My ship is safe, my captain strong, my devotion secure. My question, my word, my image is now a song sung over and over until I am no more my waking self, and the dreams begin. My trust is in the captain who guides the journey, who helps me find deeper meaning in my life, who has always helped me to do this.

The night sea journey fills my being. I will awake when the ship has reached that further shore. I will awake. I will awake to the dream. I will awake recalling and writing my visions of the night as they flow forth, just as the wind sweeps in from the sea. I will awake bringing a gift from the eternal depths of myself, a gift from the Lord.[35]

(A second picture has replaced the first. It is the same scene, but the ship has moved much farther away; it is out to sea and the sky above it thick with the darkness of night.)

Betsy:
In the silence of this night, may God bless you. Good night. *(Slowly, some of the people move off to their rooms for the night. You may choose to remain in your chair a little longer as others are doing, to be with the picture of the sailing ship headed off into the dark night. The last strains of the music are fading out, and the remaining candles are snuffed out by the two facilitators. And—when you are ready—you go to your bed where your dream request waits for you, and you set off on your own night sea journey.)*

The Second Day

Morning Prayer

(In your journal or notebook write down your morning notes: of a dream, of thoughts or sounds on waking, of prayer that springs from the morning's gifts.

At 7:30 you hear a gentle bell ringing in the halls and soft music playing. When you're ready, you go to the large meeting place—a bank by the lakeside at the foot of the Center property—to join the others. It is a beautiful, clear morning, and the lake ducks and geese are busy diving for their breakfasts.

The group remains in silence until all are together.)

Tom:
Good morning everyone. *(General greetings are exchanged)*

Betsy:
There may be a few of us who are still getting in a last minute dream, but now we'd like to begin our day together with prayer, so would you form into a circle here, please? *(The group does this. You find yourself picking out a few familiar faces from last night. The morning air is still cool, and you're glad to have brought along a jacket.)*

Tom:
Now, we have plans for a short time of prayer together, all of which may be short-circuited by a goose. I came down here earlier just to make sure our spot was dry, and there's a goose—well, more likely, a gander—who told me that this was *his* turf. I got hissed at and he attached himself to the leg of my pants, and when I backed off, he went off a little too. Anyway, he's gone out for a dip now and I'm hoping he heard me telling him that we aren't going to stay, and that we're very peaceful people who mean him no harm.

Betsy:
And if he didn't get the message, he'll let us know—in which case, we'll finish our morning prayer while double-timing it up the hill!

Tom:
Here we are now in a circle, the symbol of totality and eternity. We've come from a night in which we invited the God of totality and eternity to be with us in a special way. Let's begin with words from the scriptures; in Psalm 127 we hear that

the Lord gives to those who are beloved in sleep.[1]

And here is the opening of Psalm 63 *(he passes the bible to the woman deacon, who reads):*

O God, you are my God whom I seek;
    for you my flesh pines and my soul thirsts
    like the earth, parched, lifeless and without water.
Thus have I gazed toward you in the sanctuary
    to see your power and your glory,
For your kindness is a greater good than life;
    my lips shall glorify you.
Thus will I bless you while I live,
    lifting up my hands, I will call upon your name.
As with the riches of a banquet shall my soul be satisfied,
    and with exultant lips my mouth shall praise you.
I will remember you upon my couch,
    and through the night-watches I will meditate on you:
That you are my help,
    and in the shadow of your wings I shout for joy.
My soul clings fast to you:
    your right hand upholds me.[2]

Betsy:
God of all creation—of the dreams of the night and the newness of this day—we come together this beautiful morning after our night-watches. We have sought to remember you on our couches, in our beds, during our own night sea journeys—and we ask now that, with the light of day, you help us understand the gifts of this night just past.

I'll invite you now to round out this prayer with just one or two words, if you like, to be clearer about just what the gifts of the night may have been for you. Anyone who would like to participate, just chime in—but please don't feel you have to do so.

You are our help, O God, just as the psalm tells us, and we thank you this morning for these gifts of the night: *(Assorted voices mention special gifts of the night, such as rest and peace and wisdom. What would you say, either aloud or in your heart? Jot this down in your book.)*

Tom:
And we'll close this prayer to start the day with a song that seems to have been written just for dreamers. You'll recognize the words of scripture on which it's based, and if you know the song, join in. *(From a portable tape player comes the music of* What You Hear in the Dark[3] *with its words of ministry and outreach: "What you hear in the dark, / You must speak in the light."[4])*

Tom:
We're going to go back up the hill now for breakfast, and then gather together again at 9:30—in about an hour—in the large room where we were last night. It looks as though our timing is just right, because our grey friend is coming this way. I'd *think* he'd be glad to have a spiritual group like us here, seeing as how geese were sacred birds to many people in the olden times. But—maybe he doesn't know about that![5] *(A "honk, honk" makes it clear that the large gander has had enough of this intrusion into his territory. Shaking his feathers, he heads toward the group, which respectfully retreats and heads back up the hill toward the dining room of the old house. On the way you notice a large tree with a hollowed-out trunk, large enough for a person to fit inside. Some people actually try it out, in fact. One comments that it would have been in a tree like this that some of the bygone hermits of religious history might have lived.*

In the dining room there is a country breakfast of eggs and pancakes waiting, with juices and homemade breads and preserves. This first meal together is a good opportunity for the conference participants to get to know each other.)

The Morning Sessions

(Just before 9:30 you hear strains of a familiar song from the large meeting room. It is Neil Diamond singing (from Jonathan Livingston Seagull) "Dear Father."[6] You remember that the song with its soaring melody is an invocation to the Father from those who dream. It plays on and, coming into the room, you find a table covered with books about the dream in religious traditions. In addition, large pictures (which are the same as many of the slides you saw last night in the dream ceremony) are on display in one corner. There is Jacob, asleep with his head on a rock as an array of angels ascend and descend a ladder to heaven; there is Ursula sleeping with her hand cupped to her ear so that she won't miss a word of the message coming in on the soft voice of the angel at her door; there is Jane of Aza, the dalmatian with a torch sitting on top of her as she lies under her patchwork quilt. You recognize others, and join with a group of people who are trying to identify the many dreamers pictured here. Betsy is helping them, pointing to a list of the pictures on the wall that identifies both the scene pictured and the artist.

The music tapers off, and Tom is asking the participants to settle down in their seats for the morning.)

Betsy:
Before we begin, I want you to know that I did a little investigating about the feathered friend we met earlier. He doesn't have a name, but the sisters who run the Center call him "our arrogant pet," and his nap time is after lunch—so, if you want to take another turn around the lake, that's probably the best time to go there without upsetting him. He's all bluff and sound and fury, according to those who know him, so you really needn't worry that you'll be attacked by a grey goose—someone asked about that!

Insurance agent:
Well, it might interest everyone to know that I had a dream about a goose last night—and I've never been here before, and didn't know there was a goose here. Maybe he was honking in the night.

Betsy:
Aha! Now that's an example of what Jung calls *synchronicity*. And it's the kind of "coincidence" that says, "Pay attention to this symbol." We'll be talking about that a little later.

The first thing we want to do this morning, as it says on your schedules, is to debrief our ceremony of last night, and also anything that happened during the night.

Now, this is important: while we want to savor and share any fruits of the night that *you* are willing to share—and for some of us there may have been no dreams at all, but just a regular night's sleep—we aren't going to go into the details of anyone's dream. There are a couple of reasons for this: the first, of course, is our time limitation, but that's not as important as the second, and that is because the dream is such a fragile, ephemeral gift. One of our basic rules of thumb is that the dream should be kept to ourselves—or only shared with the other special persons with whom we share the contents of our soul's life—until it has begun to give up its meaning. That's what we call "honoring the dream," and when we don't do that it's as though we let it out too soon and all its power can just be diffused. It's like having something precious inside a closed bottle, and then taking the stopper out before the brew—or whatever—is ready.

So, we'll compare notes on both the ceremony and the fruits of it—if any—but we'll ask you not to go into *specifics* about any dream.

Tom:
On the other hand, if some of you are really on fire to talk about a dream you've just had—really *need* it to be shared, for whatever reason—we don't want to shut the door on that need, either. So, you could see either of us when we have a break and we could talk things over a little more if you're finding yourself with that kind of need this morning. Is that o.k.? *(General agreement from the participants.)*

Tom:
Let's reflect back a little on last night's ceremony. We didn't give you much introduction to dream invocation (or incubation, as some speak of it) because we wanted to use all the energy here for the actual act of calling for a dream.

Betsy:
And also, both of us come from that wing of education that says the best learning comes from *reflection on* our experiences, rather than from-the-top-down input on theory. So, reflecting on what we did to-

gether, can we have some general reactions from you about the whole process?

Youth minister:
Well, my first reaction is to say that whereas I was a little doubtful that I would dream, even after all the preparation, I did dream about the very thing I'd put under my pillow. I haven't quite figured out just how the dream speaks about that matter—but it does.

Tom:
Good! And the figuring out is what comes next.

Carpenter:
I really want to thank you for the last part of the ceremony—the ship going off into the night, and the pictures of it. When I got back to my bed, that was so impressive to me that I never did get around to thinking about the note under my pillow. And I know I had a dream, but I couldn't remember it when I woke up. What I did remember was that I had some new appreciation of dreams in general.

Betsy:
And that may be the best fruit of this conference for many of us. Let's take a little survey of results, just by raising hands. How many people didn't remember anything at all upon waking? *(About a quarter of the group raises its hands.)* And how many remembered something from their night's sleep that—in some way—seems to connect with the phrase or words or whatever went under your pillow? *(More than half of the people respond to this question)* And how many had some dream or dream fragment—but it didn't seem to have anything to do with the subject you were using as a seed? *(Another quarter or so of the group falls into this category.)*

O.K., thanks—that gives us a cross-section. Before I forget, I just want to suggest that you continue to watch your dreams for the next few nights, or even the next few weeks, for *something* connected with your dream concern of last night—especially if you didn't have a full-blown dream response.

You know, we're not in charge of this process of dialogue with the as-yet-unrevealed parts of ourselves—and we have to be listening for the soul's response *whenever* it comes, even though it may not be on *our* timetable.

Tom:
Yes, I'd like to emphasize that too. In anything dealing with the soul, the "add-water-and-stir" approach is too simplistic. You'll remember that we mentioned not having any expectations, but just being open to the word of God. For many of us, last night may have just been the initiation of a process that will cover several days, or weeks, or even more.

We're going to pass out, now, a handout called *The Ancient Art of Dream Invocation*. It will give you the steps of our ceremony of yesterday, and you'll be able to repeat the process for yourself when you have something on which you'd like some dream-input. This is really a summary of what we said and did last night, and when your copy reaches you, just take a few minutes to look it over to see if it's clear. *(Papers are handed around. Here is your copy of this handout.)*

Tom:
Let's just run through this together: You can see from the first point that this skill of invoking the dream is something to be used when we really have a serious concern—it's not a parlor game. On the other hand, many people have learned to ask for enlightening dreams as part of their evening or night prayers, in a simpler way. The longer ceremonial invocation, however, is a serious matter for serious times.

Betsy:
And you see our note there to only use as a dream seed something about which we *really* want accurate information—please, just jump in with questions and your comments as we go through this together.

Choir director:
Well, I'm glad you said that to us last night, because I *am* wrestling with a really large problem in my life right now, and that was the first thing that came to my mind. But then, after I heard you say that, I decided I might not be ready to hear from God first-hand about that part of my life—so I chose something else.

Tom:
Yes, and the word "readiness" is really important here. We need to listen to our hearts, to our intuition and our feeling about the next step we're being called to.

Sister:
You know what you know when you know it.

The ancient art of
DREAM INVOCATION

Peoples of many ancient cultures—Greece, Egypt, the American Indians—had techniques for "incubating" or "hatching" a dream when they needed to be in touch with the Giver of Dreams: their God. In the Greek Orthodox monasteries of the Aegean, this has been a practice for centuries and still is today.

STEPS FOR DREAM INVOCATION

1. Clarify the Issue for Incubation:

We can use this sort of dream skill when there is some concern of ours that is not clear at a conscious level. It might be

- a current problem (inner or outer)
- a need for direction (inner or outer)
- an event whose meaning we want to explore more deeply
- a sense of shifting in our life, a rearranging of priorities
- a fear whose cause is hazy
- the meaning of a previous dream
- any decision that needs to be made
- a question about a relationship

(For a first attempt, it might be best not to pick some enormous, life-changing issue—but we don't want to water down the technique by focusing on something trivial, either. Best choice: something that seems to be asking to be considered, "pushing the psyche.")

BE SURE you only ask the Dreamer Within for something you *truly* want honest information on! The dream may not tell you what you *want* to hear, but may come back with a "you asked for it!" answer. The desire for self-knowledge takes courage.

The subject matter for incubation can be decided upon in a quiet, reflective way. One concern will usually present itself and be seen to be the obvious choice. Your readiness will attract results.

2. Write About the Matter at Length:

a) In your journal write for as long as necessary about the matter you have chosen. Describe it in detail: its major aspects, causes, your hopes and/or fears about it, why the matter is important to you, various alternatives in connection with it, which of these you have already tried—and their results, your feelings as you write this, etc. This is done to get the static out, to unclutter your mind about the matter.

b) In quiet, listening to your heart, allow all the above to distill itself into a PHRASE or a QUESTION or even an IMAGE that has to do with the matter at hand. Write the words or draw the picture in bold letters or form in your journal. Let go of all the words you wrote about the matter—just focus on the words or image in front of you.

3. Prepare for Bed:

—as quietly as possible, holding the image or words in your mind and heart. Turn down your bed; put your journal under your pillow. In imitation of the ancients, there are many extras you might add at this point: special bathing rituals, special sleepwear, special pillows (the herb mugwort is supposed to have special dream effects!). You might bless your bed, sprinkle it with holy water, stand by it in silent prayer.

4. The Ceremony:

Dream incubation ceremonies have several possible ingredients, with which one can experiment. Some of these are:

- fasting from the evening meal
- body relaxation techniques/yoga practices
- looking at pictures of dreamers
- scripture that seems appropriate, especially on listening to God
- re-creation in guided imagery of one's "perfect place," the *ideal* spot in which one would like to sleep
- music
- meditation on the phrase or question, as on a mantra, or by focusing on the picture (this is called "seeding the dream" or "symbol injection")
- special prayers or dream invocations

BE CREATIVE! WHAT WORKS FOR YOU? TRY DIFFERENT THINGS.

5. Going to Sleep:

Gently, return to bed and repeat the words you have chosen (or focus mentally on the symbol you have drawn). Place yourself in the presence of God. Ask for an enlightening dream in response to the matter you have incubated. Give it to God . . . have no expectations.

6. On Awakening:

Allow yourself to waken slowly, and try to be still so you may capture anything that is with you. It may be a complete dream—or a fragment of one. It may be just an image, or a feeling, or a color, or a sound. Lie quietly to see if something more appears. Perhaps a song will play itself through your mind—or you may first notice a ticking clock, or a bird's song, or a pet's noises.

When satisfied that you have whatever is going to come, record it in your journal after last night's entry. You may find that writing triggers more recall—or leads you to write a poem or a story or sketch a picture.

Take time for this step. Take time now to pray, to thank God for your sleep and whatever its fruits have been. If possible, stay still for a half hour or more, and keep recording anything that comes to you. Even if there is nothing to record, be still and rest in the Lord.

7. Working on the Material of the Incubation:

See the handout "6 Steps for Honoring Your Dreams" and work through the steps, or use the contents of your journal in any other way you have developed to see if something from the night throws light on your question or concern. You may have to stay with this for many days; "carry it in your pocket."

IF the night material seems to speak to you in relation to your concern, honor it by giving the whole process a special place in your journal, perhaps with color and picture. Thank God for it!

Tom:
Yes! That's it.

Now, don't try to shorten step two. You remember how much time we gave you last night to write as fully as possible about the topic you picked. Getting our thoughts out like this—or, at home, onto a tape recorder perhaps—sort of clears the channel. It helps us focus.

Betsy:
Then, we came up with something *very simple* that capsulized all of this outpouring. This is what we used to zero in on—it's called the "dream seed."

Salesman:
Now I had trouble with that part of it, until you said something about drawing a picture. I couldn't get any words, but a little stick figure came to me.

Betsy:
Oh, good. And, of course, you realize that we're doing this under artificial conditions. If you were home and decided to have an invocation for a dream and no words or picture came that seemed right, you'd figure it wasn't the right time and then you could wait until it *was* a good time. For many of us, last night might just have been a time to learn a skill or be exposed to it for the first time—you may need a few more practice sessions on your own before this becomes more natural.

Tom:
Now, steps three and four can go together when you're on your own. And we really encourage you to find the things that best help *you* ceremonially. You might do all the things on the paper under these two steps, or just one or two of them.

Nurse:
I like the mugwort under the pillow. Where can I get that?

Homemaker:
Do you sleep on it or eat it?

Nurse:
Oh, don't eat it—it makes you perspire like crazy. It's a folk medicine, but I wouldn't recommend eating it or drinking mugwort tea.

Betsy:
Well, believe it or not, there are mugwort pillows you can find from time to time in some of the bookstores and places that carry herbs and health foods. And we put that in more or less as a joke, but there's something to be said here for the power of suggestion too—if you really found a mugwort pillow you could say that you were honoring an ancient tradition that dreamers down through the centuries have created, and that sort of unites you with those who have come before us, like the people on our slides last night and in the pictures over there.

Parish secretary:
That's what I liked best last night—all the pictures of the dreamers in scripture and history, and even in the eastern religions.

Betsy:
And we're always on the lookout for other good dreamers to add to the slides, so if anyone comes across a good picture, please lend it to us to copy. We'll leave the big pictures up through lunch time, so you can see them again. There's a list of the paintings by the door over there. How about step five?

Tom:
The important thing there is "no expectations." We aren't the ones in charge of the process. You'll read articles today, and books, about *dream control*. They tell you that you can take charge of your dreams and make them be nighttime adventures to suit your taste.[7] Well, from our standpoint—which is that God is the author of the dream—that would be called "dream *manipulation*." It's an activity of the ego, which sets itself above the higher power within each of us. That's something that we spend most of our lives trying not to do as it is, so why should we put the ego in charge of the one time when it *is* on hold, when we're sleeping?

Business man:
So, there are different approaches to dreaming then, depending upon one's theology?

Tom:
Yes, and one's psychology too. If the ego is the supreme good of your psychology, of course it makes sense to have it run things day and night. But if there's something more—C. G. Jung called it the Self,

or the image of God in us—it needs to be heard from as often and as much as possible. The ego needs to get out of the way.

Business man:
And there are some psychologists interested more in the physiology of dreams, isn't that so? They're measuring rapid eye movements in sleep labs and so on.

Tom:
Yes, and often for a variety of reasons. This research has been going on now since the 1950's or so. It's very well documented by this time—and what we're interested in, of course, is the content and purpose of the dream in a spiritual framework. We're talking about a God of love who wants to communicate with us, and chooses this as one way of doing that. So, yes, one's psychology *and* theology are part of a framework for the dream. We'll be getting back to this point.

Betsy:
Now, the next step is crucial too. You know how often we wake up and feel that a dream has just slipped "off the hook," like the fish that "just got away." Well, I find that if I lie still without moving when I wake up, I can usually catch a dream and then I run through it again like a movie, to set it before I try to write it down.

Grocery store clerk:
And the alarm clock really kills it off!

Betsy:
Oh, you bet! We can train ourselves to wake up without an alarm by just picturing the clock at wake-up time as part of our night prayer. After a while, we'll find we wake up at the time we've picked and pictured. No, alarms and dreams don't go too well together.

Tom:
And anxiety about recording or catching the dream just interferes too. If we don't capture a dream one night, the message will usually come again until we get it. Remember—we don't have to be in control of any of this.

Pastor:
We're cooperating with grace.

Tom:
That's it exactly.

Betsy:
And the last step is something we'll talk more about later this morning. When we do receive a dream—especially one we've made a real plea for—then we need to work with it. We'll give you the handout mentioned after the break, in about fifteen minutes.

Let's talk just a little bit about your experience during the night and this morning when you woke up—not specific dream details now, for the reasons we mentioned earlier, but just general reflections on the process, or questions, if you have some.

Graduate student:
Well, I woke up several times during the night, and that was O.K. Each time, I felt as though I'd just missed a dream, but what really got me was how I felt as though something important was going on.

Betsy:
Can you tell us a little more? How would you describe what was going on?

Student:
Well, I was listening for the voice of God—that's what was happening. I remembered the reading about Samuel, and how he kept waking up. So, even though I didn't remember any dream at all, what I still have is a sense of paying more attention to God speaking to me.

Betsy:
Well, that's wonderful—and that's what it's all about, whether we get a specific dream image and message, or just an increased awareness that God is present to us. Both come under the heading of "revelation."

Teacher:
And, for me, it wasn't a dream I remembered, but a sound from outside. I woke up very early—it was just dawn—and I heard the birds just beginning to make their noises. Now, that does connect with my question under my pillow last night—as a symbol, I mean. So I want to work with it as I would with a dream symbol.

Tom:
Yes, we don't want to limit God to just sleeping images and messages. Sometimes the first thing we see or hear when we wake up is very powerful.

Betsy:
Usually the first thing I see when I wake up is my little cat. She sleeps on my bed and sometimes ends up on top of me if I'm on my back. Then she stares at me until she sees my eyes begin to open, then meows for her cat food! So I've learned to keep my eyes closed until I can go through a dream at least once in my mind. Anyone else?

Counseling center director:
Well, this may sound funny, but I didn't really remember anything in particular from the night—I just knew I had had a wonderful night's sleep. You see, my husband snores very loudly . . . *(audience reaction to this bit of news!)* and I have a hard time catching any dreams unless I'm alone, as I was last night.

Tom:
So, we're coping with alarm clocks, and snorers, and cats, and what else?

Young mother:
Babies!

Minister:
Midnight phone calls!

Aerobics instructor:
Someone else in bed who tosses and turns.

Tom:
And, in spite of all this, God finds ways of getting through—if not in our dreams, then in God's own way. And our task is to have our antennae out, to be good receivers, right?

Betsy:
Can I take just a few minutes before the break to tell you a little more about dream invocation or incubation or whatever name you like to call this procedure? When we were first preparing this conference—

and that would have been several years ago—I did a lot of research on the subject, and it's been just fascinating to me. On the board I've put the names of some of the best references on the subject, including Jung,[8] and you might want to look these up for yourself. But here's just a little more—I know, for me, to be aware that a spiritual practice of my own has deep roots in history makes it much richer.

So, what we did last night is also called by other names. Some people call it "dream induction" or speak of "induced dreams." And then you read about "meeting God half-way" as a way of describing dream invocation, or "dream hatching," which I like. In fact the word *incubation* comes from the Latin for the act of hatching (whether that be a dream or baby chicks or birds); it means "to sleep or lie on." And it also has to do, in Latin, with "brooding upon," in the way the spirit of God brooded over the chaos in the opening of Genesis[9]—so it's God as *ruah*,[10] hovering over the formlessness. Isn't that a good image of how it is when we're asleep and God is active within our dreaming?

Religious education director:
That would be a good picture to use as part of the induction process, wouldn't it? I can just see God hovering over my bed, about to transform the dark formlessness of the night into something with shape for me.

Tom:
And I've used God as potter as a meditative image for dreaming too.[11]

Betsy:
Yes, and both have the kind of power we're asking for when we call on God for the dream. Any other images of God that fit here?

Priest:
How about God as mother hen, clucking over her chicks and protecting them? It's the "shadow of your wings" idea we heard this morning.[12]

Waitress:
I like the pillar of fire by night image too—light in the dark night, God leading us.[13]

Betsy:
Yes. Again, here's where our own creativity comes in—we can each find the image of God as giver of the dream that works best for us.

And that will change from time to time, as we change and shift and grow—or go on hold.

Let me give you just a little more of what I dug up about dream incubations; you already know that this is an ancient practice, very widespread. Some of the peoples who have practiced dream invoking are:

- peoples of the early Christian churches, especially in the east, in places like Cyprus and Constantinople. These practices continue today in the Lebanese church, and in North Africa, and in Ortho-dox monasteries on the Greek islands;
- in the more rational western church, there was still dream hatch-ing until the eighteenth century in Italy and France and Austria;
- the most famous dream rituals were conducted in Greece, as long ago as the fifth and sixth centuries B.C. in the temples of the god of healing, Aesculapius. This was part of Greek culture and, in fact, Sophocles gave his home to be the first shrine of Aesculapius in Athens. People would go to these temples and pray for a healing dream—you can read about this in the books on the board if it's not familiar; it's a fascinating subject;
- in all the other ancient cultures, we find the same thing: in Egypt the god of dreams was Serapis (note the similarity to *seraphim*), and throughout India and Tibet there are dream temples—and even dream mountains in the Himalayas of Tibet;
- the Eskimo shaman, or primitive priest, would pull a dreamer who was seeking a dream on a sled to a secluded igloo and leave him there for a month—somehow the Greek temple sounds better to me;
- and, very important, the American Indians' lore is filled with vi-sion quest and dream quest stories, as you probably know—these were often part of the rite of passage into adulthood for braves and Indian maidens, and they would go off and seek a dream that would give them their life's mission and show them their special gifts that were to be used for the good of the tribe. One story I like is about the Ojibwa Indians—near the Great Lakes: they would not only go off into the wilderness on their vision quest, but pre-pare a ritual nest in which to sleep—and dream.

Sister:
Can I cut in for a minute? I just want to say that I worked in southern New Mexico in the 1950's—a long time ago—and at that time people were just beginning to appreciate how much we had lost as a country

by not respecting the traditions of the American Indian. First, we "discovered" their beautiful art work, and then the customs, and now the earthy and simple spirituality that's so profound—and for me, it was a wonderful balance to all the heady training I'd had all my life. I'm just so glad to see people who aren't native Americans finally appreciating our country's original spiritual heritage.

Tom:
I was at a Roman Catholic Mass not long ago where an Indian medicine man waved smoke into the four corners of the universe three times during the Mass. It was a marriage of two traditions that really did justice to both.[14]

Betsy:
And all the dream invocation practices of all these peoples, east and west, basically had four ingredients—with their own variations, of course. And we included them as we called on the dream too. The first: a belief that God—or the gods—uses the medium of the dream, and a desire for this kind of communication; the second is preparation—sometimes for months ahead of time. How many of you planned to be here, say, more than three months ago? *(More than half of the participants respond to this.)* Then there's the immediate preparation—or proximate, as the Jesuits would say: getting ready, traveling—or making a pilgrimage to a sacred spot. You did both of these, and for other people it has been a trip to a mountain or a well or a spring or a cave or a temple or a church or a monastery. Then there's the offering: food or monies or animals—whatever was appropriate. You did that too.

And, finally, the ritual—with many variations, usually including some kind of purification by fasting or bathing, and some kind of prayer or calling on the god or goddess who would send the dream. We did the latter, but not the former.

Temple religious school director:
You know, all the time you've been talking I've been thinking about my dog—and he dreams and snorts and chases rabbits or something at night. Before he goes to sleep, he finds his special spot, and he has his own ritual—he paws the ground and arranges his blanket, and then he circles around three times. I've watched him for—let's see— six years now, and every night it's the same thing, ever since he was a puppy.

Tom:
Saying . . . ?

Temple school director:
Saying that the instinctual or animal part of us—and of animals and primitive peoples—finds all this very natural, and that we've gotten so sophisticated and above-the-collar that we've lost something very basic.

Betsy:
Yes. And one of the exciting things happening in our time is the reclaiming of many of the basic and most elemental aspects of life—the dream being one of these.

Tom:
And, to carry that idea a step further, another of the exciting things I've seen happening—just in pockets, really—is appreciation of the animals and how they can teach us about these elemental and basic aspects of "religious living," if you will. You know, Jung spoke of the animals as being *pious,* because they were so true to the nature God had given them. So, your dog teaches you about sleep rituals, and our goose this morning taught us about being true to its goose-nature. The animals are about the instincts, but they're also about something that is "other"—which is what the spiritual realm is for us.

Therapist:
So, they help us see that animal instinct and spirit can co-exist.

Betsy:
Yes, exactly. They teach us about bridging that gap that we've lived with so long. And there are those among us who won't eat animals just for that reason, because they're not *inferior,* but live in a *superior* way. They're our teachers. Well, that's sort of an aside. You'll notice we're good at diverting.

Let's take a break for about ten minutes. You might want to look over some of these books, or the pictures—and I'd invite you to find the pictures which are especially about combining opposites, in just the way we're saying the animals do. Jacob's ladder is an obvious example, for instance; it unites heaven and earth. What we're about here in these three days is letting two parts of *ourselves* be in dialogue: the part of us which is conscious, and that which is not yet conscious. The dream is one way in which that joining is promoted.

(The break is welcome, for you're still caring for the events of last night within yourself and have also been wanting to get back to the pictures which were on the slides. Remembering Betsy's suggestion to look for images of the opposites joined, you study the pictures again, finding the sun and moon in one, and the sacred tree in another. William Blake's picturing of Jacob's ladder is especially powerful; even Dominic's black cape over his white habit is an opposites-uniting image, as is the cross in the painting of Helena's dream.

Neil Diamond's voice sings "Dear Father" once again, and this is the signal for a return to your chair. Waiting for you is a second handout with the heading "6 Steps for Honoring Your Dreams.")

Tom:
During the break, a couple of people came up with good questions about the process of dream incubation, so let's just take a minute to stay with that subject. One question was, "Are there ever times when it's *not* a good idea to invoke a dream?" And my thought about that is that the *right* time is when you're really up for something that we're saying is a sacred practice—and so the less suitable times would be when you're not: for instance, if you're over-tired, or rushed, or have been sick and not all there, or if you've even eaten or drunk too much. This isn't something we would want to take lightly.

And someone else asked if we can repeat a ritual like the ones we've been talking about if we don't get an answer at once—yes, we can. This is—as we're sharing it from our perspective—a form of prayer, isn't it? So, just as you would repeat a prayer of petition, say, when worshiping alone or with a community or your family, we can repeat the prayer of petition for a dream on a specific subject. Just as in any other prayer, we trust that God has the timing for the answer.

Good questions—thanks. At lunch we can talk more about any other questions you have. We want now to move along a little and take a look at the handout you found on your chairs. We also want to get in a little theory about where the dream comes from and how and why this works.

Betsy:
First, we want to thank Paulist Press for allowing us to reprint this handout. It's material we developed several years ago and now it's in our book for them titled *Coming Home*. There are different approaches to working with a dream, and we'll talk of some other ways

6 Steps for
HONORING YOUR DREAMS

1. Record the dream: Write down all the details, feelings and fine points of each dream. Dating them is helpful.

2. Write down any associations you have for anything in the dream: What connections or memories do the people or things or places in the dream have for you? (for example: a dream of my grandparents' home might stir up memories of peace and security and love—or it might have completely different associations.)

Perhaps the dream seems to parallel some story you know (for example: a dream about being sent out into unknown territory might remind you of stories as different as those of Abraham or the voyages of the Starship *Enterprise*.)

There are books of symbols that can give you background about how people of all times and places have used various images which may occur in dreams. (e.g. *Dictionary of Symbols* by Cirlot)

3. Do something with the dream—Draw it, or write a dialogue with one of the characters or symbols from the dream, or use a picture (drawn or mental) of something from the dream as a prayer-starter.

This will help unlock the meaning of the dream.

4. Listen to the dream as if it were a play or a movie or scripture story: If I saw this on the stage or in a theatre, what would it be about? Can you state the *theme* of the dream in a sentence?

Viewing a dream objectively in this way often helps it to release its meaning.

5. Try to discern what the message of the dream is: Dreams have a purpose; they inform us about things we aren't conscious of in waking life. (This is called the *compensatory* function of the dream.)

What does the unconscious/what does God want me to become conscious of through this dream? You will know you have it right when there is a feeling of sureness, a "click".

6. Response: What action can I take to respond to the dream message or teaching? If we do something in response to a dream, we will often experience a release of energy; the dream shows us another step in the process of spiritual growth.

Throughout the process, prayer and sharing with one's spiritual guide help greatly.

From: *Coming Home: A Manual for Spiritual Direction.* Copyright © 1986 by Betsy Caprio and Thomas M. Hedberg, S.D.B. Used by permission.

later, but these basic steps are those we've found helpful, especially when one is just beginning to tend the dreams.

Oh yes, also, during the break, someone asked which was the best primer on dreams in a religious context, and I think we'd both recommend Morton Kelsey's little book *Dreams: A Way to Listen to God*.[15] We really owe him and John Sanford a tremendous debt for bringing back our awareness of the dream and its religious roots.

I know we have a lot of Kelsey-Sanford groupies here with us, right?—especially since we're fortunate enough to have them both here in California, and we get a chance to hear them speak off and on. They have both been deeply influenced, as you know, by Jung's thought, as have we, so the psychological theory we'll be sharing with you has that base. And, please, those of you with that kind of background, just chime in as we go, O.K.? Note that we're not saying one can just accept Jungian psychology in one gulp without any discernment about how it fits with our faiths, just that it's a tremendous help in the how-to's. Up here we also have a good issue of *New Catholic World* from 1984, and it has articles that really pinpoint these differences.[16]

Tom:
And it would be of interest to believers of all faith traditions, don't you think?

Betsy:
Oh yes.

Tom:
Taking just a few minutes for basic theory now, I've got a picture here of Jesus and the fishermen letting down their nets—you may remember it from last night. According to the Jungian view of the soul or psyche that we're working from, each of us is like an island: the part of us that we call consciousness has emerged from the seas—but most of us is below water. Now, that's like Freud's iceberg model—but with this difference: at the deeper layers down under the waters, all these islands are joined. They're not islands after all. That deeper level is Jung's collective unconscious, the part of our humanity we share with all peoples of all times and places. No man or woman or child is an island, psychologically speaking. It's another way of understanding the mystical body.

And, as things come up from below the water line—things like dreams, and projections, and fantasies, and unexpected behavior that just pops out—we can assimilate them, make them part of our consciousness.

Homemaker:
But we don't always do that, do we?

Tom:
Actually, we *rarely* do that—unless we've made some sort of commitment to the inner life and to increased consciousness. And that's where this picture comes in; every night we get an opportunity to "let down your nets," as the words of scripture go. The dream can—if we let it—bring up something of the contents of the depths that are hidden away.

Private investigator:
But you have to haul it in, or else the fish just goes back down under the water line again.

Tom:
Right.

Seminary professor:
So you're saying that our dreams aren't just a rerun of what we've done during the day, but they're about something else, something we don't know yet.

Tom:
Yes—the dream is usually considered to be compensatory to our waking or conscious attitude. It tells us about things we need to balance out our conscious approach, which is usually very one-sided. Remember: from the Jungian point of view we're using, there's an inborn impulse within us toward wholeness that's trying to be manifested—that's a very consoling idea and one that certainly fits with our faith perspective.[17] We're continually being sent what we need for balancing out.

Betsy:
Here's the way we usually draw our map of the inner world:
  (At the board, she sketches Diagram A):

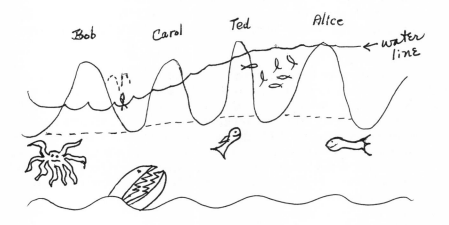

And the separate little tips of the islands are individual people's awareness or consciousness—the part that says "This is me," with the ego as its center. And just under that, the personal unconscious, with each one's own memories and so forth. And below that the collective unconscious, where everyone is joined and shares the same ancient matrix of archetypal energies. (Dr. Joseph Henderson of San Francisco also postulates another layer—a "cultural unconscious"— between these two layers.)

Repairwoman:
And the fish, then?—they're what can come up at night . . .

Betsy:
Or in the day, but especially at night, in the dream. And each time we haul one in, the water line around our own island of consciousness gets a little bit lower—you see that the people here, the islands, aren't all the same size.

Student:
No, "Alice" is almost drowning!

Betsy:
Almost completely unconscious. One more thing—note that not all the contents of the depths are necessarily delightful; there're sharks and squid and so forth—but they're much less harmful once beached.

Tom:
A good reference from Jung on the balancing out, in case you'd like to look it up, is paragraph 653 of Volume Ten of the *Collected Works*.[18] Jung's writing about the struggle of the—and I'm quoting— "most important of the fundamental instincts, the religious instinct for wholeness" to free itself and become conscious. He goes on about how the other two basic instincts, the drive for power and the sexual instinct, so easily overwhelm the religious instinct, and concludes that "the right hand does not know what the left is doing!" Sounds familiar, doesn't it?

Melkite deacon:
Then, the main purpose of dreaming is to redress the imbalance of our conscious attitude?

Tom:
Basically, yes—we could say dreams are sent to make us more whole. And, of course, this process is never finished, at least not here on earth.
  (There's a quiet over the group which seems to signify a soaking-in of this vast idea. Tom's questioning look asks if it's all right to proceed. He decides it is.)

Tom:
Let's go on now. What we want to do until lunch time, or just before, is divide ourselves into two groups. Take a look at the handout about the six steps again, and see if you think you need to be in the beginners' group which will go over these points in detail and give you a chance to ask questions on the nuts and bolts of working with a dream. And those of you who would like this will meet with me in the next room. If you have the mechanics down pretty well and want to talk about a next step in working with dreams, then stay here with Betsy—and we've got about an hour, so we can really go into each of these topics in some depth. O.K.? How many will join me next door? *(The group divides almost in half, with about thirty going with Tom into the adjoining lounge room.*
  You decide to stay with the advanced group, knowing that, al-

*though the basic review is always helpful, it is easily-found infor-
mation in the many dream books available. Betsy asks the remaining
twenty or so to gather together in one part of the conference room in a
circle for easier communication.)*

Betsy:
Well, here we are. It's really more my style to sit in a smaller group
like this than to stand up in front of a crowd and play teacher. I like
this better. Let's just keep it informal.

Let me tell you how I thought we'd spend this time—and if you'd
rather go somewhere else with the dreams, that'll be fine with me.

I've got a pile of blank books here, as you can see—some are
bound, and others are looseleaf, and some are small and some are
large. And this one is mine *(she points to a large looseleaf notebook
with a dark blue-designed padded cover, rather elegant)*. It was a
Christmas gift from a special friend, several years ago—in fact, she
and her daughter made it themselves *(she opens the notebook to show
that the inside covers are also covered, in a lavender fabric; there is
heavy unlined art paper for pages, and a ribbon to tie the book together)*. Isn't it nice? And when I opened it, I knew I was supposed to
do something special with this book, but it was a while before I had
any clear idea of what that was—and even longer before I got around
to doing it.

Nurse:
When I saw all these books here, I had a memory of Jung's famous
"Red Book" that he wrote in and painted in—is that your Red
Book?—actually, it's a Blue Book.

Betsy:
That's right—that's just what it is, though not as artistic. How many
of you know about the Red Book? *(Only five or six people have heard
of it.)* Well, I have a picture of it here in this very beautiful volume
titled *C. G. Jung: Word and Image.*[19] And the story behind it is that
in the early 1900's—1913 to be exact—Jung began a tremendous period of encounter with the unconscious (his own, that is) that lasted
about six years. Later, he went on to say that all his later work had
its roots in that period, which would mean his work for the next fifty
years, almost. He died in 1961; and since he was born in 1875, he
would have been almost forty when this six-year period began: married, the father of a family, a well-known psychiatrist with a practice

and favor with Freud (soon to be cut off), a published author in his field, and a faculty member at the University of Zurich.

Parish secretary:
A man in mid-life, like a lot of us. Did he have a mid-life crisis?

Betsy:
Well, yes, that's really what it was. And when he gave up much of his outer position to go within, the fruits of that encounter over-flowed into the Red Book which you see pictured here. It's one of those old-fashioned, leather bound, beautifully engraved volumes we only see in libraries now.

And here are some of the incredible drawings and paintings and script writing he put in this volume *(the following pages of* Word and Image *are turned to show drawings in brilliant colors of strange fig-ures and scenes in art nouveau style)*.

Sister:
If you've ever seen the Laurens van der Post movie about Jung, the book and some of the drawings are in it.[20]

Betsy:
And there's a more recent film called *Matter of Heart*—it's a collec-tion of interviews with Jung's closest colleagues that people from the Los Angeles Jung Institute have helped to put together—which also has some shots of the pages of the Red Book.[21] If you've never seen these films, I really recommend them both—they're quite different, and both will help you get the flavor of this remarkable man.

Anyway, I began working on my Blue Book the fall after I re-turned from studying in Zurich at the Jung Institute. I think the most important thing that happened to me there was that my appre-ciation of this man shifted from focus on his ideas—which had been of great importance to me for more than a decade—to a new appre-ciation of how thoroughly Jung himself lived out his commitment to the life of his soul. Being on his turf, and seeing his home and meet-ing his daughter,[22] and getting the feel of the big lake on which this man had sailed and so on, all made him much more human for me—and helped me be even more aware that we are *all* called to that same kind of commitment to the interior life.

Pastor's wife:
I had that same reaction when we went to Switzerland, too. There's a tendency among many of his followers to divinize Jung, you

know—something he particularly didn't want—and I guess we did that too, in a way *(including her husband with a gesture)*. It was good to see him more as someone who lived his life fully and well.

Betsy:
Yes. A good model for us in that respect, isn't he? Well, to go on, I began to think about some sort of version of the Red Book that was possible for more people—especially, for me, since I felt a need for a special sort of storehouse of that kind, but hadn't gotten around to the right format for myself. By this time I had been logging dreams and doing things with images and symbols from dreams for, oh, twelve years or so—long enough so that I felt I had a dream history.

And I had increasingly upgraded my journals from spiral pads into more lasting blank books filled with pictures—mostly cut out of magazines—and colored inks and paints, so that I felt they were doing justice to my soul life. Something was still missing. The *special* dreams of this whole time had gotten lost in the pages of the many journals and dream logs, and I had this nagging feeling that I had neglected them and not kept their meaning alive.

Pastor:
You mean you hadn't worked on them enough?

Betsy:
No, not exactly that—more that after treasuring them and attending to them and even using their meaning in different ways, *then* they had no place to go. And maybe that's O.K.—but it was more as though a final step hadn't been taken yet, and I didn't know for sure what it was.

And all this time, there was something about Jung's Red Book that spoke to me.

Teacher:
It sounds as though you're headed to some sort of autobiography based on special dreams.

Betsy:
Yes, an inner autobiography, the story of a soul. Not that that's a new idea, but I knew it had to be something visual, because that's the *language* of the soul. And at the same time, I don't have that artistic talent that would make such a project easy.

Now, maybe someone here has done something like this—let's hear from you so I'm not the one doing most of the talking.

Teacher:
Well, I do have a special place for my Big Dreams. A good while back I got into the habit of typing out my dreams separately—at least, the ones I had time to work on. And I'd take one copy to the spiritual director I was with then, and keep one for myself. Then I put together a bunch of folders and divided them up into categories of dreams, like nature dreams and action dreams and animal dreams and special people dreams.

Professor:
So you could trace different themes in your dreams over the years and see how they shifted or grew.

Teacher:
Yes—and it's been very helpful. I have a whole folder now on snake dreams—there were so many I pulled them out of the animals' folder and gave them their own!

Betsy:
And do you put some sort of pictures on the front of the folders—like a snake or Mercury's staff with the snakes or the snake in the Moses and Aaron story?[23] Or does the folder have a snakeskin-print cover?

Teacher:
Well, no, I haven't done that, but I do draw little sketches on the side of the pages, in the margins.

Betsy:
Yes, to stay with the images and not get too abstract and heady. Thanks—a very good approach. Anyone else with ideas on dream— ummm, what's the word? preservation? celebration?

Aerobics instructor:
How about dream appreciation?

Secretary:
Or dream commemoration? or conservation?

Betsy:
All of those, right? Has anyone else had any ideas on how to do this? Or maybe you don't feel the need to save the special dreams or honor them permanently the way I do.

Choir director:
Oh, I have—and I've sort of found a way to keep parts of the special dreams before me. I have a couple of pieces of poster board that I've kept adding pictures to—there's one with the important masculine figures all together, and I keep putting new ones on. Some are dream men, and some are real people who hook that part of me. And the other has women and girls that are special, and some of these are dream people and some come from TV or the movies or books, and others are real women, like my Mom, who's a big part of my feminine side.

Betsy:
Well, that's a good idea, isn't it? And you just keep adding to them—they're your inner family, aren't they?

Choir director:
Uh-huh, and animals are in there too, like a brown bear on the masculine page, from the story of *Rose Red and Snow White*.[24]

Betsy:
So, you got to that place the same way I got to my Blue Book—which was from a feeling that the special dream figures were *too* special to be left behind, even after their message had become clear. It's like, for me, having been given a beautiful gift and then putting it away in a drawer after the newness has worn off, and never appreciating it again. That's what didn't feel right to me.

Pastor:
So, each of you was after a way to string the pearls together.

Betsy:
Yes.

Pastor:
Yes, that seems important—it's like the next step after we learn how to do the things on the handout about working with dreams one at a time.

Betsy:
That's how it has been for me. Now, should we stay on this topic? I thought I could show you some of the ideas I've collected on how to do this—from many people, actually—but I'm also very happy to be as responsive as possible to *your* particular needs. What do you think? *(General consensus is definitely to stay with this idea.)*

Betsy:
O.K. That's what we'll do. And I've brought along some blank books that we keep at the office for people who want to buy them, in case anyone liked this idea and wanted an especially beautiful journal. We just keep them in stock and sell them at cost, so you're welcome to take a look at them later.[25] They're not always easy to find.

Sister:
You know, I wonder if a scroll would work—you could start at the left end of the paper, and just keep adding dreams and pictures and in the end you'd have it all together. And the shape is holy; the scroll itself says: "This is sacred material."

Betsy:
Oh, yes—that would do it, wouldn't it? And Jung even painted figures on the *wall* of his house at Bollingen.[26] That way they would live with you—well, you could do that with the posters too, couldn't you?

Before we keep on brainstorming, I don't want to forget to tell you what I've found to be the *greatest* fruit of my rescuing the special dreams from their resting places and bringing them all together, in addition to being more comfortable about treasuring them. What's emerged is a sense of my own inner journey in a way that's new to me—and I've been using that kind of language for a *long* time, folks, so it's not as if I haven't told my story or seen how my life is part of salvation history, or any of the ways we've been phrasing that idea since the 1960's. But I had never told it in dreams—and when I got the special ones together, one after another, they told my inner story in a new way. It was clearer than ever that God has been with me at the key times in my life, not only in its outer events, but in the dreams I've been sent. The dreams touch me at such a deep level that, well, yes, it's like stringing pearls or jewels on a thread.

Religious education director:
Will you show us what's inside your Blue Book—or isn't that a good idea?

Betsy:
Well, you know, I thought about that. It's a question that has two sides to the answer, doesn't it? But my bottom line and vote is usually on the side of educating, and that means sharing when it's appropriate. I thought I'd show you a few things in here if you're interested *(general interest is expressed)*. Since many of you are professionally involved in others' lives, I know you're going to see the possibilities in this sort of dream record with others too. That's part of tomorrow, though—we don't want to jump too soon into all the what-can-we-do-with-this-stuff? thoughts and skip over what we might do with these ideas for *our own* soul's unfolding.

Pastor's wife:
Just one more question: have you found that pulling together all the Big Dreams helps with your dreaming *now?* I mean, are you remembering more, or having more dreams, or . . . ?

Betsy:
Not *that,* as much as just enjoying them more and appreciating the process more. My guess, if I continue at the rate the book shows, is that each year might bring me, oh, maybe six or seven really special dreams. Maybe not even that many. I'm getting selective now. Actually, my pace is slowing down. But what I do have is a very *strong* feeling of satisfaction, or maybe "delight" would be a better word. It's just so clear now—even more than before—that the guidance I've needed is there when it's needed.

Pastor's wife:
Which helps you trust that it will be there in the future.

Betsy:
For sure—we're in the same valley that the Valley Girls come from, you know, so I can say "for sure."

Bank teller:
The Valley of the Dolls?

Aerobics instructor:
No—the San Fernando Valley!

Betsy:
Well, here's just a few of the things in this book that I'd like to show you. First, there's a title page—but I don't have a title yet. I'm still not sure what to call it.

Parish secretary:
The Blue Book?

Betsy:
Maybe that's what it'll be in the end.

And I put in a table of contents next, because I give the important dreams a title, and this helps me recognize them. And, then, I was looking for some kind of opening theme, and in my first dream log I came across three dreams that were about six months apart each time—so, a year and a half for all three. And each one was about water, and my relationship to it.

Pastor:
Isn't that Jung's only symbol that *definitely* means something?

Betsy:
Yes. Well, the sea, actually, is such a strong image for the unconscious, just as we used it earlier today with the fishing and nets— that was his thought, although he was supremely cautious about reducing any image to a single meaning.

I put pictures of these dreams all on one page from top left to bottom right, so I could see them as a series. *(Betsy holds the book so the group can see the first pictures. There are three sketches within a border, each having a stick figure woman and a few waves.)*

Now, I hope you're encouraged by my art work—if I can do this, I *know* you can. I've had the reverse happening recently in studying art therapy—the majority of people in that field are artists to begin with, and they can just whip out beautiful drawings, which has intimidated me. So, take heart!

The first drawing is a dream in which I was standing on the beach looking at the water. And the second shows me wading into the ocean, just up to my ankles. And the third shows me swimming in the waves.

Bank teller:
And these came just when you were beginning to record your dreams?

Betsy:
Yes, the very first dream log.

Bank teller:
So, you were looking at the unknown waters. Then you began testing them—very cautiously, it appears. And then you were able to feel at home in them. I like that.

Betsy:
This isn't an uncommon sequence—has anyone else had this kind of "getting into the swim of things" dream?

Student:
Well, do surfing dreams count? I've had a series of those, where I was in close to the shore and sort of scared, and then got farther out and more confident, and then got sunk as well.

Betsy:
Oh, yes—that's the same theme, isn't it?

Student:
A lot of my dreams are about water and the ocean, because I live at the beach and spend a lot of time there—I have all my life. It's always been a powerful symbol for me.

Betsy:
So, the image was working on you long before you had any ideas about dreams and symbolism and all that?

Student:
Yes—I've always gone to the ocean to think and get myself together, since I was a little kid.

Teacher:
Betsy, I see you've got the dreams written in next to the pictures, and I see dates and numbers—what are the numbers? And do you always date your dreams as you go along?

Betsy:
Oh yes. I use a plain spiral notebook by my bed to catch the dreams when I wake up, and of course they come out scribbled and just jotted down. But when I finish one dream, I always put the next number to

invite another dream—and then I date it when it comes. So then I have the date and number—which often have some significance too.

Mailwoman:
I've always dated my dreams and I notice the dates. Sometimes a dream will be on someone's birthday who's special to me, or on a holiday or some kind of feast day.

Betsy:
And you look for a connection of the dream content to that date?

Mailwoman:
Yes. It's not always there, but sometimes there's a link.

Betsy:
Yes. The water dream dates are here. Let's see, the first was almost exactly fourteen years ago, and I could look at that as the real beginning of my relationship to the unconscious, to the waters.

Here's another dream I thought I'd show you. It came about two years after the last water dream. This is one I've shared publicly before, so I feel O.K. about doing it again—but there are only a few that I've done that with. It's important to wait till they've been worked through, and aren't "hot" anymore, or else we can lose the dream's power by getting it out there too soon.

This will give you a better idea of what I'm trying to do with the special dreams in my life. You can see I've drawn a picture of it. Let me tell you the dream or read it to you so you'll get a clearer picture.

I am with some people in a car and we need to stop for gas. I'm not driving. We get out of the car and I wander off to the side of the gas station, where there's a huge old stone wall made of large, dark, reddish-brown stones or blocks. I follow a path to the right of this wall, and it turns into a very narrow lane that hugs the wall and drops away to a cliff. The gas station is far behind me now.

Suddenly, I come out into a clearing. It's a beautiful park on a summer's day, and people are picnicking and swimming in a small lake in the middle of the park. I know that the lake is called "Silver Lake." There are flowers and shrubs in bloom and the air is warm. I stand there admiring the park, and then I notice—far in the distance—a very modern, space-age city being built. It's still under construction, but it has towers and a lot of glass and is sparkling in the sunlight.

And that's the dream that's written down here. I titled it "Silver Lake." And—you know—even as I read it again, and it's over ten years old, I still have a sense of awe and wonder at this dream.

Secretary:
Well, I could feel that as you were reading it.

Bank teller:
And that explains why it's important for you to keep it in this way and not let it get lost in a ten year old journal.

Betsy:
Exactly! And we *all* have dreams like this that never lose their power for us—life-transforming dreams. Sometimes I type up the dream on colored paper and put it in, or I write it in—I keep trying to practice calligraphy so even the way the dream's written down will do it justice.

Priest:
Getting back to the Red Book, I was amazed when I saw Jung's beautiful writing—it's like the medieval manuscripts he collected.

Betsy:
Yes—let's look at that again *(she opens* Word and Image *to a page with a drawing of one of Jung's early dream figures and much writing, and passes it around)*. It's medieval looking, very Germanic.

You can see that I've got both a written and a picture version of my dream. I sketched the part of the dream where I'm just rounding the wall and coming upon the lake and the city in the distance. And then, under these, I put down all the associations for each image in the dream—just the way we suggest on the handout you have. Let's just take a couple as an example. What would be possible associations for, let's see, the stone wall?

Graduate student:
Oh, barrier, resistance.

Elderly minister:
Fortress.

Counseling center director:
Blockage, locking out.

Betsy:
All of these—and, I forgot to tell you, I had the sense in the dream that this was the wall of *an armory,* a place where people get ready for war. And it pretty well described and felt like my outer life at that point. So, the bottom line was of an unfriendly, inhospitable place, but in the dream I'm leaving it behind or going around it. I'm being called by "the narrow path"—which makes me think of Jesus' words[27]—the path only wide enough for one person, the individual path.

Priest:
Which looks pretty risky, from your description—and the picture.

Betsy:
Yes, it was a tight squeeze. So I'm leaving behind a way of being where I'm not even driving myself on the road, and where the people driving have run out of fuel or energy, and then being invited into this beautiful, serene place. And I knew in the dream that the lake was named "Silver Lake." What sort of associations would come with that?

Secretary:
Well, silver's the color associated with the moon, so it's the feminine energy waiting there.[28]

Aerobics instructor:
And it's the water again, like a continuation of the water dreams at the beginning of your book. But this water is safer and calmer than the ocean. It's a new body of water to explore.

Pastor:
But it's farther away. You have to go a way to get to it.

Student:
And other people are already in it and enjoying it.

Betsy:
All these things, yes. You can see I listed them here next to "lake" under the picture. It was also clear to me that this was an inner lake, like springs of living water inside me. The whole dream, once I got past the wall, was very quiet and still, even though there are people playing and eating in the park.

Professor:
But, best of all, there's the city in the distance, just going up.

Betsy:
Oh yes—a long way away, but definitely under construction, and shining in the sunlight. What associations might I have listed for that?

Choir director:
Well, I thought right away of the holy city, the new Jerusalem.

Nurse:
A final destination.

Bank teller:
Your new home or dwelling place—since you're leaving the old way behind.

Betsy:
That's about what I put down under associations for the city—and they're all true. Strictly speaking, some are personal associations

and some are what are called amplification, which has the overtone that the association comes from universal lore or the scriptures or folk tales and customs, and so on. "New Jerusalem" would be an amplification of the symbol. It's not just my personal association, but one that many people familiar with the scriptures would come up with.

I see we're going through the steps on the handout, even though I hadn't planned to do that. The next thing I have in my book here is a summary in just a few words of the theme of the dream—what would you have put down if you had been doing this?

Student:
Well, maybe, something like "I'm being called to a better place."

Teacher:
Or, maybe, "There is a place of quiet and rest within me."

Pastor's wife:
"A new home is underway."

Betsy:
Yes, each of these; mine was "I discover the place where I belong." And I've found that coming up with just a short phrase like that, or a sentence, is really helpful in getting perspective on a dream. After I spend time with all the details, this helps put it back together again and brings in some objectivity—that way I can understand the dream better.

And under all this you can see I wrote what I thought was the message of the dream—that's the fifth step on the handout, and the message I put here was that I am supposed to dedicate myself more fully to the inner life. Finally, our step number six, which is some action step or response to the dream message. For this one, I decided upon an increase of time for prayer.

Graduate student:
It's a dream about the kingdom within.

Betsy:
Yes.

Graduate student:
Now, did you do all this as carefully when you first worked with the dream?

Betsy:
Yes, I did it as carefully—I mean, in as much detail. But now in this book I've done it more artistically, more slowly, in a more savoring way.

Pastor:
It's like going back to read over a passage of scripture that grabbed you and got you all worked up when you first stumbled on it, but now it's an old friend—and you can let it soak in more. It goes deeper.

Betsy:
Right, that's it exactly. There's a quality of reminiscence that goes with the dream now. In religious education we talk a lot about reflecting on our faith stories, the way the people of Israel reflected on their history. They had to do this for a long time before it jelled for them. So, what they did in a collective way, we can each do in an individual way.

Two more things go in here, as you can see. By now, I'm up to four pages just on this dream, and the last one has a summary of what was going on in my life at this time, and how the dream sprang out of that context. That's the faith story on an outer level, isn't it? Jacob might have written down his angels-on-the-ladder dream (if he'd had a Blue Book), but then if he had also put in the context of where he was—having just left home after cheating his brother and deceiving his father, separated from the mother who loved him so much, and just *before* he met Rachel—it would take on richer meaning.

The other thing is that special symbols—like the lake and the city and the wall in this dream—have a way of popping up in other places. They can come back in dreams, of course, and then you call them a "recurring dream symbol." But they also come up in our everyday life, and in reading and movies and so forth. They hook onto the dream.

For instance, almost eight years after this dream about Silver Lake, I was working with a therapist and making sand trays.[29] And one of the sand trays turned out to be a representation of a half-built city with a small figure of a woman inside it. Well, it took me about a month to realize that this was a continuation of the dream, and that I had moved—in eight years!—from just seeing the city at a distance, to being *in* the city and helping it get built. The sand tray is like a waking dream in some way, and it was a powerful experience to realize this connection between the two things. I took this picture of it, and put it on the next page *(she shows the photograph of the small sand box and the construction in it)*. And then, you can see, I've been adding lines from reading and poems and so forth that are about the same theme. Here's a note about Alan Hovhaness' piece of music, *The Holy City,* which is a beauty. And listening to it helps me stay connected to this inner holy city.

College student:
I have a question about time—this kind of thing takes a lot of time, I can see.

Betsy:
Yes, it does—I haven't done it all at once though. When I began this book, I decided to just let it write itself at its own pace, and every so often—maybe once a month or every six weeks—I feel like adding another dream to it. I've been going over my early journals and dream logs, and have only gotten through about three or four years of them. It's a kind of prayer for me.

College student:
But you have to have some sort of history in order to be able to see it from this perspective.

Betsy:
Yes—and even if that's just a couple of years, that's a history, isn't it? And, remember, I was almost forty when I began writing down my dreams at all. You're way ahead of me.

Elderly minister:
And I just began a few years ago, when I retired—but already I have a dream history that I think is very rich.

Betsy:
So we're back to the subject of timing, and God's timing being O.K., whenever it unfolds.
   Just a couple of other things I wanted to mention before we stop for lunch—by the way, this Center is famous for its wonderful food, and I smell one of their tamale casseroles already. Those of you who aren't from the southwest, do you know about Tex-Mex food?

Teacher:
Well, I flew in from Philadelphia, and we have it there too—not as hot as Mexican food, right?

Nurse:
Right—you might want to try some of our blue corn meal tortillas before you go, if you don't have them back in Pennsylvania. They're a specialty.

Betsy:
You mentioned earlier *(referring to the teacher who had kept the files on her dream subjects)* the idea of recurring images, and you have files for different topics. Another way to do that, which I probably will add to this book, is a dream glossary or dictionary in the back of it. That can be a summary of your own personal dream images that are most important.

And you know, as you read dream books—like the ones we've referred to and others (I also like Ann Faraday's work a lot, and got lots of practical ideas from her early on[30])—you come up with other ways that could make a collection of dreams even more useful.

There's just one more thing that I want to mention, and it's really important, we think. In fact, for a thorough going over this point, I'll refer you to Jack Sanford's tapes titled *Dreams: Your Royal Road to Healing* from Credence Cassettes in Kansas City.[31] While getting at meaning is certainly what the so-called "dream work" is about, he points out that there's something even more important than meaning, which is very much an ego activity. One reason our dreams aren't always so clear is because meaning is secondary, and the important, primary thing is that the ego may need to experience something greater than itself (especially if it hasn't given recognition to anything greater than itself as yet).

So, my point is that—yes—of course, we do want to be able to grasp some meaning from our dreams, but it may be that the wrestling with them, like Jacob, is what really matters. It moves us away from egocentricity, and points to the ego being the servant of that which is greater than itself. And the symbols may need to stay just symbols, pointers to something beyond, rather than images analyzed to death.

Therapist:
So the dream that leaves us saying "I haven't a clue" may be the most helpful of all?

Betsy:
Yes, if we've stayed with it in one form or another. Just like a good disciple of C. G. Jung, I've presented you with two quite different

ways of being with the dream now—and I end up saying both are valid, and can co-exist, and that the whole process is full of such paradoxes! Confusing?

Other Therapist:
Well, yes and no! How's that for a paradoxical answer? *(His answer is appreciated by the group.)*

Betsy:
Remember, Tom was hinting at this whole idea of the balance of opposites when he asked us to look for images of that in the pictures. And we'll be getting back to this point later today and tomorrow.

So, *un*knowing can be just as valid and necessary as knowing. It's that whole eastern idea of "the one who knows really doesn't know at all" or "those who know are not learned—the learned do not know."[32] Taoist thought and the classic texts, like the *Tao Te Ching* and the *I Ching,* can teach us so much.

Teacher:
That not-having-to-know attitude about the dream reminds me of the fool in the Tarot deck.

Betsy:
Yes.

Homemaker:
And for me it calls to mind all those youngest brothers in the fairy tales—they don't know what to do, and so they can listen to the advice of the fox or the frog or the cat or the dwarf. They know that they *don't* know and that's O.K., whereas their older brothers always think they know what to do—and they lose in the end.

Betsy:
Yes. There needs to be something of the Dummling in us even as we study the meanings of the dream symbols for ourselves. I appreciate your input on this—and I have to admit to you that, as a thinking type rather than an intuiter, I fall back all too easily into the "let's figure it out" mode—thinking types like these neat little outlines with Step One and Step Two and so on. I've learned the most from the friends and people I work with who are feelers and highly intuitive.

Therapist:
So typology plays a role in how we approach the dream, then?

Betsy:
Yes, of course. How could it not? Let's back up a minute here and take a look at how that works. If you know Jungian typology—the four functions of the psyche that the Myers-Briggs Type Indicator supposedly tests out: feeling and thinking, and sensation and intuition—you're aware that we each have all four of these but that one is dominant, or most used. And its opposite is what's called our inferior function, and although we never really have terrific access to this one it is our link to the unconscious part of the psyche or soul, which is why we never have terrific access to it!

Anyway, could it be that those who have, say, thinking as their inferior function are very well served by doing a lot of *thinking about* the dream, and breaking it down into symbols and researching these, and so on, just as our "Six Steps" handout suggests? Then, perhaps, those whose inferior function is intuition might be well-advised to sort of float with the dream, and soak in it, or let it soak into them until their hunches about it become hits. How about those people with little access to sensation?

First Therapist:
They might be the ones for whom art materials and pictures of the dream images would be most helpful.

Her Spouse:
Or working in clay, or even experiencing it in the body.

Betsy:
Yes. And how about the low-feeling folks—what would you suggest for them in being with their dreams?

Pastor:
They might first note their reactions to the dream, which things stood out as important and of value, making a judgment about the dream on that basis.

Betsy:
I'll just invite you to consider this approach, which would root each of our approaches to the dream in our typology. That might be helpful.

Mailwoman:
I hope you don't mind my asking, but after all the work you're putting into that book, what plans do you have for it when you die? I mean, will it be left to someone, or what?

Betsy:
That's a good question—but I don't know yet. I have several grown children, and maybe one of them would want it, but I'm not really sure. Right now, it's the doing of it that's so helpful to me that's important, and I haven't thought about where it will end up; but wouldn't any of us love to have a grandparent's life story like this someday? I have some old letters of my great-grandmother that I treasure—she lived during the Civil War in Virginia, but I don't know much about her inner life from them.

Teacher:
It could be a family history album, in a way.

Secretary:
A *Roots* log.

Betsy:
Yes! Well, so much for my Blue Book, for this morning, at least. What do you think? Is this a usable next step for anyone else?

Pastor's wife:
Oh yes. I want to look over the journals you brought and start one for myself.

Parish secretary:
I have a big scrapbook someone gave me last Christmas, and I've never used it—it would work for a dream collection journal.

Graduate student:
This is a very busy time in my life so I know I can't do something like this now, but hearing about it makes me want to save my dreams and really earmark the special ones so I can get them together sometime.

Professor:
And I'm seeing it as an extension of the personal journaling ideas I use in my psych classes.

Religious education director:
So, you really take seriously all the things about giving time to your own inner life. I'm always torn between the need to do that and all the outer needs that are so pressing. It's a constant battle.

Betsy:
Well, it is, and that's probably never going to change completely, but I guess I've really learned (the hard way) the number one ministry truth, or maybe it's the number two truth—there are two that are so basic. Anyway, it's the old "you can't give what you ain't got." I've learned through experience that the quality of my ministry is directly proportionate to the quality of my own relationship to God. And when I *forget* that, I can fall into activism—the heresy of good works—so easily. It happens all the time.

Now, there're always those people who use introspection and the interior life as an escape from the responsibilities of life. They can be so busy going inward to the kingdom that they forget about the need for the kingdom of God to be growing all around us too. And that's something else, not spiritual growth, isn't it?

Priest:
Escapism.

Counseling center director:
Or just plain selfishness.

Sister:
What's the number two truth you just mentioned?

Betsy:
Oh, well, for me it's "you've got to start where the person you're serving is"—even if that's not what you've planned to do or where you want to be. Do you agree?

Sister:
Oh yes—I'm not sure which one is number one and which is number two. *(Tom appears in the doorway between the two meeting rooms and asks if we can wrap up the morning sessions. We signal that we're through, and he stands where both groups can hear him.)*

Tom:
Lunch will be in a half hour, folks, and then we're going to have a time of silence until three-thirty. You might want to take a nap, and

you could renew your dream intention of last night if you do that. Or it might just be a good time to process this morning's sessions. If anyone would like to talk to either of us alone, let us know and we'll work out a time.

This afternoon, when you return to this room, we're going to move on to the search for our dream guide, the *spiritus rector* (if you like Latin). Some of you have already found such a channel to the dream life, and we hope this will strengthen it, and others may find this a new topic completely.

Betsy:
(moving to the doorway) And if you'd like a last look at the pictures of the dreamers, this would be a good time to get that. We're going to replace them with another set of pictures after lunch; we felt that having both sets up at once would really be an overload.

Tom:
So, *bon appetit* everyone. Enjoy! *(During the lunch time, Tom decides to tell this "naptime story":*

Tom:
When we start to explore dreams it can lead into all kinds of interesting by-ways, and one of them is the whole world of sleep. I'm wondering if many of you know that the church has canonized "Seven Holy Sleepers"—and even given them a feast day, July 27.

Just to give you their tale briefly, and because we might call ourselves "the fifty-seven holy sleepers," let me tell their story:

> Once upon a time, in Ephesus, there were seven leading men in the emperor Decius' household, and they were Christians. When the emperor ordered them to worship idols and deny their faith, they refused, and went off to hide in a cave on a mountain.
>
> Every morning, one of them would disguise himself as a beggar and go to town to beg for the daily food for all. One day, the one who had gone to town returned to the cave in terror, reporting to the other six that the emperor was in a rage about them, and was determined to seek them out and kill them. So, they ate the food he had begged with tears and sighs, and then fell into a deep sleep.
>
> The emperor was furious and learned that they were in the cave, which he then ordered sealed over with stones so that they might perish of hunger on awakening.
>
> However—three hundred and seventy-seven years passed!

The Seven Holy Sleepers awoke one morning and thought it was the very next day. They greeted each other, and got ready to face the evil emperor Decius, who was, of course, long since dead. One of them disguised himself as a beggar, and went into town as usual. There, much to his astonishment, he saw a much-changed Ephesus, with a cross over each gate of the city, and he said to himself, "I must be dreaming!"

Going into the marketplace, he heard people talking about the Christ, and his wonder knew no bounds. When the food vendors saw his few ancient coins, with which he tried to buy some bread, they determined that he must have stumbled on some hidden treasure from the olden times, and so the Holy Sleeper was brought before the bishop. After hearing his story, the bishop realized that some miracle for the sake of the people of Ephesus had indeed taken place, and so he set out with the Sleeper to the cave, after promising not to harm him or his companions. A whole multitude of the townspeople followed them.

There, at the cave, all saw the Seven Holy Sleepers with their faces like "roses in bloom" (the old text says). Falling down, all glorified God. The then-ruling emperor, Theodosius, was called and when he arrived, the faces of the Seven Holy Sleepers "shone like the sun."

Everyone glorified God, and proclaimed that this miracle had been sent to refute the heresy of those who denied the resurrection of the dead. The emperor cast off his hair-shirt which he had worn for penance. One of the Sleepers said to him, "We were alive, lying asleep and feeling naught."

Then the Seven Holy Sleepers bowed their heads to the earth, and fell asleep again, surrendering their souls to God. The emperor wept over them and kissed them, and ordered that seven golden coffins be made for them. However, that very night the Sleepers appeared to him in a dream, and said that they should be returned to the earth, where they had been all this time. And so the emperor was content to seal over the cave once more, this time with gilded stones, and there the Seven Holy Sleepers found their eternal resting place.

And this is the end of the story.[33]

Pastor:
The church's own Rip Van Winkles!

(The next three and a half hours are yours for lunch, reflection, prayer, rest and sleep and dreams—if desired, or for seeking out in-

dividual guidance from one of the conference leaders. You might make notes in your journal or notebook about your reactions to the conference thus far, then use some unscheduled time as you like. After this break, you will be ready to continue with the rest of the second day's schedule.)

The Afternoon Sessions

(When the participants return to the gathering room, they find an art exhibit waiting for them: in one corner are almost thirty colored pictures of a famous scriptural scene, the annunciation to Mary. There are prints of fourth and fifth century icons, illustrations of the scene from medieval books of hours, examples from stained glass, mosaic work and frescoes in many churches, and reproductions of the masterpieces of Renaissance artists from both Italy and northern Europe.[1] In each, an angel has landed before the virgin (who is almost always on the right-hand side of the picture), and in many the very words of the angel are written out: "Hail, full of grace, the Lord is with thee . . ." The group takes time to look at the pictures carefully, while music plays in the background. After about ten minutes, you settle into one of the comfortable arm chairs in the seating area, and the others find their places in preparation for the afternoon session. Again, the signal that it was time to regroup has been Neil Diamond's husky voice singing out Dear Father, *with its statement that we all dream . . .)*

Tom:
Well, welcome back everyone. Let's move along now. I wonder if anything interesting has happened since we were last in this room—does anyone have a story to tell or a question that's come up?

Sister:
I was thinking about the slides of famous dreamers in church history that we saw last night, and wondered if Saint Patrick shouldn't be included in that group. I seem to remember a story about him dreaming that he should return to Ireland as a missionary. Does anyone know about that?

Retired candy-shop owner:
I remember that story too. He did have a dream that changed his life.

Annunciation (1431–1435) painted by Fra Angelico, now in the Prado Museum, Madrid.

His wife:
I think we have a picture of him dreaming at home. Would you like to have it?

Betsy:
Oh yes, that would be a great help. Again, if anyone comes across other pictures of "spiritual dreamers" and can lend them to us to make a slide, we'd really appreciate it.

Tom:
Anyone else with something to ask or tell us?

Young mother, away from her child for the first time:
Well, after lunch I went back to my room to lie down for a while. That's the only time of the day my baby naps now, so I usually nap along with her. I fell asleep and found myself dreaming about last night's topic.

Betsy:
So the incubation took a little more time, but apparently it was at work.

Young mother:
Yes. Can I tell you what it was about?

Betsy:
Would you like to?

Young mother:
Yes, I wrote last night about being concerned that I wasn't doing a good job as a mother. My little girl was born when I was seventeen, and after her birth I realized I didn't know the first thing about babies and how to raise them. I've worried about it all year. Then last night, I made that the subject of my incubation, and came up with a picture of myself holding her in my arms to focus on. I don't remember dreaming at all last night, but when I woke up from my nap this afternoon I just had a flash of her face smiling at me.

Tom:
And how do you feel that was some sort of dream message?

Young mother:
Oh, I just knew from the way she looked so happy that I must be doing a pretty good job after all. *(Group applauds the young woman spontaneously, and those around her offer words of reassurance.)*

Tom:
Well, that's a *very* good example of how the incubation process works, and also of how the unconscious and our consciousness can dialogue with each other. It's as simple as that, really. Thanks for telling us about your little girl and your dream picture.

We're going to shift gears a little now to begin a preparation for this evening's incubation ceremony, which will have a slightly different focus. You've all had a chance to look over the pictures that are on the wall and the tables over in the corner, and they'll be out for the rest of the seminar. Let me tell you a little bit about why those pictures are there:

First, would you think back to the slides we saw last night of the famous dreamers? In many of them, there was a messenger of the dream, wasn't there? What kind of messenger can you recall?

Choir director:
Well, it was often an angel.

Tom:
Yes, which angels can you remember?

Same woman:
There were angels speaking to Joseph a couple of times, and one coming to the wise men.

Business man:
And there was an angel in the picture of St. Ursula.

Elderly minister:
And in the very first picture, Jacob's dream—there were many angels going up and down the ladder to heaven.

Tom:
Yes, and others too. "Angel" comes from the Greek word meaning messenger—and in terms of the dream, which comes from the "other world" of the unconscious, it's appropriate that there be some sort of

link or connection or messenger from that other world, isn't it? What is an angel's most noticeable feature?

Many voices:
The wings.

Tom:
Yes, the wings—and beautiful wings are what the artists whose work we've seen have given them. The simpler peoples of times before ours thought of heaven as "up," and so someone coming from heaven (which was assumed to be the origin-point of the dream) needed to be able to fly, to rise above our earthly level. Wings on a person—or birds, in general—say that they come from the spirit realm, or that they bring a message from God.[2] Do you think we've gotten too sophisticated today for angels?

General murmurs:
I hope not.

Probably!

Who knows?

Tom:
Well, we want to focus now on what is the connecting link for *each of us* to the spirit realm. For some of us, we may like to think in terms of an angel, a winged being, but for others, it may be something quite different. Where we want to head, for this evening's ceremony, is toward delineating for ourselves what our own link or channel to the kingdom of heaven—which *we* know is also within each of us—is like. If we have a strong sense of that link, that channel, it helps us to be better receptors of our dreams, and also of all the other things that come from the kingdom within: touches of God in our daily life, inspirations, prayers that bubble up, and so forth. Are you with me? *(General spirit of being with Tom moves him on.)*

Tom:
Now, getting back to the picture of the annunciation, which has—as you so clearly can see—the angel messenger as one of the two leading characters in the scene, I'm going to let Betsy pick it up here, because these pictures are very special to her and she's been collecting them for, how long?

Betsy:
Oh, at least fifteen years. Maybe even longer. Let's spend a few minutes talking about the ingredients of the annunciation scene. It's certainly not a new picture for any of us, but we want to approach it in a somewhat different way than most of us are used to. In the past, we've often been invited to identify with a figure in a biblical scene—for example, Roman Catholics have strung fifteen of the episodes from the life of Jesus into the rosary, and have usually been encouraged to use Mary as a model for receptivity; most of us think of Jesus as a model for enduring pain and, later, for overcoming death. Those familiar with the Ignatian *Exercises* know about the suggestions to enter into the scene, listen to the conversation going on and so forth.[3] More recently, Lyman Coleman has repopularized what's often called "relational bible study," in which we identify with one character in the episode from scripture: for example, we might be Peter, with Jesus asking us "Do you love me?"[4]

We're going to suggest that we approach the particular biblical event that we have here—the annunciation to Mary that she has been chosen to bear the Son of God—as though all the figures in it are parts of ourself. This is just a translation of the way we work with dreams.[5] We can use the same skills that were on our *6 Steps* handout with the outward picture (it didn't have to be this one of the annunciation, but you'll see why we've chosen this particular story—and it's just as effective for Jews or people of other faiths). Everything in the picture can be seen as some aspect of our own soul; the image is an archetypal one that would have probably found its way to canvas and stained glass even if it had never been recorded in scripture.[6] Another way to say that is: within us, something corresponding to the announcing of new life—God's life—takes place, no matter *what* our belief system. This event can stay unconscious, or we can explore it, live with it, make it ours, consciously. If we do the latter, we'll be in a better position to really live out our own time of annunciation. Now, I'm getting really wordy. Hang in with us, and I think you'll find that where we end up will give us not only a stronger connection with our inner world, but will also provide a broader frame of reference, a rationale for paying attention to our dreams in such detail. We're going to do a little theologizing along the way, to help us see the dream from a wider perspective.

Starting with the angel, then—both the angels of last night's pictures, and the angels in the annunciation scenes over there, for they all perform the task of bringing the message from the other world—what details do you notice about them?

Priest:
In almost all the pictures of the annunciation, the angel is on the left. I believe that's traditionally supposed to symbolize the unconscious, the unknown.[7]

Betsy:
Yes, that's true. Occasionally, the angel is on the right—and it seems that in these rare cases the design of the altarpiece or window or whatever had something to do with the positioning of the figures.[8] Of course, when the first artists painted the scenes, they weren't consciously thinking "I'll put the angel on the left to show him as a messenger from the spiritual realm," but they came out that way because the artists were following a natural tendency within themselves. And once the rules of iconography got fixed, as they did—really, "codified" would be an even better word—the idea stuck. We're implying, however, that it was no accident this messenger from the other world comes from the left.

Priest:
And in some of these pictures today, and in the dream slides last night, there would be God the Father in a little cloud in the upper left-hand corner of the painting, which makes it even clearer that the angel links heaven and earth.

Tom:
That upper left-hand corner, then, would be the farthest possible distance from our world or the world of the dreamer or Mary—that is, the most unconscious. And the angel then becomes what's known as a *hieros gamos* image, from the Greek for "sacred marriage." Let me put that expression on the board here; you can see the root words show up in our words like "hierarchy" and "monogamy" and "polygamy." The sacred marriage in these works of art is between . . . ?

Priest:
Heaven and earth, or spiritual world and material world.

Tom:
Yes, and also between the unconscious and consciousness. This is how we've been describing the dream so far, as something that comes from the unconscious and to which consciousness then has a chance to respond.

Betsy:
So the angel is a *hieros gamos* image in these examples, one of many such images. Just a few of the other common ones are the sacred tree, the ladder (as in Jacob's dream), and even the cross itself, with one arm pointing up to heaven and its crossbar representing the horizontal plane of the earth. This meaning of the cross pre-dates Christianity by centuries. Remember, you were looking for these this morning. And it's good to remember that any of these transcultural, archetypal symbols can have several meanings; we must never limit them to just one. The angel can also stand for the human being at his or her most radiant, letting our light shine—an "earth angel," as they say in Islam.[10]

College student:
Do you remember the old song *Earth Angel?* These ideas even get into our pop culture.

Tom:
Can you sing it for us? *(He does so, hamming it up a little. Applause and laughter.)*

Betsy:
What else did you notice about the angels—or what else is part of your own idea of angels, from scripture or from anywhere else?

Teacher:
Well, don't most of the ones you've shown us have something in their hand? Is it a rod or a staff?

Betsy:
Yes, that's it—a scepter, really. And the scepter would show . . . ?

Teacher:
Well, authority I guess—they're not rulers, but they come from the ruler, from THE Ruler.

Betsy:
That's it. It shows they have the power of the ruler behind them. In some pictures, it might be an olive branch, to indicate that they're on a peaceful mission, or a lit taper, to show that they come with a message from the One who is light—or, to switch back to the psychological language—the source of consciousness. This staff we see

held by the angel evolves in fantasy literature into the wizard's magic wand.

Teacher:
Where it still means the same thing: power, authority.

Betsy:
Right. Oh yes, just for the record I might mention that you will occasionally see a picture that looks like the annunciation, but the angel will have a palm with stars coming from it. Those are pictures from the story of the dormition of the Virgin, and the angel—this time, Michael—is telling Mary her death is approaching. Some of the Sienese artists of the High Middle Ages and a little later used this device.[11]

O.K. What else is there about the angel? Remember, we're heading toward some more clarity about the link between consciousness and unconsciousness in *our* lives, and we hope that by examining one of the most traditional religious images of that link—the angel—it will help us get to know our own connecting link better.

Tom:
Is that called "The Psychic Connection"? *(Laughter.)*

Betsy:
Sure. Why not?

Minister:
Well, something about the angel's gesture—in the dream pictures I noticed that the angel was often touching the dreamer, and maybe when the dreamer awoke he would say something like, "I've been touched by God."

Tom:
And if they aren't touching, they are often pictured as *reaching out* to the dreamer, aren't they? And then in these annunciation pictures, you can see that in the earliest ones the angel is pointing to Mary or extending a hand to her. In a later period, she becomes more like a queen on her throne, as Mary gained a more prominent devotional status in the Christian world, and then the angels often have their arms folded across their breasts, as if they were paying homage to her.

Betsy:
And then the reaching out is shown by words coming from the angels' mouths, either painted right into the scene, or on a scroll—it's called a banderole. Occasionally, Mary's words of "Yes, be it done unto me" are also painted in, to show the dialogue between her and the messenger—but they're put in upside down, so that God the Father up in the corner can read them! If you look closely at the print of the large picture by Jan van Eyck which hangs in the National Gallery in Washington, D.C., you can see this. It's the tall one with the beatific, smiling angel on the table over there, called "The Annunciation in a Church." And look closely at the other pictures: in one you'll notice the angel reaching out to Mary with a letter sealed with a heart—a Valentine![12]

Sister:
Isn't Gabriel the patron saint of mailmen?

Tom:
That's right, sister, and Gabriel is also the patron of communication in general—and of the dream. So all this touching or reaching out—either physically or verbally—on the part of the angels indicates the desire of the unconscious contents to make contact with us, through their carrier. And when the words are actually written into the scene it seems to stress the point that *this message is very real.*

Graduate student:
Well, another thing saying that is the setting of so many of these pictures you've shown us. Often the dreamers were dressed in the costume of the time of the artist, not the traditional clothes of their real time—I'm thinking of the one of Joseph dreaming that he should take Mary and Jesus and run off to Egypt to escape Herod. Joseph is dressed like a man of the Middle Ages, and Mary is in the same sort of clothing.

Homemaker:
And sometimes the pictures are set in buildings of non-biblical times. If you look at all these annunciation pictures, see how many of them look nothing like Nazareth would probably have been—Mary's house has leaded glass windows and brass chandeliers, and there's one over there with a fancy canopy bed all hung in red velvet or satin.[13]

Betsy:
Yes, you've really discovered an important clue here. What is all this "modern" dress and architecture and furnishing saying to the people who look at these pictures?

Homemaker:
Well, it's saying, "This can happen in our time"—or the time of the artist, that is. It says, "This scene didn't just happen once upon a time, but could be happening today."

Betsy:
To . . . ?

Homemaker:
To us.

Betsy:
Yes, and that's very important. Let's put a mental star next to that idea and hold onto it. The angel—or whatever connecting link each of us has to that other world—is part of *anyone,* of *everyone.* The contents of the unconscious of each of us—or, to say that another way: God's revelation (small "r")[14] to each of us—is available as part of our daily life. And, here in this dream seminar, we've been saying that the dream is one of the primary ways in which this revelation is sent. And, *last* point, it's the strength of our link to that world of the dream that can help us hear or not hear the message. (I know we'll be repeating that over and over, but we just want to be sure we stay with the primary purpose of our time together, which is the whys and wherefores of dreams.)

Tom:
You see we need to keep pulling ourselves back—both of us have been known to wander far afield! One last thing on how the angels in these pictures reach out and touch someone—I wonder if they work for the phone company? Look carefully at the annunciation pictures again, and you'll see one Byzantine mosaic over there in which the angel is handing a sphere to Mary, and another one—an icon from Russia—with a transparent sphere that has a cross in it. What's that about?

Bank teller:
Well, the circle is one of the signs of psychological wholeness, isn't it? So, wouldn't the sphere be an even greater sign of that? The angel is giving Mary the key to her wholeness.[15]

Betsy:
Exactly, that's what it's about. Let's wrap up the angel qualities now: we've said the angels are winged, suggesting the ability to transcend—and to transcend swiftly—the barriers between the two worlds. They are sent from one with power—God, who often appears in these pictures too, just so we won't forget the source of the message. They reach out to us, and the message can come in our everyday surroundings; the connection with the world of spirit isn't something obscure or extraordinary, but very homely and natural. And the totality of the message, the end result, is our psychological and spiritual—I like the word "psychospiritual"—wholeness.[16] Now we probably won't achieve that while we're here on earth, but it's what each of us is headed toward.

So, whether or not all of this communication from the other world reaches us depends upon our own connectedness to it, and the strength of that link. And *that's* what all these powerful and beautiful angels are about.

Tom:
I'd just like to point out one more aspect of this idea. You'll notice in the dream pictures last night that contained angels, and in all these of the annunciation today, the attitude of the angels. Always, they are reverent, gentle, respectful; they kneel, or walk in softly, or hover in the air as though they're about to come in for a three-point landing—but very gently. If they touch someone, it's just barely, usually with one finger. This correlates to the attitude of God toward us. *Usually,* the interior life isn't forced on us; we are invited to it, sent messages from it, but not pushed into it. However, any such archetypal idea has its opposite side, and there is the "hound of heaven" concept, or the angel wrestling with Jacob—the image of God pursuing us relentlessly and grappling with us.

There are even flip sides of the annunciation scene, such as the story of Danaë from Greek mythology, where Zeus impregnates her by a shower of gold without her permission. She becomes the mother of Perseus.[17] Then, in the strange pictures that come to us from the world of alchemy—the process which C. G. Jung compared so thoroughly to the individuation process—there is one you might come across called "Gilding the Queen." It has the same idea, impregnation with lumps of gold, this time—and it's very different from the reverent attitude of the angels we've been looking at.[18] However, the result is the same: impregnation with that which is from the world which is "other."

There's a point here about listening intentionally to the inner messages so they don't have to be forced on us.

Betsy:
The basic Jungian principle of "the unconscious treats you in the same way you treat it". . .

Let's stop for about ten minutes now, just for a stretch break. It'll give us another chance to look at all the annunciation pictures. But let's just close this part of our afternoon with a short prayer. Will you join me?

"God, Author of dreams, Creator of angels, help us each to strengthen our own connection to your world within us, the world of spirit. Whether that bridge be angelic, strong like the archangel Gabriel whose name means "God is my strength,"[19] or whether it be completely different, help us to develop it, become aware of it, pay attention to it. We thank you for the way you have made us. Amen."
(You drift back to the corner containing the pictures of the annunciation. Sure enough, there are several angels with scrolls coming from their mouths, and what variety is found in their wings! The artists have used all their colors here, from black lined with white to multicolors which make the angels kin to the peacock.[20] One by Fra Angelico has a finger to his lips as if to say to Mary, "Be still and listen."[21] The angels of the icons, from the eastern church, look as if they're performing a dance step; they are true petitioners for the "Lord of the Dance." Different people find a favorite annunciation scene; others are overheard to say, "I can't find myself in this picture at all."

You notice that a variety of art supplies are being set out, which leads you to speculate with others on the second half of the afternoon session.)

Tom:
Let's begin again, shall we? You can see we have something creative (well, we hope it will be) planned for today, so we want to be sure to leave enough time for it. *(You take your seat again. By now, it's beginning to feel like your own turf.)*

Betsy:
I think I'd better tell you where we're going just so no one catastrophizes. Not so long ago, I know I used to freeze when the crayons and paper came out, but since I've been doing what is sometimes called "active imagination," that seems to have passed. If you're still at the freezing stage with art supplies, just hang in—I know you'll find it's worth the effort to try to visualize for yourself some of the things we're now using words alone to describe.

Later on, we'll ask you to take time with the paper here and the coloring materials to *try* to depict your own link or *hieros gamos* image, that which is in you that joins consciousness and unconsciousness. There are so many possible ways to picture such a link or connection, and we've been exploring the angel in depth because it's just one of them. The valuable thing will be for each of us to picture *our own* channel in *our own* way; having examined one possibility—the angel—will help us understand links in general better.

Student:
Should we start coming up with our own link now?

Betsy:
Well, yes and no. Let's just call this a germinating time. In fact, since this part of us is usually much more unconscious than conscious, we'll do best to let it arise from the unconscious. What we'd like to do now is stay with the pictures of the annunciation just a little longer. This particular scene contains some other very helpful clues about receptivity to the contents of the inner world, and among those contents, of course, the dream is foremost.

Tom:
And the annunciation, because it is the beginning of the actual story of Jesus, leads us to another, much more theoretical way of understanding the entire inner growth process. We'll talk about that tomorrow morning.

Betsy:
O.K. Let's look just a bit at the second major figure in this scene, which is Mary, of course. We want to remember that we're approaching these pictures as, somehow, pictures of an event in *our* lives—and, as we saw, the artists who painted them understood that too. That's why they used contemporary settings and clothing for their figures.

How about Mary? All of you are familiar with the scriptural description of this scene from her life. What would you want to point out about her either from the biblical version in Luke or from any or all of the art work we have here today?

Carpenter:
Well, we talked about the angel coming from the left. In almost all the pictures, Mary is facing left; she's watching to hear—or to see— what's coming at her from that other world you're talking about.

Betsy:
Yes, she is. She's *almost waiting* for something to come to her from "the left," isn't she? Good. What else?

Sister:
Well, for years her "fiat" or "yes," Mary saying "Let it be done unto me according to your word," was used as the model for a lot of us. It has been seen as the proper attitude toward the Spirit, another way of saying "Thy will be done." She's a good model for that all her life, but perhaps especially so at this moment.

Tom:
That sort of fits with the idea of receptivity, of really being ready to follow the impulses of God within us, no matter how unusual they may seem. I think if I'd been in her shoes—or sandals?—my response would much more likely have been "Oh no!"—or, at least, "I'll have to think about that."

Of course, we don't know exactly how the scene went; what we have is the distillation of its essence, and the receptivity of Mary is what comes through. Maybe she really did say "You've got to be kidding," or "I hope it's a girl," but the story has lived in a certain form— with her receptive "yes," that is—because that's how *we* need to recall it. We need to know about that part of us which is potentially *that open* to the movement of God's life in us.

Betsy:
So, you're saying it's no accident that the story of this encounter has come down to us in this form, then? It's as though the human soul has retained verbal and pictorial descriptions of what *it* needs from the earliest times, just to remind ourselves of the basic attitudes that are essential to life. The exactness or the historicity of this story or

scene, or any story, isn't the point when you're seeing it as a mirror of something in the soul. Did I say what I think you were saying?

Tom:
Yes, that's it. A good example is the way you retell the story of St. Barbara, who was sealed in a tower. She probably never existed, but people needed to keep her story alive because it corresponded to something within their psyches.[22]

Betsy:
And her story is also an annunciation story: she is impregnated by God. Let's just note then that receptivity is one of the qualities associated in Jungian thought (and many ancient traditions in which that psychology is rooted) with *the feminine principle*—and, along the same lines of thought, both men and women contain energies that we can characterize as "feminine."[23] Looked at that way, Mary can stand for the receptive side of both men and women. This isn't just a picture of *a woman's* soul. Do you see the fine distinction we're making here between the older, familiar approach of "Use Mary as a model," and a sort of psychical photography approach that says this scene (or any scene that attracts us) is a snapshot of our soul—and all the ingredients of the scene represent something in us? It's an intrapsychic approach.

So, rather than saying "Be like Mary," we're saying "What does the Mary of the picture correspond to in you or in me?" It's not completely different, but there is a distinction that's very important—because the first approach asks us to change consciously, by using our egos, to act and think more like Mary (or Ruth, or Jesus, or whoever), and the second approach says that Mary or whoever *already* lives in us; she stands for something in us that's—perhaps—not yet conscious and available to us.

Tom:
But can potentially become available.

Betsy:
Yes, that's it. Edward Edinger, whose work we'll keep referring to, puts it this way: he says as long as we're just relating to the holy figures as other people, their power is covered over by the art. The art keeps the image safely locked in the picture.[24]

I don't want to labor the point, but do you see the difference?

Salesman:
Can I try it again?

Betsy:
Try it again.

Salesman:
Using your example of the annunciation then, when I look at Mary in any of these pictures, I need to see her as standing for something in me, a part of me. And having heard enough Jungian talk over the years, that would be, for me, the feminine side of my personality, the anima.

Betsy:
Yes. If you speak classical Jungian, that's exactly what we're saying. Of course, there's also neo-Jungian and post-Jungian—but we won't get into that! And for a woman?

Salesman:
Well, for a woman those inner feminine energies are closer to the surface. They might be very up front, or they might be shadow women still waiting to be discovered.

Betsy:
That's really a perfect description of what Mary in these pictures is about. Thanks. Is there anything else anyone wants to mention about her—remembering that "her" is really part of you and of me?

Aerobics instructor:
In many of the pictures, she has a book on her lap or on a prayer stand in front of her, as though she's been reading or saying her prayers.

Betsy:
St. Bernard of Clairvaux, back in the 1100's, said that Mary was reading the Hebrew scriptures when the angel came to visit her, particularly the prophecy about herself: "A virgin shall be with child . . . who will be called Emmanuel." The reference is Isaiah 7:14. She was thinking about how special it would be for whoever that woman was, not knowing it was about herself.[25] The point for us and for our finding of ourselves in this picture is that Mary is a woman rooted in her history and tradition. She's done some homework. Let's talk about her as "virgin," in general.

Same woman:
I remember a book by Esther Harding, in which she writes about the image of virginity. She says, I think, that it stands for being self-contained, about knowing that you have what you need within you so that you don't keep on just being a reactor to those around you and the outside, everyday life. She calls it something like "one-unto-one's-self-ness."

Betsy:
That's important. The physical virginity isn't the point here as much as the psychological virginity or self-containment. Another way to say that is to talk about a healthy, strong ego or sense of "me," the "I'm O.K." of the Transactional Analysis psychologists and educators. We need to have that ego-strength if we're going to encounter the other world, the transpersonal—or, that which is beyond the personal, beyond "me."

It's as though the bearing—and you can understand that word as carrying new life and also as carrying a heavy burden, like the cross—of God within us is so tremendous an experience, that if we're not strong, we will burst with it. Dr. Edinger talks about how it will "blast us."[26]

Graduate instructor:
I have a favorite verse that's just about that. Would you like to hear it?

Tom:
Of course.

Graduate instructor:
I think it's medieval. It goes:

> Who am I, that into such as me
> —one tiny drop—should come the sea?

Tom:
Well, the source is Angelus Silesius, who wrote little two-liners like that back in the seventeenth century.[27] (You'll see later on that I've been boning up on him. He was one of that later bunch of German mystical writers that included Johann Arndt and Jacob Boehme, and they had been inspired by a revival of the fourteenth century Rhineland mystics like Meister Eckhart and Henry Suso and Tauler and

the rest.) Thanks. And yes, it shows perfectly how we can be over-powered by the contents of the unconscious (which is what we call psychosis)[28] if we don't have a strongly established ego with which to meet them. That sense of self is the "virgin" in each of us, men and women.

Religious education director:
And one of the biggest challenges I face is counteracting all the old religious teaching about ourselves being worthless.

Tom:
Yes, and I think I shouldn't get started on *that*—one of my pet peeves—or we'll really go far away from our twofold topic of dreams and connecting to the world inside. By the way, the book you referred to by Esther Harding was *Woman's Mysteries*,[29] wasn't it?—just in case someone wants to pursue this. Another excellent book with more on the idea of psychological virginity is Jean Bolen's *Goddesses in Everywoman*.[30]

Betsy:
The idea of putting ourselves down comes from a misunderstanding of teachings such as "I must decrease that he may increase," and many others—and you're right! if we go off on that ship we may never see our dream port again! Tom and I have a book out titled *Coming Home*,[31] in which we do go into the idea of ego and beyond-the-ego thoroughly, just in case you want to explore the ideas on that topic further.

(For myself, I have a favorite teacher about the virgin archetype, and that is my cat—and other people's cats as well. You know how self-contained and self-sufficient they are, don't you? It's no wonder cats have been worshiped as goddesses in some past times, especially in ancient Egypt.[32]) Is there anything else about the Mary of the annunciation you'd want to mention? Remember, we're zeroing in on how this entire picture is about ourselves, especially about the link to that inner cosmos we keep talking about, and now we're just taking a look at the ingredients in the picture other than the angel, who stands for that connecting link.

Insurance agent:
The words in the bible say she's troubled by the message she gets, and the angel has to tell her not to be afraid. That says to me that

the encounter with the transpersonal, as you call it, is scary. Some of my dreams are very frightening.

Betsy:
Dreams can be terrifying sometimes, and the encounter with the divine can be terrifying. Remember Jonah? And many other of Mary's ancestors? All through the Hebrew scriptures we have stories about this. After all, if we listen to God we may have to change our lives, which can be very scary. We're going to be talking more about the work of Dr. Edinger of Los Angeles tomorrow; he points out that the words in the *Jerusalem Bible* translation of Luke's story have the angel saying " . . . the power of the Most High will cover you with its shadow . . . " and how that is indeed terrifying. He gives the example of the baby chick, which will run if a shadow crosses its path; this instinct is part of the infant chicken's inner reality, and a built-in protection against predatory birds like hawks that do "overshadow" it. "Overshadowing" means to cast a cloud over something—a cloud just like one of the earliest biblical descriptions of God.[33]

Young mother:
And the end result of this scene is that Mary conceives; she becomes pregnant with new life that's going to have the name "God with us" (Emmanuel). So, are you saying that if we say yes to this sometimes scary linking up with the other world within us, we can have the same thing happen?

Tom:
That's exactly what we're saying. And the dream, once we connect to it, is one of the most powerful of all ways we know that "God is with us." So then, Mary's attitude—as she is presented in the biblical story and in Christian art down through the centuries—is what must surface from within each of us who would also *knowingly* carry that divine life.

Betsy:
You know, I've lived with this idea for a long time now, but it still moves me to hear it spoken of so personally. And I *still* am hooked by these pictures and keep coming back to them. It's no accident that this is probably the third most-pictured scene in Christian art. What do you think are the two scenes most often shown, just for the record?

Voices from the group:
The crucifixion.

Christmas, the nativity.

Easter, the resurrection.

Betsy:
The birth and death of Jesus, yes, and then this scene, the annunciation. There are more representations of this initial moment of the feminine being filled by the Spirit of God than of Easter. Isn't that amazing? But, maybe it's not; it's the beginning of the inner odyssey, and maybe many of us never get to resurrection.

Here's what we're going to do now. We've moved into the premise that the annunciation can happen to each of us, that these pictures represent something in our own inner life, potentially, at least. We've taken a good look at the two major figures in the pictures and biblical telling of the story, the angel and Mary, and we've talked about how they each correspond to something in each of us. And we've also seen how they picture the attitude we need in order to harness and make use of the contents of our dreams.

On the walls of the room we've put up large pieces of blank paper, and at the top you can see there are headings. The first here is "Spirit of God," then there's "Plant Life," and "Signs of Old and New," and then "Enclosed Space," and "Mood," meaning the general mood or tone of the setting in these pictures. Let's take another ten minutes, and we invite you to come up and jot down on these pages anything you see in the paintings over there that fits in one of these five categories. If you want to take it to the next step and add a note on what it corresponds to in the soul, do that too. You may want to go back and forth and look at the pictures again or reread the scripture—it's Luke 1:26–38 here in the bible—and you'll want to see what's already on the paper so we don't have fifty people repeating the same idea.

We know there are some people in every group who may not want to speak out, and this will give each of us a chance to have our ideas woven into the fabric of this weekend—so go to it and then we'll pull them together. *(You study your picture(s) of the annunciation, and in your notebook write something down under as many of the headings as you can:* Spirit of God, Plant Life, Signs of Old and New, Enclosed Space, *and* Mood. *The room is full of activity, as people go back and forth to study the pictures. The papers on the walls begin to fill up with many people's ideas, including your own.)*

Tom:
Well, let's see what we've got here. How about if I read the main ideas on each of these pages, and let's remember that this entire scene is like a directive to us about how to allow God to conceive new life within us. For some of us, God may have been experienced only as "out there"—and here comes a call to know that God's also available to us "in here." Most of us have probably already lived out that second reality somewhat, or we wouldn't have come to a dream workshop, but we may need a reminder of this powerful truth, or a fine-tuning of the skills that help us stay in touch with God "in here."

O.K., on the "Spirit of God" page you've listed the dove, the traditional emblem of the Holy Spirit. The bird stands for rising, for spirit. Someone added "white"—again, the idea of light, consciousness penetrating us.

You found the rays of light in many of the pictures, always coming from that upper left-hand or most unconscious part of the setting. Again, consciousness is what's being communicated to and encased in Mary. Someone put down "cloud," as we mentioned earlier, and then added, "cloud in the desert, at the tabernacle—Mary is a tabernacle here, we are tabernacles."[34]

Betsy:
That idea could also go on the "Enclosed Space" sheet, couldn't it?

Tom:
Oh, yes. Here's one more thought about the Spirit of God: a couple of the icons have not a dove descending from heaven, but a circle with a dot in the center. Yes, and here's someone who noticed one with God the Father sort of throwing out a ball or a sphere. In both, Mary is being sent that which will make her total; we met that idea earlier when we saw the angels holding out spheres to her. Now, she's having them rained down on her. Be careful what you pray for, we're told—you never know what's going to come down on you. I'm surprised someone hasn't painted this scene with a lightning bolt zapping the mother of God!

Elderly woman:
Maybe that idea was so tied to the ancient pagan gods that the Christians didn't want to use it.

Tom:
That's probably just what happened. I'm glad you thought of it. Let's take a look at the "Plant Life" sheet now: the plant that stands out, of course, is the lily. Sometimes the archangel holds it, in which case it stands for religious illumination, which we know comes with angels. Sometimes the lilies are in a vase, and we take them to represent Mary's kinship to the bride of the Canticles, who says, "I am the lily of the valley."[35] The picture is about a spiritual marriage, isn't it? Remember—this is our picture too. Lilies are usually associated with purity or virginity, which we've talked about, and with Easter—so they say, here, many things, including the thought that from this event in Mary's life, in our life, rebirth can come about. Oh, good, someone noted that the feast of the annunciation is celebrated on March 25, just nine months before Christmas, but also at the time of the spring equinox, a time when more light begins to come on the earth, more consciousness. Springtime: the time of rebirth (think how often Easter comes at about March 25).

Betsy:
"Lilies in a vase," someone wrote. Again, the idea of the vessel or container or enclosed space. Sometimes the vases are clear glass, translucent—"Let your light shine" from within that container.

Tom:
There are pages of lily-lore in the good symbols dictionaries, like Cirlot.[36] You might want to do more research on all of these. Here's one more thing: someone wrote "field of flowers outside Mary's home." Yes, some of these are what's called a *millefleurs* picture, with just an abundance of spring flowers carpeting the landscape. Again, these tell us that it's springtime, that new life is occurring.

Betsy:
The outer world mirrors our inner world.

Tom:
The olive branch, when it's in the picture, shows that this is a time of peace—or something that can lead to peace. I like that. And you noted that some of the pictures have trees, but always in the distance. Well, the tree is another connector of heaven and earth, but what else does it stand for in Christian art?

Waitress:
The cross, the tree on which Jesus was crucified.

Tom:
Yes, and so with this special moment of being filled with the Spirit of God, there's also the awareness or even the warning that down the road, somewhere in the distance, the cross waits too. You don't have the joy without its opposite as well. Shall I talk about *enantio-dromia?*

Betsy:
Oh, please don't! I'm just kidding—that's a favorite word of Tom's, and he always finds a way to get it in—but it's a good word, and we can talk about it if you'd like.

Tom:
We'd better go on! Let's look at the "Signs of Old and New" page. Why don't you take it over, Betsy, so I can collect my thoughts on *enantiodromia?*

Betsy:
You know we're going to hear about it now, don't you? O.K., oh, you found three of these: there's one picture by Petrus Christus of Flanders that's in the Metropolitan in New York. Yes, that's it *(someone is holding it up)*. Mary is in the doorway of a church, in a gown with ermine trim on it (this is a long way from Nazareth, folks), and behind the angel facing her is a crumbling wall. That stands for—well, what do you think?

Another Sister:
Is it for the old way, the life of living the law only, as contrasted with the new life of the spirit?

Betsy:
Yes, that's it.

Sister:
And the old way is crumbling.

Betsy:
Yes. We no longer need it. Not that we don't need the law, but just that the spirit is a higher law, if you like. It's Paul saying, "The letter kills, but the spirit gives life."[37] The old way is outer-directed; you let someone else tell you how to find God. The new way, symbolized

for us by Mary here—but remember, she is standing for our feminine, receptive side too—is inner-directed.

The other scene that shows that even more clearly is the van Eyck picture we talked about before. Would someone bring that over?—it's the tall thin picture with the smiling angel that has such gorgeous wings. *(A middle-aged man brings it before the group.)* Here it is, and someone looked carefully and saw that Mary is standing on a floor of marble, in which are scenes from the story of the people of Israel. Here's Samson, and here's David. This says that— well, what *does* it say?

Teacher:
It could say that she—or, rather, what she stands for, this new way— is taking the place of the old, or it could say that the Old Testament is the foundation for the New.[38]

Betsy:
Or both, couldn't it? Let's go with both, rather than an "either-or" choice. There are always different facets and layers of meanings as we begin to contact the contents within. ("When I was a child, I thought as a child . . . " and so on.) Jung talks about how we need to turn around in the middle of our lives and look inward, but that the first half of life is needed, by most people, to adapt to the world and find one's place.[39] And why? So we can develop that healthy and strong ego we need to meet the contents of the unconscious—or, as we put it earlier?

Young mother:
To become "virgins." Gee, I get a second chance! *(Laughter)*

Tom:
All kinds of miracles in the new age, right?

Betsy:
But, again, if these pictures of the annunciation are being looked at by us, for now, as inner snapshots, what does this juxtaposition of old and new mean in our lives? What is *my* "old way"? If I face the left, the unconscious, and hear the message, and say "yes" to it, what might that mean in terms of change in my life? We don't have to answer that right now—I just throw it out to us so we can remember our point of view.

The third old-and-new pair is found in a couple of the Fra Angelico paintings we've brought pictures of,[40] and also in the one with the strange house of Mary that looks more like the pleasure dome of Kublai Khan.[41] It's that one in the middle, with the angel's arms folded very sternly, if someone would bring it over.

Grocery store clerk:
This one?

Betsy:
Yes.

Same man:
It looks more like the Pussycat Theatre in Santa Monica.

Betsy:
(amid laughter) You can tell us about that at dinner! Actually, it does look like the Pussycat—I'm just guessing, of course. *Anyway,* you can see here that Adam and Eve appear in the background of the picture; in all three of these examples, they're leaving the garden, and are despondent, even weeping.

Same man:
I felt that way when I left the movie last time too. No, seriously, they're in the picture to show that the new is fixing up the old, right?

Betsy:
Yes, and Paul talks about it too, comparing Jesus and Adam. Dr. Edinger mentions in his talks on this topic that he has pictures with Eve and the serpent in the background; again, examples of that old comparison of Eve and Mary, which we can look at not in a derogatory "women are the cause of evil" way, but more as two sides of the same story. Both Eve and Mary are facing the numinous, a greater power, that which is "other."[42] There are many layers here. We might even compare Eve's serpent with Mary's angel—there is a similarity, zoologically speaking—between scales and wings, between snakes and birds. It's as though we can't have the light side without the dark side, or the new without the old. Eve lives within us too.

Tom:
Now I have to talk about *enantiodromia!* It just means the tendency of the psyche to fluctuate between the opposites, or for an opposite to be constellated when we spend a good deal of time with the other op-

posite. And, certainly, in history we've had plenty of examples of that. It's a good word, isn't it? It's from the Greek words for "a running" and "the opposites."[43] So, these pictures show the opposites of Adam and Eve running into Mary and Jesus, just being conceived. What is that picture's background, Betsy? It looks a little older than Santa Monica.

Betsy:
Yes, it is a little older, from the fifteenth century, in fact. This is also in the National Gallery in Washington, and if you send to them for their catalogue of color reprints you can get it for almost nothing. Notice that the angel is *pushing* Adam and Eve out of Paradise! And in the landscape below them are rabbits, hares—often in these *millefleurs* pictures to symbolize fertility and new life, just as the flowers do. It's by Giovanni di Paolo, one of the great artists of early Renaissance Siena. This is one of my favorites.

Tom:
So it's really a picture of paradise lost—and paradise regained, then.

Betsy:
It certainly is, just that. Later, I'll put the addresses of some of the museum catalogue stores from which these prints came on the board so you can have them if you want copies.[44] We have wonderful art treasures right here in the United States, as you probably know. Now, we have two more sheets to look at. Let's talk about mood for a moment.

Tom:
I'd like to do that one, because it's another favorite subject of mine. Let's see, you wrote down words like "calm" and "still" and "peaceful" and "holy." Here's "quiet," and here's "reverent." How would you translate this mood into *your* daily living?

Secretary:
Well, it's like setting apart some time for prayer, and just for being quiet. You have to be still to hear the message.

Tom:
Yes, that's it. In so many of these pictures, and in the dream pictures we saw last night, it was as though time was standing still, don't you think? We have to build that kind of time into our lives if we're going

to do the inner work well. I should add that I keep trying to find other language than "inner work"—that makes the spiritual life sound so arduous.

Same woman:
Well, how much time do you recommend spending on your inner . . . whatever we want to call it?

Tom:
That varies, but I certainly recommend trying for an hour a day— that hour to include whatever kind of prayer works best for you, attending to whatever important dreams have come along, writing in your journal, doing active imagination. Many people would say an hour isn't nearly enough. I know, I know. You have to make a living. It's as though the interior life is a vocation too, and if you're called to it, you make the time. Don't try to *find* the time, though—it'll never be there just lying around.

One of the best and most comforting things I've learned is that if you don't get a dream message the first or second or third time around—either because you haven't had time to work on the dream, or because it just won't let itself be unlocked—the message will keep coming until you do get it—IF you've made the time commitment we're talking about.

Student:
Maybe this should be a thirty day seminar.

Tom:
Maybe it should be—but our scene also tells us that the Spirit comes in the middle of everyday activities. Now, Betsy will do the last sheet and then we'll have a pre-dinner break.

Betsy:
Let's look over here on the "Enclosed Space" page. We've got "church" and "house" and "cloister" and "monastery." Remember, we also need to add "Mary" as another example of the enclosed space; she stands for us as tabernacle. Even the vase that is so present here is a sign of that enclosure or containment. Now, one of the favorite words in Jungian circles is another Greek word, *temenos*.[45]

Tom:
My word is longer.

Betsy:

That's right, but I've got another one coming up tomorrow that puts *enantiodromia* in the shade! Anyway, *temenos* means sacred space or precinct, set-apart space, like a temple or sanctuary or sacred grove.

Sister:

Or the paradise garden.

Betsy:

Yes, or Jerusalem, the holy city, or the new Jerusalem in the Book of Revelation, which is a mandalic-shaped *temenos*.

Our dream logs are also enclosed spaces, aren't they? A journal is a set-apart space. The idea is that in such a place, the message can take root; it's like a pot or a plot of ground to a plant. Close relationships can be containers too—relationships with a spouse, a special friend, a spiritual guide or therapist or counselor, a prayer partner. Just as we need set-apart or sacred time to hear the inner messages, we also need set-apart and sacred space. That's what the virgin is doing in these buildings. We never see the annunciation taking place out in a field or on the main street of Florence or Ghent, do we? No, it's always in some set-apart space or place, and that says something about our need for the same in our lives.

If you read the apocryphal books of the bible, the ones that got left out, you learn all sorts of interesting addenda to the biblical stories. I'm sure many of you are familiar with them, especially the more recent finds at Nag Hammadi in Egypt.[46] Well, for a longer time we've had a book titled the *Protevangelion,* a Gospel ascribed to James the Less, who was the first bishop of Jerusalem, you recall.[47] In chapter nine of this book is a fascinating sidelight on the annunciation scene. We read that Mary had gone to the well for water, in the evening. She heard a voice addressing her, but couldn't quite get the message, nor could she find the messenger. Trembling, she went back into her house and picked up her spinning, and once inside—in her enclosed space, her *temenos*—she was able to hear the message and to dialogue with the messenger. She needed to be contained in order to become container. Do you like that? I do. *(General agreement)*

Homemaker:

It certainly makes me think again about the value of creating a home for others, and for myself.

Betsy:

Yes. Yes, indeed. And even without a quiet *place,* we can learn to experience our *selves* as enclosures, as Catherine of Siena did.[48]

Tom:

How about pulling all this together now? Are you all still here? Are you with us? *(General agreement)*

Tom:

We spent last evening and this morning on the dream, specifically. This afternoon, we've broadened our viewpoint to get a look at a whole way of living that starts, for each of us, in a way that is—somehow—like the annunciation of the angel to Mary. Listen to Thomas Merton's way of describing this experience when it happens to you or to me:

> We awaken not only to a realization of the immensity and majesty of God "out there" as . . . Ruler of the universe . . . but also to a more intimate and more wonderful perception (of God) as directly and personally present in our own being.[49]

Merton is talking about the contemplative life. And here is Dr. Edinger's succinct summary of this moment of annunciation in an individual's life; he is using the language of Jung's psychology:

> . . . it symbolizes the soul's impregnating encounter with the Self. It is a moment of immense danger and ambiguity.[50]

We will, as I said, explore his work a little more tomorrow morning, and I think you will find it profoundly interesting. Dr. Edinger also uncovered an unpublished quote from C. G. Jung in which he says that if he were to choose *one* image of a person's original experience of the autonomous psyche—we would say, perhaps, the spiritual realm within or the transpersonal—he would choose the annunciation image. This was in 1925.[51] *The dream* finds its place in a spiritual life that is focused on the immanent God, in the way Merton describes. It is the most numinous contact many of us ever have with the God within. And switching back to the language of psychology, we can see the dream as the major way in which the Self—the living image of God within us, Augustine's *imago Dei*—communicates with us, a form of prayer. Without this sort of framework that the annunciation picture or some other theoretical schema gives us, we may not have a very good idea of the purpose of the dream, or from whence it comes, or what the goal of the process of spiritual growth is. So, we've stepped back a bit to get some perspective, using this very special and familiar scene of the angel and the virgin to picture ourselves. You can see that we've applied to the annunciation scene some of our steps for honoring a dream that we discussed this morning.

Betsy:
We'll be seeing that this picture, the first in the story of Jesus, is also the first in a process within our soul's life—whether we're Christians or not. And, we must remember that—just as in physical pregnancies—the new life that is conceived can also be miscarried, or even aborted.

Let's get back to our starting point of this afternoon—the idea of discovering something more about that connecting link to the life of God which our pictures represent by the angel. That will be a less solemn note on which to close the afternoon. We have, as we said, some art supplies all around. In the three quarters of an hour before supper, you may want to rest or refresh yourselves, but we'd like to encourage you to use what's here and begin to let a picture emerge from within you. *(Barely audible music can now be heard. It is restful.)*

Each of us might have a completely different way of depicting our own connection or link or bridge between the two worlds of heaven and earth, or between the unconscious and consciousness. Let's try to keep a silence, so that whoever does want to draw or doodle can get into a reflective state and allow whatever wants to come up from inside do just that. What we're after is some representation of our own *hieros gamos* channels—and maybe, for some of us, the angel will surface. Our link, however, might look quite different, and I don't want to make any suggestions because the important thing is for each of us to get to know what *our own* bridge or messenger part is like. You may feel more moved to write than to draw—perhaps a letter or a poem or just journal-type entries. You might prefer to stretch out and listen to the music that will be playing, and let your imagination take you off somewhere—somewhere where you may find an image for your own messenger of dreams.

The important thing will be to become more aware of how this connection, which is the dream connection, works or feels in yourself—and any way you can do that, even just to a small degree, will be helpful. So, we'll stop talking now and let the silence and the music take over. You may want to just sit quietly where you are for a while. The bell will ring for dinner in just under an hour, and we'll be here if anyone has any questions about the active imagination work. *(The group disperses around the large room, and some go off. Quiet music fills the room, as you choose materials with which to work. In your notebook or journal draw or write about your own angel—or its equivalent. You have almost an hour to allow any image or words about your dream connection to emerge.)*

The Evening Sessions

(The evening has come. It is after suppertime, and the group—now becoming a community—is re-collecting in the large meeting room. You join them, finding your now-staked-out spot, bringing with you the work you did during the afternoon session. Spend some time letting it speak to you, as the Dear Father *music calls everyone together.)*

Tom:
We're about ready for our second evening together, and its shape will be very much like what we experienced together yesterday evening. This time, we hope you're a little more rested and relaxed. Friday nights usually aren't our best times if we've been working all week long. By the way, let's forgive Neil Diamond for his exclusive language—it's an old song, you know.

Betsy:
Do all of you have your work of this afternoon with you? We meant to remind you at supper that it would be good to have it for this evening. If any of you need to go back to your room to get a drawing or something you wrote, there's time now to do that.

Let's talk a little about your experience of creating an image or description of that part of you that's the connecting link between the two worlds of consciousness and unconsciousness. Any reflections? feedback? problems? questions?

University professor:
I went back to the pictures of the annunciation we were talking about this afternoon. I had a feeling that I wanted to draw my own link in some way that was *sort of* like an angel—but not exactly. Then I noticed one of the modern versions of this scene, the picture inside a little country house, with Mary at her sewing machine.

Tom:
Why don't you get it and bring it over here?

Professor:
This one *(holding it up to the group)*. I don't know where it's from, but it's obviously drawn by someone from our time.

Tom:
Yes, it's by a contemporary Nicaraguan artist, sort of a primitive or Grandma Moses style. The woman who painted it was part of the Solentiname community of Ernesto Cardenal.

Professor:
Well, Mary has on a red dress, as you can see. And the angel is a man in a white suit—but you know he's not just a human being because he has sort of a neon-lights halo around his head, just little dots. He's walking in like an ordinary guest and he looks as though he's saying "Hi there!"[1]

Betsy:
Did this picture help you get a handle on something inside yourself?

Professor:
Yes. As I looked at it I got a sense of my own link being less magnificent than all the beautiful winged angels in the other pictures. For me, this picture gave me a lead on how my own bridge is represented better by a gesture: a hand reaching out, just as the man in the picture has his hand reaching out to Mary. I drew an outstretched hand, and I spent some time trying to feel that inside my own psyche, and it began to change into a swinging door, one that opens to let something through and then closes off again. So, that's what I finally came up with and got down on paper. Here it is. *(The professor shows the group his swinging door picture, drawn very precisely, as though for a floor plan blueprint. The little arrows indicating the swing are there; later you discover he is on the faculty of an engineering school.)*
Is this the kind of thing you had in mind?

Betsy:
It's exactly the kind of thing we had in mind—and it's important to stress that there's no right or wrong way to have envisioned this important part of ourselves. Maybe some of you have *no idea* of that component in you that joins the worlds of "I" and "not-I."[2] That's O.K.

too; if we want to know about this part of ourself, it will come, in God's time, not ours.

Tom:
What you really want to say is "don't sweat it," right?

Betsy:
Right! While you're up here with the picture of the swinging door, why don't we see if anyone else came up with something similar? You went from outreaching hand to swinging door, in fact. Does that tie in with anyone else's discoveries? Incidentally, please know that whenever we ask questions like that, we also have an unspoken rule that says "Please feel free to keep quiet about what you're doing and not share it with anyone, if that's better for you."

Nurse:
I began with a door, but it was a Dutch door—you know, with a top half and a bottom half. That way, I could open just a part of it if I wanted to, or open it all the way. Then I felt I should change to a window as my image, because that's something I have a little more control over. For example, you can see *through* a window, but not necessarily let in what you see on the other side.

Tom:
And how does that translate in terms of your inner life?

Nurse:
Well, long before I began to experience the parts of myself that are what we'd call archetypal, I read about them.

Betsy:
You looked at them as though through a window.

Nurse:
Yes, but of course just reading about, say, the shadow or the animus[3] isn't the same thing as actually experiencing them—or letting them in.

Betsy:
That's for sure! With a window, then, you can raise it a little or all the way—or you can just look through it. That brings us back to our point of this afternoon about the need for one to have a strong ego or

sense of self (small "s") before too much connecting with the inner world is undertaken intentionally.

Tom:
Which is not to say that the numinosity of God's life within us can't overtake us and shatter right through the window or door or whatever, at any time.

Betsy:
Paul on the Damascus road is a good example of that, probably the favorite example of spiritual clobbering.

Jung points out that it's not uncommon for those who are beginning to encounter the unconscious to assume that it knows more, knows better than consciousness. The pitfall here is that we then allow ourselves to follow the input from the unconscious—whether that comes to us in dreams, or some other way—as though it had the last word.[4] A person with a strong ego (or consciousness) won't allow that to happen; he or she will initiate and continue a dialogue with the contents of the unconscious, and act out of that dialogue. That's like being in charge of the door or the window, isn't it?

Tom:
But there's always this tension when you deal with any pair of opposites. The annunciation gives us a good example of it. On one hand, we could say that Mary *was* being zapped—"overpowered" is probably the word we'd choose—by this angelic visit, just as we can feel brought to our knees when we have a powerful message from the unconscious. On the other hand, she isn't taken, like some of the mythological women we talked about this afternoon. She has an option to listen or not listen, to say "yes" or "no." So, when the story tells us that she said "yes" and was still a virgin, we can translate that to psychological language and say she dialogued with the contents of the unconscious, and her strong ego or sense of self remained intact. She wasn't overpowered. To get back to your examples, she kept her hand on the doorknob or the window frame.

Teacher:
I don't want to labor the point, but just let me be sure I'm with you. You're saying that when we take the annunciation story psychologically, the matter of Mary's virginity is *very* important, even though the exegetes are still arguing about whether or not that's a question or a non-question historically, physically, factually.

Tom:
That's right. O.K. now, is there another type of image that surfaced as you spent time alone this afternoon?

Assorted voices:
I liked the idea of bridge, and I drew that.

My picture came out like a canal between two levels—sort of a channel.

I wrote instead of drawing, and came up with a description of an elevator that stopped at different floors until it arrived at the roof or penthouse.

I had a ski lift operating, from inside a shed on the ground to the highest peak of a mountain.

Betsy:
And *all* of these images are two-way images, aren't they? They illustrate just what we've been talking about, the need for dialogue between "I" and "not-I."

Retired teacher:
When I thought about it and prayed about how to describe my own inner link, the angel kept coming back to me. There have been times when I've felt some sort of presence that I could almost say was like an angel—the swiftness, the gentleness, the power all rolled into one. So, I drew an angel and I'd like to show it to you. *(She holds up a beautiful drawing of a multi-colored angel, wings wide-spread and filled with strength. Many appreciative remarks from the group members.)*

Betsy:
And you happen to be an artist, as well! It's *really beautiful*. Well, that gives us a good lead into the next part of this evening. We want to begin to create an atmosphere for the incubation ceremony which we'll use to close the evening, and since we've begun with the concept of the angel as one representation—just one of many possible representations—of that within us which links the worlds of knowing and not-yet-knowing—let's stay with it a little longer. From now on, though, when you hear or see "angel," see if you can substitute whatever image *you* have discovered that is your connection for now between these worlds. And, if you haven't come up with anything yet (or, I should say, if nothing has come up yet), why not use the angel for this evening—and keep listening and praying to see what your

particular image will be? It may *be* the angel, or it may be something we haven't even mentioned yet.

What we're going to do now is learn a song to sing as part of our ceremony later on. This is an English folk carol from long ago, from the Devonshire region, which is in the far western, Celtic tip of Great Britain, just before Cornwall. It comes from *The Oxford Book of Carols*,[5] it's number thirty-seven in that collection, which is the standard reference work for these Anglo-American folk carols.

Tom:
(as song sheets with the carol and its music are passed out) Betsy and I are pretty good at some things, but we're not great song leaders; you'll have to help us out with this. It always makes me feel better when I hear someone say that folk songs are best sung by the untrained voice.

Betsy:
And one of the important things to note about this carol, like so many of the late medieval and early Renaissance folk hymns, is that it's didactic. Whoever made up these verses was a teacher. Many, many of the old carols have as a closing stanza a direct appeal or message for the listener, a real instruction that says—just like the pictures we saw where the artist made an ancient scene look contemporary— "This is about *us,* folks. It may have happened originally way back when, but it's also happening today to you and me." We've revised a few words of the last stanza (which is something folk tradition has always allowed for) so it will fit our own meaning here as fully as possible—but, basically, this is the way the carol has always been sung. In the printed version it has a few more verses too; incidentally, this is just one of six carols for the feast of the annunciation (or the feast of the incarnation, as it used to be called in the old calendars).[6] These are songs that have their origin in pre-Reformation Britain, but were, ultimately, kept alive by the Anglican Church and Protestantism in general.[7] So, they're ecumenical, just as this group is.

Minister:
And our similarities are much greater than our differences!

Spontaneous reaction from many:
Amen!

Tom:
So, here's the carol, and please, just join in as you get the tune. The chorus melody is very much like the stanzas, so it will be easy to pick up: (see music on p. 118).

(Applause for the group from Tom and Betsy.)

Betsy:
Great! Do you like it? *(General agreement.)*

Betsy:
We've added the guitar chords, in case you want to play it for yourself later. Remember, if you were to copy this music for any sort of performed use, you'd have to get permission from the publisher, which is the Oxford University Press, with offices in New York City.

Good! We've got all the ingredients for our ceremony of induction this evening. Is there anything else to be brought up before we go over the instructions for that? Any loose ends? Inspirations?

Temple religious school director:
Just that when we first began talking about this image of Mary and the angel, which is, of course, a Christian mystery and not part of the Jewish tradition, I wondered whether or not I could connect with it. I know you're saying that these long-lived scenes have stayed alive because they live in all of us, whether one has a Jewish psyche or a Christian one, but I did wonder, since I'm Jewish.

It does work for me, though. I think all those who have ever been invited to a closer union with God can find themselves in this particular story.

Tom:
And if you were doing something like this with an audience that was largely Jewish, is there some similar story that would be even more familiar to them, which could be used to make the same point?

Temple director:
Oh, I'm sure there is. Let's see—maybe Abram responding to God's call to leave Haran and go west,[8] and Samuel, of course.

Betsy:
One reason we like the annunciation scene is because the feminine—in us, in the story—is the one receiving the message. It's the feminine energy in us that is, perhaps, more likely to hear and attend to these

The angel Gabriel from God
Was sent to Galilee
Unto a virgin fair and free,
Whose name was called Mary.
And when the angel thither came,
He fell down on his knee.
And looking up in the virgin's face,
He said, "All hail, Mary":
THEN SING WE ALL, BOTH GREAT AND SMALL, 'NO-WELL, NO-WELL, NO-WELL'; WE MAY REJOICE TO HEAR THE VOICE OF THE ANGEL — GABRIEL.

2. 'Mary,' he said, 'be not afraid,
   But do believe in me:
   The power of the Holy Ghost
   Shall overshadow thee;
   Thou shalt conceive without any grief,
   As the Lord told unto me:
   God's own dear Son from heaven shall come,
   And shall be born of thee':
   THEN SING WE ALL, ETC.

3. Good people all, both great and small,
   All ye who hear our voice,
   With one accord do praise the Lord,
   And in our hearts rejoice;
   For God may come to one and all
   While we our lives do spend;
   With hearts transformed, We'll be reborn--
   And so, let my carol end:
   THEN SING WE ALL, ETC.

inner invitations, whether we're men or women. The hero stories of the Hebrew bible are harder to use in this way, although they're excellent on *responding to* the message, on doing something with it. Abraham née Abram picks up his family and tents and all those camels and *does something,* doesn't he? That's an example of what's called "the masculine energy" in Jungian language.[9]

Tom:
And at seventy-five, one would have to have a lot of masculine energy to do all he did!

Betsy:
Well, that brings us to one other loose end, which is, how do the men who are here feel about Mary standing for a part of themselves? Is that workable for you?

Tom:
Especially, is it workable if the idea of feminine energies being part of a man's soul is new to you?[10]

Youth minister:
The idea is pretty well in circulation today, don't you think? When I was growing up in the 1960's, it was in the air, so it has always made sense to me.

Elderly minister:
Still, our culture really hasn't done a whole lot to encourage men and boys to live this out. I think it's been more of an idea than a reality. Look, I'm seventy-one years old, and while the idea of having a feminine side makes sense to me intellectually, it's really only been in the past five years that I've been able to call on it—or would you say "her?"—deliberately.

Tom:
You're saying, then, that it's been there—and I'm sure you've had plenty of opportunity to use those qualities of receptivity and listening and holding within yourself over the years—but that you weren't aware of the feminine within.

Minister:
Yes. To go back to the language of Jung, the anima was just a concept until I began listening to my dreams and doing the active imagination work with them. And it's work; it takes time.

Betsy:
And a commitment to the reality of the psyche.

Minister:
Yes.

Private investigator:
Well, I'm new to the whole idea, but I'm here to learn, so I'm trying to be open. I'll let you know tomorrow.

Tom:
O.K. Let's move on then to our immediate preparation for the cere-mony. Maybe we should use the churchy expression "proximate prep-aration." That comes after "remote preparation," as you'll recall if you ever learned meditation in a step-by-step way. (Actually, I'm trying to show you that I can speak Ignatian as well as Jungian.)

Our purpose in this evening's ceremony is twofold:

First, we want to have you re-experience the technique of dream evoking or invoking, so that you'll have one more experience of it. Then, when you want to use this procedure at home, you'll have a couple of live memories on which to fall back.

Second, whereas last night we were calling out for a dream about a particular concern in our lives, tonight we'll all focus on the same matter: the strengthening of that part of ourselves that is the link between consciousness and the unconscious. Some of us have an im-age of that link; others don't have an image yet, and can use the an-gel or any of the several which were mentioned earlier until their own image emerges.

Betsy:
Would you put in front of you, if they're not already there, the papers you drew or wrote on this afternoon, before supper?

And, now, let's settle down just a little, getting as comfortable as we can here. I'm going to ask you to focus on what it was that you drew or wrote. *(Restful music begins in the background.)* At this time, see if there's anything more you'd care to add to your image— or take away from it. If you had no response earlier, if nothing at all came, choose now any one of the images you like, something that symbolizes "linking" or "bridging" to you. Just sketch it or write down the name of it: bridge . . . channel . . . elevator . . . angel . . .

(Now is the time to make any refinements in your earlier drawing or verbal description of your inner connection. It has grown dark out-

*side; the lights have been dimmed and candles are being lit around
the room. The music is ethereal and soothing. Night has come, and—
soon—the time for dreaming.)*

Tom:

It's time for our ceremony to begin. Let's start with prayer, with the
giving of this evening to our God.

"Creator, we come together this night once again. Our hearts are
like Samuel's, saying 'Speak, Lord, your servant is listening,' and
like Mary's: receptive, open, waiting, trusting. We come with song
this night, song about an event long past yet always happening—
even in our day. And our prayer is that the song may mirror our souls
and our lives; that the waiting and listening part of ourselves will be
as open as the Mary of our song; that we may each know and have
strengthened that part in us which is the channel for your revelation."

Would you all join us now in the carol we rehearsed earlier? And,
this time, let's sing it prayerfully, seeing the image of Mary in the
carol as that receptive, feminine part of each of us. *(All join in singing "The Angel Gabriel" softly, the words on the song sheets just visible by the candlelight.)*

Betsy:

This afternoon we heard a verse from the seventeenth century by the
man who was called Angelus Silesius. Tonight, we read from him
again; *he* knew that the annunciation scene we've been soaking in
was not just about a woman of Nazareth:

> "Hail Mary!" so thou greetedst Her:
> Yet, Gabriel, what doth this avail
> To me, unless thou likewise come
> And greet me with the self-same "Hail!"?
> I must be Mary and myself
> Give birth to God, would I possess
> —Nor can I otherwise—God's gift
> Of everlasting happiness.[11]

Tom:

And now, a dream from someone who prayed, as we are doing this
night, that his link with that world of spirit be strengthened. The
ultimate dream of this sort is probably Jacob's ladder dream, which
we saw last night, but this is one from someone of our time and mind,
a construction worker who has given us permission to use his dream:

I am in my house. One door is ajar, a door I never noticed before. It leads from my bedroom to . . . I do not know where. Something tells me I must look on the other side of the door. When I do, I find there a dark corridor, which I enter.

At first, I can see nothing, and then—as my eyes grow accustomed to the darkness—I begin to make out closed doors along the corridor, and at the far end, a very dim light.

Although I am still in a building, I have an overwhelming impression of being in a birth canal.

(There is a pause, time to absorb this dream.)

Betsy:

Now, let's focus on our own written work or drawing about our own inner channel once more. The purpose of our incubation tonight is the development of that connection. This is the bridge to the place in us from which comes the dream, and the awareness of God's life within us, and our creativity, and all the inspirations that bubble up from inside our souls. *(Dreamy music begins again.)*

And, as you're focusing on what you've got before you, let me give you the directions for the rest of the night and the morning. They are the same as last night's, so won't be so strange this time.

In a few minutes, we'll ask you to leave this room, keeping silence. Get ready for bed—as much as you feel you want to before coming back for the deeper part of the ceremony. Before you return, place the paper you're holding now under your pillow. Stand by your bed and pray or bless it in whatever way is natural for you, asking that it be that set-apart space where the dream will come, and that the night's rest will also be a time when your own connection to the inner world is made even more firm than it is just now.

Be sure your dream log and something with which to write is by your bedside, and when your place of sleep feels as though it's ready to receive you later, come back to this room, quietly. We'll maintain the silence until we meet before breakfast tomorrow morning.

Those of you who are commuting, just relax here and visualize your room and bed at home—your sacred space. As you drive home later, you can keep your picture or words before you as much as it's possible to do and still drive safely. Then, you'll want to get to bed as quickly and quietly as possible once you're home. *(You follow the directions, preparing for bed and then attending to your place of rest. About fifteen minutes elapses, and then you silently return to the meeting room. A familiar hymn is being played and sung softly, repetitively; you join in:*

"Breathe on me, Breath of God,
Fill me with life anew
That I may love what Thou dost love
And do what Thou wouldst do."[12]

Tom:
It seems as if we're all here together now, so I want to welcome you to our dream invocation ceremony. *(The music changes to harp chords, slowly plucked.)*

Let's help our bodies relax even more, so they'll be ready to sleep—perchance to dream. Tonight, I'll ask you to do this by focusing on your breathing, just being aware of the breath coming in and out. Slow down the rate of your breathing, and allow any strain or tension within you to flow out with each exhalation.

Betsy:
We are gathered here, God, your holy people, asking that our means of hearing you, receiving you, being filled with you, deepen. We give this night's rest to you, expecting nothing, but watching and waiting for whatever gift you would send. We pray together that our hearts be like Mary's who, so long ago, was open to the message which came through *her* messenger, the angel. May we find ourselves in this story; may the annunciation be our story too, in many variations. *(Onto the wall of the dark room in which, now, just a few candles are burning down, is projected a picture of the annunciation. The virgin is in a simple room with a gold and white tiled floor and small casement windows on the left. Dressed in white, she is supported by two miniature angels as she listens to the words of the archangel—a youthful yet regal being in a brocaded robe of red and gold. The dove which represents God's Spirit hovers over her head, its halo beginning to penetrate her. The painting has a hushed quality to it, as though time is standing still.)*[13]

As the familiar scriptural lines are now read, will you place yourself in this scene, allowing the annunciation story to be a still photograph of something that is happening in your own life, in the way we've been discussing it this afternoon and this evening? Let the "Mary" of the story stand for that which is receptive in you, and that which is virgin or strong. *(The slide changes to another artist's rendering of the annunciation, then another. Before the scripture passage is completed, there have been projected over thirty versions of this scene, as envisioned by artists from east and west, yesterday and today.)*

Tom:

(reading slowly, and saying the name of Mary in a very low voice so that retreatants can substitute their own names)

> The angel Gabriel was sent from God to a town of Galilee called Nazareth, to a virgin betrothed to a man . . .
>
> and the virgin's name was Mary. And when the angel had come to her, he said, "Hail, full of grace, the Lord is with you. Blessed are you among women." When she had heard him she was troubled at his word, and kept pondering what manner of greeting this might be.
>
> And the angel said to her, "Do not be afraid, Mary, for you have found grace with God. Behold, you will conceive . . . and shall bring forth a child (who will be) great . . . and of his kingdom there shall be no end. . . . The Holy Spirit shall come upon you and the power of the Most High shall overshadow you . . . for nothing is impossible with God."
>
> (And) Mary said, "Behold the handmaid of the Lord; be it done to me according to your word." And the angel departed from her.[14]

Betsy:

As the music continues to play, we invite you to focus again on your own link, your own "angel." Rather than thinking *about* it, just be with it and let the symbol or description you've come up with soak into you. As you're doing this, we want to go around the room and bless you, as we did last night. Tonight we'll be laying on hands instead of using holy water, and—again—just raise your hand if you'd rather we didn't. *(You sit in stillness, focused on your own inward channel. The last slide of the annunciation is still projected on the front wall of the meeting room. The candles have burned even lower, and the music, now, is more dreamlike than before.*

Down your row of chairs comes Betsy, wearing a long blue oriental robe. When she reaches you, she places a hand on your head and says, "May your time of sleep this night be a time of deepening and strengthening of your access to the kingdom within. _____ (your name), may God be with you.")

Before Tom gives a final dream invocation, I want to remind you of the next steps. Just go to bed as quietly and swiftly as possible. As you lie in bed, let whatever is on your paper stay with you. Ask God for a dream that will—somehow—connect with your image, at the same time letting go of any expectations. Our hope is that you will fall asleep with the image you have chosen in your mind and heart.

In the morning, do just as you did this morning. Maintaining si-

lence, write whatever comes to you. Perhaps there will be a dream—
a complete one, or just a trace, a fragment. Perhaps no nighttime
memories will remain; lie quietly, and record whatever occurs to you.
It may be sounds from outside, or from others in the building. It may
be a memory that seems to have no connection at all to our topic. It
may be a song, or a visual image.

If there's time, continue with morning prayer in whatever way
is best and most natural for you. There will be music at 7:30 to let
you know that we're about to gather, and we'll meet back *here,* still
in silence, at 8:00 tomorrow morning.

Tom:

(over the dream music)

> I am quiet. I come apart from the larger group, my companions, to
> go within . . . to that place of rest and quiet, of stillness and peace—
> my innermost chamber, set apart from the busy world which sur-
> rounds me.
>
> Here, I can listen. Here, the receptive part of me is at home.
> Here, I wait for whatever will be sent to me.
>
> Sometimes I am afraid. How do I know what may come to this
> silent place that listens? What message may penetrate my heart?
> my soul? my life? Perhaps it will be something that brings change.
> If I really listen, my life may never be the same.
>
> Wait now! There is a stirring! The messenger comes . . . the
> link to my God, to the greater life within me. What manner of mes-
> senger is this? How will it speak to me? How shall I greet it? What
> form shall it take?
>
> I welcome this link to the world within me, the deeper well of
> peace and riches, the kingdom within me. Yes, this way of knowing
> has been with me since childhood . . . though I have often allowed
> it to be covered over. This night I ask that my link, my bridge to
> that place be clear. I thank God for inner knowing . . . for annun-
> ciation.
>
> Gabriel! angel of salutation![15] angel of annunciation! be with
> us as we sleep! You who are called "the supervisor of dreams" in
> the Jewish mystical tradition, you who are "the spirit of truth" to
> the people of Islam,[16] you who came to Mary, interceding for the
> God who longed to dwell within her, be with us! You, of whom it is
> said your wings stretch from east to west, and your hairs each have
> the brightness of the moon and stars, patron of dreams, be with
> us![17] This night, may *we* be strengthened in whatever it is in *us*
> that speaks of the other world, as was Mary . . .
>
> Let me say "yes" to the message I am sent. Let me say "yes"

to being filled with spirit. Come, Emmanuel, God with us. This night, may you find a dwelling place in my heart . . . and bear new life in me.

(As the final words are spoken by Tom, the projected slide of the annunciation changes to one of the pregnant virgin, great with child. It is a picture of a statue from Gothic times, perhaps something that might be in the Cloisters in New York City.)[18]

Betsy:
The Lord speaks to those who are beloved in dreams and visions of the night. May you have a blessed sleep. Good night and sweet dreams. *(The room is still, except for the final, fading notes of the dream invocation music. There are some muffled sounds—a sigh, some tears being wiped away—and, then, the members of the group rise and move silently to their rooms. You do the same, taking a last look at the woman filled with God's life whose picture is still on the wall. Quietly, the candles are snuffed out and this part of the workshop comes to a close. Silently, you go to your bed and lie down to enter sleep.)*

The Third Day

Morning Prayer

In your journal record any dreams or dream fragments of the night; . . . and write down your first impressions upon waking (awareness of sounds, colors, objects in your room, etc.).

Take some time for further elaborations on the gifts which may have come during sleep. In your notebook you may draw, make associations to dream images, pray in word or picture, or write about the night-gifts. (A bell, followed by sweet sounds of music, tells you it is 7:30 in the morning. The day will open for the community in a half an hour. You finish up your journaling and prepare for the day, arriving in the gathering room at 8:00 to greet the others. By now, many seem to be old friends, not because you have spent much time with any one, but because you have all shared in experiences that touch that deep layer of the human being where all are alike.

You notice both Tom and Betsy quietly talking with individuals, some of whom have in their hands their pictures from the day before—pictures which have spent the night as seeds under their pillows. In the center of the end of the room is a lectern, on which is a golden icon of the annunciation. Going up to it, you see that it is different from any of the other representations of the day before, all of which still circle the room. This painting, with Mary on a red-cushioned throne and the Holy Spirit encircled by a gold disk, has across its base a stream. In the water of the stream are fishes, many-legged octopus-like creatures, and seaweed; water fowl wade in the stream and find their way up to the land under the angel and the virgin.[1])

Tom:
Good morning!

General response:
Good morning!

Tom:
If you haven't had a chance to greet those around you, why don't you do that now? (*This sharing of greetings for the new day takes almost*

five minutes, as people who were strangers two days ago shake hands and embrace. You seek out those who have made some special impact upon you.)

Tom:
Let's form a circle around the icon on the stand here. *(You end up facing the icon, which is at an angle. In the background, Neil Diamond sings once again to the Father. The music takes precedence over the conversation, and a quiet circle is formed. The music recalls the night that has just passed.)*

Tom:
(reading from Psalm 108):

> My heart is ready, God,
> I will sing and chant praise.
> Wake up, my soul!
> Awake, lyre and harp!
> I will wake up the sun!
> I will give thanks to you among the peoples, O Lord;
> I will play music to you among the nations;
> For your love is high as the heavens,
> and your faithfulness as the clouds.
> God, show your greatness in the sky,
> and your glory over all the earth!
> Save us by your might; answer my prayer,
> so that the people you love may be rescued!

Betsy:
O God, Creator of night and now of day, we come together this new day in thankfulness for the hours since last we met. Each of us has our own prayer, and those of us who wish to speak of their thanks do so now . . . *(A time of spontaneous prayer follows, with thanks offered for sleep and dreams, for the new day, for the community of like-believers. You too formulate your own words of thanksgiving, which can be recorded here. Whatever your faith expression, join in as it seems appropriate.)*

Tom:
On Christmas Eve of 1978, as the Christian churches anticipated once again the birth of divinity, Archbishop Oscar Romero preached these words. They were among his last:

"God's eternal purpose has thought of all of you, and that thought is incarnated in the womb of God, as Mary incarnated the Word."[2]

Last night we asked our God to make us more mindful of just how closely we are bound to him or to her—or however it is you envision God. We are each incarnated in the womb of God, and have been and will be for eternity—just as God is incarnated in us. As a reminder of where we left off before we went to sleep, let's sing together again the last verse of the carol—the words are still posted on the wall here: *(You join in with the others to the words*

"Good people all, both great and small,
     All ye who hear our voice,
With one accord do praise the Lord,
     And in our hearts rejoice;
For God may come to one and all
     While we our lives do spend;
With hearts transformed, we'll be reborn—
     And so, let my carol end:
Then sing we all, both great and small,
     'Nowell, Nowell, Nowell:'
We may rejoice to hear the voice
     Of the angel Gabriel.")

Betsy:
Our song, our subject for dream invocation, our reminder from Bishop Romero are all about one thing: union with God. Here in the twentieth century in the United States, we are still as restless as Augustine was back in the fourth century in Africa when he wrote his famous words. Who would like to speak them for us?

College student:
"You have made us for yourself, O Lord, and our hearts are restless until they rest in you."[3]

Betsy:
The religious life, the contemplative life—even if it's lived out driving a truck or nine to five behind a desk—is what we've been praying about; this is what *the dream* is about.

Tom:
Let me say a word about the icon on the stand. In the eastern Christian churches, the icon of the feast is often put before the assembly

in this way, and people venerate it by walking up to it, entering into it reverently, sometimes kissing it. They often approach with their arms folded across their breast, like this *(demonstrating)*, bowing before it in the fashion of the eastern rite churches. Since this is the icon of the feast we're centering upon, we invite you to do the same if that seems suitable to you. It will be here throughout the day—and you will want to take a look at the differences in this icon from the other pictures of the annunciation.

Deacon of Melkite rite church:
Do you know that the annunciation is the scene that is specified for the folding doors on the iconostasis—the screen before the sanctuary? It marks the entrance into the holy of holies—and that's how we've been regarding this scene too, as an entryway into our holy of holies.[4]

Tom:
No, I didn't know that—but it fits perfectly, doesn't it? I'm glad you mentioned that. Well, it's almost breakfast time, and we wanted to be sure to say that there's space here to display your pictures or whatever you slept with under your pillow, if any of you would like to put yours up after breakfast.

We've encouraged, as you heard yesterday, keeping special inner contents (like dreams and active imagination projects) in a contained space—your journal and/or the relationship between dreamer and guide. There's, somehow, a lack of reverence for these inner contents when we just leave them around or show them to just anyone. But this room and this group *are* containers, just as the temple or the church can be a container. And it seems that we've established that sense of community that makes it appropriate to share things from our inner world with each other—if that feels right to the sharer. So, for those who'd like to grace our day with their work from yesterday, there are cork strips on the wall and push pins on the table.

Betsy:
Also, it seemed prudent to meet here this morning so our icon wouldn't be attacked by a goose! Let's sing a verse of our dream song as a closing to morning prayer. Then we'll eat—the coffee smells wonderful—have a break and return here at 9:30. *(All join in the cho-*

rus and first verse of What You Hear in the Dark, *onto which a spontaneous "Amen!" is added. Before breakfast, you look at the icon once more. Mary's throne is before a palace, all very Byzantine; in a "roof garden" of the palace grow trees and plants, amid which two birds are nesting.)*

The Morning Sessions

(After breakfast you return to the large room and see that several people have posted their drawings and symbols from yesterday. Instantly eye-catching is the retired teacher's brilliant angel. There are also much simpler sketches: a door, a gate, a tunnel with a light at the end, a window, a canal, a ladder, a tree. One page has just the words DRAW ME TO YOU *on it, written boldly in red. Another has blank verse with a border of vines surrounding it; reading it, you discover that its author has asked God to connect him to the main vine with its life-giving sap.*

Several people enter and venerate the icon in a variety of ways, pausing before it for as long as a minute or two.)

Betsy:
Here we are again. I really feel as if we've become old friends at this point. Let me give you an overview of the rest of the day, so you'll know where we're going.

Our first session this morning will be spent on debriefing last night—both the ceremony and, more important, what it led to during the night. Now, again, I want to make clear that we're not asking you what you dreamt. In fact, even if it *were* appropriate for everyone to share their dreams, we wouldn't have time. Remember too that the purpose of this retreat is much more to share *skills* in dreaming than to set up any demands that we be sent a specific sort of dream. You all know all those expressions about trying to move faster than grace, and pushing the hand of God—presumption, we used to call it in the ancient times (that was pre-1962)!

On the other hand, some of you may have had extremely interesting nights that you are willing to let us know about, and this will add to our experience of the workshop and our knowledge about how the incubation process works. So, if this container seems "tight" enough and you fall into that category, we welcome your contributions.

134

After the morning break, which will be about 10:30, we want to come back and put all the pieces together. There's a theoretical aspect to all this that we haven't gone into in much detail, and those of you who need theory to support your experience may be feeling the lack of it so far. So, we hope we can step back a little and provide that theory before we have our noon meal. We'll have dinner at 12:30 and then have our closing session and ceremony here at 1:30, which means the seminar will end at about 2:45. Then, we re-enter the real world—do you remember that place? *(A groan from the back of the room)* But let's not get ahead of ourselves. Let's stay with our experience of last evening, and of the nighttime. We prayed for something specific in our ceremony: the deepening or strengthening of that link that connects us to the God within. And here are your pictures—some of them—and your written words that helped you clarify just what that might be like for you. I'm glad so many of you brought them to put up. Is there anything you'd like to bring up?

Deacon:
Well, I found a feather on the floor by my bed this morning—it was probably from the pillow, but I kind of wondered if Gabriel had paid me a visit. After all, we invoked him last night!

Betsy:
Hmmm. Well, Gabriel is called the presider over birth. You remember that he was the angel who came to Zechariah, John the Baptist's father, as well as to Mary. And he's also supposed to have been the angel who foretold Samson's birth, which is another interesting story.[5] So, perhaps he was there to help something be born last night, or maybe it was our goose!

Deacon:
Well, I can go with that. I woke up this morning not with any dream memory, but with a strong, strong picture in my mind of the picture under my pillow. I had wondered yesterday when we were drawing if I really needed a picture, or whether my connection to God hadn't been pretty well formed already over the years. But I went along with you, and—as I said—when I woke up, my picture was almost hanging in the air in front of me. And now, it seems very important to me that I try to visualize that connection in this way.

Tom:
Yes, the waking image seconded your work of yesterday, didn't it? It's as though the unconscious said, "This is valuable. Pay attention."

And you come from a liturgical tradition that's full of that sort of statement. Doesn't the deacon come out at different times in the eastern rites and say to the people, "Pay attention"?

Deacon:
Yes, he does—I do. And when I call the people to prayer, I lift the end of the stole I'm wearing. Now that I think of it, St. John Chrysostom says this gesture is in imitation of the announcing angel.[6]

Betsy:
Hmmmmm. Seems like things are hooking together here. Maybe you should save that feather on the floor! Do you see how we're also talking about the difference between apophatic spirituality—or imageless prayer and devotions, the emptying, "cloud of unknowing" approach—and kataphatic spirituality? The latter is not in opposition to the former, but can be a complement to it—the word comes from the Greek for "with images." And the approach that we're pursuing, which is so rooted in Jung's psychology, is largely kataphatic, because we know the power of the symbol and how it is the language of the dream.

Now, depending upon your own religious tradition—which may range from iconoclastic to veneration of images of the holy—you may or may not be at home with this idea of the visual as a connector to the inner kingdom. In a broadly ecumenical group such as this is, we're bound to have a wide variety of reactions to the idea of image in general.[7]

Could we get back to the deacon's picture? What I want to ask is, what next step do you see yourself taking with your own image?

Deacon:
Well, I think I just want to take the picture home and live with it.

Tom:
And see what birth may come from it.

Deacon:
Yes.

Tom:
That's a good example of how this process we've been going through works. We don't have to have tremendous breakthroughs or blockbuster dreams. What we are called to do is to listen—and to respond,

to whatever is sent. Thanks! Do any others have something they'd like to tell us, or perhaps something that was sent as a gift for the group?

Retired Teacher:
Well, I feel I want to tell you all about my dream. First, I should say that I've been using my dreams for many years, so I don't really expect neat answers in them all the time—although I've learned that that can happen. And last night it did. I had such a beautiful dream that I just want to tell you about it and use it as an example of God's goodness to me.

Betsy:
Please do—*if* it's not too soon to share it.

Teacher:
Well, I slept with the angel over there under my pillow. And I was very moved by the slides you showed last night, especially the ones by the artists who put the annunciation scene in their own time so people would know it kept on happening. This is the dream I had last night:

> I am in my living room watching a television program. A famous woman singer is introducing her latest song, and it is just a repeating over and over of the line, "I need you."
>
> After she finishes singing, she announces to all the television audience the name of the person who has been chosen . . . it's not clear what the person has been chosen for or by whom, just that this is an important moment. And she says my name. I am the chosen one!
>
> When I hear my name, I drop whatever it is I've been doing (I think I had some mending in my lap), and get up immediately. It's perfectly clear that I have to go to do whatever it is I've been chosen for, and that nothing in the world is as important as this is. I am absolutely thrilled to have been chosen! And—somehow—the singer is really my angel!

(The group has listened very quietly to the dream, and there is a sense of wonderment at it when the teacher finishes. She wipes away tears, and her face is changed by the telling of her dream. The room is still for a bit after she sits down.)

Betsy:
I almost hesitate to go on after hearing your dream. *(She speaks softly and slowly. There is another pause of appreciation.)* Thank you. *(Those near the teacher reach out to speak to her and touch her in thanks.)* There's much we could say, but there are times when it would be sinful to dissect the butterfly—or, in this case, the dream. We'll just appreciate it and be happy for you.

Teacher:
And I thank you—all. And there *is* one thing I would like to add to what you said yesterday, Betsy. As I mentioned, I have been using my dreams for my own spiritual life for some years, but actually, I was in my mid-fifties when I began doing this. And I recall, at the time, I thought, "Oh, what took me so long to get here? All those years I could have been dreaming, and drawing closer to God in that way." But I just want to assure any others who are feeling that way because they're just beginning to know about their dreams that in whatever time you have, you'll be sent the dreams you need. And one dream like this one I just told you is something to live on for a long, long time. So, never think you're too late getting started.

Tom:
And that's very important. I know when I began learning about the inner world in my thirties, I regretted the years I had lived without that intimate connection to it, but God doesn't seem to be hampered by our way of understanding time, or *chronos.* Anyone else with that "look at all the time I've lost" feeling? *(Almost everyone raises a hand, and there is relieved laughter at the realization that it is a common attitude.)*

Betsy:
This reminds *us* again to remember that we're not in charge of the process of our growth, that God will send us what we need when we're ready for it—which is not the same thing as saying that there's nothing we can do, is it?

Tom:
Well, we do have time for some more conversation about last evening and the night. I think we really need to note that a special dream like the one we've just heard is the exception rather than the rule. These beautiful, rich, complete gifts do come from time to time, and we never forget them. But, who was it who said the reason we have so

few numinous dreams is because God wants us to spend time in prayer trying to figure out what the garden-variety dreams are saying to us?

Betsy:
I'm going to guess Basil the Great, and will check it.[8]

Private Investigator:
As I've told you already, this is all brand new to me. My wife here brought me along, said I'd like what you were doing—and I do, but I don't really understand it yet.

Betsy:
My own experience was that after I heard all this material about twenty times, I began to get it. It's like relearning a language we haven't spoken since we were babies. "Dreamese," it's called.

Investigator:
Well, my paper yesterday was very simple, just a couple of words because I couldn't think of anything to draw. When I woke up I heard a sound that seemed to me to be like a river going by.

Investigator's wife:
Actually, it was the water running for my shower.

Investigator:
But what I thought of was the river—so that's what I wrote about and drew a picture of before breakfast.

Tom:
Which is an excellent example of how the skill works in real life. You went with what came to you. Someone else might have been given the idea of a waterfall, or a garden hose, and that would have been the image for that person to work with. Good—you're getting it! Does the river have any more meaning for you that you can tell us about, or is it so new and fresh that it needs to be kept just for yourself at this point?

Investigator:
I sort of saw it as a picture of something that connects, and maybe I can use it for my link that we were talking about. It only goes one way, though. What really struck me was when we came in this morn-

ing and saw the icon with the angel and Mary—the new one on the stand over there—and it has at the bottom a river. It was like, "Oh, how did that get there?" and "I guess I'm supposed to pay attention to the river." That's what you call synchronicity, isn't it?

Tom:
It sure is, and a good example of it. Why didn't any of the other pictures have a river? Why should you wake up with the sound and idea of "river" and then, from across the city, we bring a picture of a river? This is the sort of thing that can't be explained as cause and effect, but is too much of a coincidence to be *just* a coincidence. I wouldn't be surprised if "river" were to come to you again before too much longer, just to make the point that this image is important.

Deacon:
"Pay attention!"

Tom:
Right, pay attention to the image of river. If you want to read up on synchronicity, Jung's work on that is found in Volume 8 of his *Collected Works,* and also is published in a small separate volume.[9] He calls synchronicity "an acausal connecting principle." And the other good and very readable book you might try is *The Tao of Psychology* by Jean Bolen,[10] whom we mentioned yesterday. I'm glad you brought that up.

Betsy:
I'll put those references on the board while you go on. Would you want to talk about what you saw in the river in the picture?

Investigator:
It's got fish and a squid in it, and some strange looking birds that are out of proportion.

Investigator's wife:
Some of the fish are gold and some are black, and there's a duck swimming along too.

Tom:
Why do you think that stream of water is there at the bottom of this annunciation? By the way, it's a very famous one, a copy of one in the Orthodox monastery of Saint Catherine on Mount Sinai.

Choir director:
Well, if water is one of the main symbols of the unconscious, as Jung said it was,[11] it's almost as though having the stream at the bottom of the picture says, "Look, folks, your understanding of this scene rests on your closeness to the unconscious."

Tom:
Or we could say that the unconscious underlies the meaning of this scene, couldn't we?

Choir director:
Yes. And in the unconscious are the gold fish, the precious ones, and the weird looking, dangerous creatures too—like in the diagram you put on the board yesterday. Of all the pictures of the annunciation you've got out here, I think this one makes it clearest that it's a picture of something going on inside us—or potentially going on inside us.

Betsy:
And in the top right hand corner of the picture is that nest of birds in the trees of the roof garden. If both "top" and "right" can be assumed to stand for consciousness, what is this little detail saying?

Sister:
Well, it's saying that growth—the trees, and new life, the nest with the birds in it—are the result of allowing this announcing to happen to ourselves. We can become more conscious.

Betsy:
I think that's just it—and did the artist, who lived back in the twelfth century, stop and think this out? What I mean is, did he say to himself, "Well, now, I'm going to put this river at the bottom of the icon to show that the contents of the unconscious are what lie under the meaning of the angel and Mary," or "When people see that little nest of birds in the trees, that will tell them that a new consciousness is the end product of this event"?

Sister:
No, of course not.

Betsy:
But . . .

Sister:
But there are universal ways of picturing things, and he just tapped into that part of himself that knew about them.

Betsy:
That's it. In the creative process, the connection in this artist to that universal level—Jung's collective unconscious—was made, and these symbols that transcend time and place and culture found their way onto his canvas. Actually, it's on a board.

Now, the artist may also have been consciously representing one of Mary's titles, the idea of the Mother of God as "grace-giving stream," but even that idea comes initially from this same substratum of the psyche or the soul. Anyone of us who gives life to God, who incarnates the life of God, can be a grace-giving stream to our world. *(To the private eye:)* Does this give some amplification to your river image?

Investigator:
Yes, it does—and now I just need to sit with it.

Betsy:
Yes. Again, we're seeing how the process of dialoguing with the contents of the unconscious works. We notice what's going on, what's being sent, then we stay with it; then something else hooks on to that, we let it rest some more, and gradually the image and the associations and amplifications that are connecting up to it form a pocket of energy that does its work in us.[12]

Investigator's wife:
It almost sounds too easy that way. I always thought we had to puzzle these things out and figure them out, analyze them.

Betsy:
That's partially true, but if that's *all* we do, then we've fallen into the opposite pitfall from the one we talked about yesterday—the mode of giving too much power to the unconscious. If we do all the work ourselves (or think we have to), we give too much power to *consciousness*. We're after a dialogue between the two, remember. And it's a skill that comes with practice, just like riding a bike or driving a car.

Tom:
One of the stories I like best about Jung is that when a dream was a puzzle to him, he'd put it in the pocket of his jacket which had his

tobacco and pipe in it. He'd actually write it down and put the paper in the same pocket, and then each time he would reach for his pipe his hand would touch the written dream, and he'd be called back to it. Gradually, the dream would do its own work. I like to write out a dream and leave my journal open to that page in a place where I'll see it often. Each time I go by and notice the dream lying there, it becomes a little more real and it sort of works on itself.

Student:
Back to Jung's example, is that what you'd call a pipe dream? *(Laughter, and a general stretching and shuffling-around time.)*

Tom:
(pulling out his pipe) Yes, we can call it a pipe dream, and we might note too that many of our dreams do seem to go up in smoke! We just don't have the time to work on all of them or attend to all of them in the way we might like to. After a while, one gets to know which ones demand attention. Do you remember what the criteria were for discerning which dreams were absolute "musts"? We went into this yesterday morning in the beginners' group.

Candy store owner:
There were two tests: either that the subject matter was very important or that the dream had a lot of feeling attached to it.

Young mother:
Or both.

Betsy:
Yes. And of these two criteria, which is the more important?

Young mother:
The strong feeling.

Betsy:
Yes, that's it. Getting back to the subject of last night's dream incubation ceremony, we were praying that our link between ourselves and God would be strengthened. Someone might have awakened today with a whole Jacob's ladder dream or something equally impressive, and also with just a tiny fragment—maybe a picture of a door or a window. If the latter had much more strong feeling or affect

attached to it, that would be the image to give prime time to, wouldn't it?

Young mother:
But the other dream would also be important, wouldn't it?

Betsy:
Oh yes, and in some sort of utopia or heaven we'd have time to pay attention to *all* of this material—but we often have to make choices and let some good ones sit on the sidelines.

Tom:
The good thing to know is that if a subject is important, we'll hear about it again and again from the unconscious, either through our dreams or in some other way. So, if we're paying attention, the dialogue will be happening. God is persistent.

We have time for one more bit of feedback from the night. Does anyone else want to jump in here?

Carpenter:
I really wasn't going to say anything because when I woke up this morning and wrote down the dream I remembered, it was almost too unreal. I guess I didn't want the rest of you to think I made it up! But I really want to tell it to you . . .

Betsy:
We'll believe you.

Carpenter:
O.K. then. This was my dream:

> I'm with a group of people in a sort of beach house. There is one wall with sliding glass doors, and I hear a knock on these doors. A woman goes to the door and a beautiful radiant young person is there. I know that it is an angel, but no one else seems to know.
>
> The angel gives her a letter, but no one is sure whom the letter is for. I go over to the door and I see the messenger sort of vanish into the sky. All I can think of is whether or not the letter is for me.

Tom:
Wow! Well, that's certainly the next question to ask, isn't it? What a very direct result of dream-seeding—not all of us would get such a

quick response! You prayed for a dream and you got one. Let's just take a minute to appreciate that one. Do you mind if I ask you this: Was the link you had pictured under your pillow an angel?

Carpenter:
Well, no, it was a carrier pigeon.

Betsy:
Close enough! And how about feathers—did you find any on your floor the way Jeff did?

Carpenter:
No! No feathers! I need to know what to do next. That's where I get stuck.

Tom:
Well, let's collect some ideas, especially from the more experienced dreamers here. What could John do next?

Elderly minister:
Well, if that were my dream, I think I would go back to it—sort of recreate the scene in my mind, and then picture myself going up to the woman in the dream and asking her if the letter had a name on the envelope.

Tom:
Yes, that would be a good next step. And if it *was* addressed to you, then what?

Elderly minister:
Then I'd take it, and go off somewhere and open it, very reverently.

Tom:
That's a good example of an active imagination technique, some-times called "dreaming the dream onward."[13] And you just do it by letting yourself quietly and meditatively re-enter the dream scene in your imagination.

Carpenter:
Isn't that like making something up?

Tom:
Well, yes—and no. I mean, where does the made-up stuff come from? It comes from the same place as the dream. When we can do this process in a relaxed state, rather than a very cognitive, let's-see-what-I-can-come-up-with state, we gain access once again to the contents of the unconscious. You can tell the difference when you do it, because the ideas and images just spring into your awareness, and you can trust these. Or, if this doesn't work too well for you, what else could someone do with a dream like John's in order to help unlock its full meaning?

Religious education director:
You might ask for another dream that would clarify the first one, or continue the first one.

Betsy:
Yes, that's another good idea. How might that sound in practice? Can you give us an example of how you might actually do that?

Director:
Well, I would probably make it a prayer before going to sleep, sort of a mini-dream ceremony. I might say something like, "Lord, you are speaking to me in my dreams, and I thank you for this gift. Please let me know what comes after the dream you sent last night. Was the angel bringing a message to me? What was the message? You, who tell us to ask and we shall receive, you alone have the answer." Something like that.

Carpenter:
That sounds like something I could do. And would I get the answer?

Betsy:
You'll have to try it and see what happens, won't you? Remember that the answer might come in some very different form than the scene and characters of the first dream. Be open.

Director:
Can I just say that this, for me, really points out the value of having someone else to share this whole process with. I know we can get along somewhat on our own, but if there's someone who can go along with us as a guide or a teacher or even just as a friend, it makes everything a lot easier.

Tom:

Well, there's absolutely no doubt about that—and the spiritual companion or guide is a wonderful help. My own experience has been that if you're seeking such a person and are really ready for him or her, that person will surface in your life.

Homemaker:

"When the student is ready, the teacher will appear."

Tom:

Yes, or the friend, or prayer partner, or mentor, or someone—that special other person for the inner journey can take different forms, and I think it's important not to have a set idea of just who it will be, but to be open to the person that's sent. And if no one is sent, that doesn't mean we can't go on alone—although it's more difficult and riskier, to be sure.

Betsy:

I know how much the guides in my life have blessed me, but there have also been times between them when there was no one to bounce all this off, and then I'd be sent a special author, or a new way of finding that guidance through the scriptures.

I guess the bottom line, for me, is that God knows when we're really seeking first the kingdom and won't abandon us if that's where our heart is.

Carpenter:

Even if it feels as though we've been abandoned sometimes.

Betsy:

Oh yes, it can feel that way! The favorite prayer of the believer is H-E-L-P, isn't it? We're out there grousing around in the desert, and it's only later that we can say, "And you were with me all the time." This is where the journal is so helpful, because it can be that kind of "other," and because we can read back in our logs and see that, of course, we were never alone.

Tom:

And that brings me to my big moment of the day! Yesterday Betsy promised she would top my word of the century, *enantiodromia*. And it's time to take a break, but we still haven't heard it.

Betsy:
Funny you should bring that up, because I was just going to ask John if the two things we've suggested he do with his dream, and the other thoughts about a spiritual guide and the journal, have affected his *weltanschauung*.

Carpenter:
You weren't really going to ask me that!

Betsy:
Well, no—I wasn't, but I knew I *would* have to get it in somewhere. It's one of those words that's used over and over in the Jungian literature and I just sort of thought I'd drop it in casually so you'd know I was on the inside. And it means . . . ?

Secretary:
It means your world view, or the way you perceive all of life.

Betsy:
Yes, and it's even better if you can say it with a German accent.

Tom:
Or a Swiss one.

Secretary:
Well, that *definitely* tops your word, Tom!

Tom:
I guess it does—three syllable words in German definitely score more points than seven syllables of Greek, and I'm going to call time here just so we can have a break of about fifteen minutes, and then we want to pull all these threads together. We want you to leave with your own *weltanschauung* fully *enantiodromia*-d. *(From the back of the room comes a voice saying, "Please . . . no more!" And with a combination of groans and laughter the group gives itself a break.)*
    (The break time ending, the strains of the now-familiar Dear Father *music are heard once more. You return to the meeting room, a place which now holds some rich memories of your own experiences and others'. Tom, at the podium, has already begun saying goodbyes; Betsy is in a corner of the room, conferring intently with one of the participants. You find your seat and settle in for the remainder of the morning session of this last day.)*

Tom:
Welcome back, everyone. Let's get started again. Does it seem to you that we've been together longer than three days? Actually, it's not even a full three days, is it? *(General agreement throughout the group.)*

Tom:
You realize that we've just brushed over the surface of this complex subject. We want to stress again that the great value of dream knowledge comes from the experiencing of the dreams themselves, not from reading about them or going to workshops about them. Jung had some strong words to say about learning that stayed above the collar. He speaks of how experience of the world (inside and out) and of one's own passions—and that's his word—will give forth richer stores of knowledge than textbooks a foot thick.[14] So, we want to encourage you to take the skills and ideas you've gathered here and put them to work for yourself.

Now, almost all here are involved in the helping fields in some way—and I mean that in the broadest sense of the words. And from your schedules you see that we've planned the final session to be a brainstorming time on "What Lies Ahead?" which will include ideas on letting these ideas spill over into those helping fields. *BUT*—and I'm spelling that with capitals—a word of caution. You can guess what that is, right?

Teacher:
Don't lay it on others until it's working in our own lives.

Tom:
Exactly! I feel an urge to let my twenty-minute ferverino on this start to roll, and something tells me to spare you that—so I'll just let the thought rest. Now, I expect many points for this display of self-control and restraint.

Betsy:
At least seventy-five points, for sure! And I want to second what Tom has just said. The best service to others flows from our persons, as we continue to deepen our own relationship of intimacy with God. Then, whatever we do in the classroom—or from the pulpit or wherever—is rooted in our own inner truth. I can feel myself about to get on a roll with this too, so I'm going to shift gears here.

We promised you some sort of theoretical framework for all that we've done, and it feels as though that should surface about now, so let's back up a little. There are two parallel developmental stage theories we can use—depending upon whether we're speaking the language of Christianity or the language of Jung's psychology. I have a little chart here that we'll pass out, and you see that it speaks about the language of conversion, on the one hand, and of individuation, on the other. *Roughly* speaking, these are different words for the same process.

Tom:
Which is a relief, knowing that we don't have to be both converted and individuated—just one is enough for a lifetime.

Betsy:
Yes, one's definitely enough to keep us busy! Now, I need to say that we're not saying these two processes are identical—obviously, when you speak the language of religion or conversion, you're able to be very explicit about the goal being intimate relationship with God (at least in the western religious traditions—it's different in the east, where the goal is usually expressed as absorption *into* God). Incidentally, we're not using "conversion" in the sense of being a convert to any denomination.

Tom:
And when you speak the psychological language and talk about individuating, to use Jung's term, or self-actualizing or self-transcending, to use Maslow's, well, then, the idea of relationship to that which is Other is still there, but it may not always be expressed as "God."

Betsy:
The important point for us is that the *processes* are parallel—what happens in the person is the same developmental process whether one is calling it "a" or "b" or "c." (This chart is also from our book *Coming Home*—thanks, Paulist Press. The Individuation line, across, is based primarily on Erich Neumann's work.)[15]

Deacon:
So I can be converted, which I understand as something that never stops happening, and at the same time the individuation process is taking place (even if I'm not using the psychological language)?

Betsy:
Yes, that's what we're saying. And the next point is that in either framework, the dream has an important function—it is the main means of access to the world within us, and the stronger our connectedness or our link is to that world, the more likely it is that the conversion process or individuation process will come about.

Tom:
Which is not to say, remember, that we can't reach the end point of our development—that state of unitedness with God—*without* the dream. Just that when the learnings of analytical psychology are overlaid onto our Christian or Jewish traditions of ongoing conversion, we have new light and new understanding about how this union can be fostered. And the dialogue between consciousness and unconsciousness—which the dream fosters so wonderfully—is the key to that individuation process. Clear?—or muddy waters?

Teacher:
Let me be sure I understand. Someone could plug into path one here on the chart—the conversion path, as described by his or her own faith—and someone else could plug into path two, into Jungian analysis and work toward the goal of individuation, and someone else could have a foot on both paths, because they run parallel to each other.

Tom:
And—then what?

Teacher:
And then he or she would have two complementary sets of skills and insights to help the growth process unfold, rather than just one way of doing it.

Tom:
Exactly. Down at the bottom of the chart you'll see that we've got some scriptural parallels to the process, and they fit either one of the two stage theories above. Now, of course, nothing as human as spiritual development is as neat at this little chart—we're always wanting to put ourselves in boxes or on this or that rung of the ladder, the holy *scala*.

THE LIFE OF

	Beginnings ——————→	Normal Life ——————→
The Conversion Process: "I" and "Thou"	Little children are naturally in a state of union with God . . . although they may not know it. We celebrate this with **baptism.**	Mainstreamed into life of institution/group; celebrated in sacramental churches by **first penance and Eucharist.** Part of Church because of parents, then out of habit . . . or fear, or need for security. Unconscious identification with the collective group.
The Individuation Process: "I" and "Not-I" (Or Self)	We are born with the "map" of totality already complete . . . in a pre-conscious unitive state. No sense of "I" or "me" (pre-ego). all is one ◯ *(participation mystique)* —no consciousness— Erich Neumann's UROBORIC STAGE, after Uroborus, the ancient circular image of the serpent biting its own tail	*Individuation: Part 1* Sense of "I" (ego) begins to emerge from womb-like state, though still contained by it. (Neumann's MATRIARCHAL STAGE) 3 stages postulated by Dora Kalff: • animal-vegetative (still very instinctual) • fighting to break out • adaptation to the collective (Neumann's PATRIARCHAL STAGE) *May* make it = healthy ego ("the hero") OR *May not* make it = ego remains weak, and compensates by defenses (Fritz Kunkel) and/or seeking new substitute "womb"
The Story of Salvation (Salvation History)	Creation of the World Paradise Prodigal son at home Annunciation to Mary	Kingdom of Israel Promised Land Jerusalem, the holy city Goes away Grain of wheat "I live . . ." "The people who Jesus' birth and life

THE SOUL

Death to that Life ⟶	HOME **New Life (Completed in Eternity)**
Separation from Faith of Child: 1. leave . . . "that's not for me" and/or 2. "there's got to be more . . . " A turning around (PURGATIVE STAGE of old texts) (Wm. James & Morton Kelsey suggest that we may skip this phase: the "once-born" or Gerald O'Collins' "smooth evolvers"; most, however, are "twice-born.")	*Adult Conversion/2nd Journey:* (ILLUMINATIVE & UNITIVE stages) *Personal* relationship with God sought, leading to intimate union of love. Church ambiguous about how to celebrate this! In *some* views, **confirmation** (as a recommitment to one's baptismal vows) could celebrate adult conversion.
	*Individuation: Part 2*
The Old Way No Longer Works: 1. Crisis leads to "I need help/change" (i.e., ego not strong enough to meet the crisis, can no longer control) (One feels like one is being "cooked" or in a furnace . . . which can burn one to a bitter crisp, *or* refine one to gold. In one case, give up and regress—in the other, go through the crisis, find higher power within) and/or 2. Respond to inner call to self- (ego-) transcendence, as (capital S) Self/image of God makes its presence felt (Jung's "religious instinct" is Self longing for *re*union).	*Rearrangement of the Personality:* Center shifts from ego to Self. (Edward Edinger's INTEGRATIVE STAGE) Ego no longer in charge, but remains strong—is servant/channel/mirror of true Center (which has always been there). Ego-Self axis established. A return to the unitive consciousness of childhood . . . but this time, aware of it (conscious, intentional). All is one . . . again. (Neumann's GREAT INDIVIDUAL)
—— Collapse of the kingdom(s) —————— —Paradise lost —————————— —— In exile ("captive Israel") —————— (earlier: the desert) —Jerusalem destroyed —————— —from home (pigs!) ———————— —— buried in ground —————— —— "now, not I . . . " —"I must decrease . . . "——————— —walk in darkness . . . "——————— "Heart of stone," "hardness of ♥ " —— Jesus' death and entombment	—— The kingdom is within —— Paradise regained —— Return to promised land ("ransomed Israel") —— The new Jerusalem, Heaven —— Returns home —— sprouts and grows ("new creation," "born again") —— "but Christ lives in me" —— "that He may increase" —— "have seen a great light" —— "become as little children" Jesus' resurrection and following events

,b. This chart is *not* age-specific; and one can stop or regress at any point

)NE CAN MOVE ALONG:
. *With the group or collective*
. *On the solo path*
, *Both (b. has priority)*

rom: *Coming Home: A Manual for Spiritual Direction.* Copyright © 1986 by Betsy Caprio and Thomas M. Hedberg, S.D.B. Used by permission.

Betsy:
If you like Abraham Maslow's work, as I have for many years, you know he talks about "rubricizing," his word for wanting to know all the rubrics or details, so that one can get it right and find out just where one is on the map. And, he says, that's no good, that's not the point.[16] In fact, in earlier times, it was assumed that only the spiritual guide had the map of growth and the grower just did what he was told or what she was told to do. But we've gone beyond that, I think, to a time when we can take an intentional part in our own growth process. Jung's huge body of work is one of the *major* factors in this shift.

Religious education director:
Well, certainly, the emphasis on adult education in the religious groups over the past generation is indicative of this kind of intentionality.

Betsy:
Yes, and that's true even about adult ed. that's not specifically concerned with spiritual growth, but about religious concerns in general, isn't it? You know, I'm wanting to get to a specific point, but I keep feeling these temptations to throw in little sermonettes about preparing for the twenty-first century, and about how many of us are involved in what I like to call "frontier ministry." One phrase I especially like is Jean Houston's description of our generation at the end of the twentieth century as "the people of the parentheses"—she means the new age isn't here yet, but the old way of seeing things is dead or dying, and we're the ones straddling the gap between these two world views.[17]

Tom:
You're back to the *weltanschauung* again.

Betsy:
Ah, *mea maxima culpa.*

Tom:
We want to share with you a bit of the work of Dr. Edward Edinger, who lives now in Los Angeles. He's the former director of the analyst training program at the Jung Institute in New York, and you may know his book *Ego and Archetype,* or his books on alchemy, or William Blake and Job, or the Old Testament, or *Moby Dick.*[18] Now, Dr.

Edinger, whom we've had the privilege of hearing, has a lifelong interest in the biblical stories of both the Hebrew and the Christian scriptures. If you read *Ego and Archetype* you'll find his early published thought on these religious matters in the chapter titled "Christ as Paradigm of the Individuating Ego," a chapter that's been reprinted more than once and is deservedly well thought of. That book came out in 1972, and in the 1980's Dr. Edinger has been refining and elaborating on his ideas in that earlier chapter.[19]

His work has had a profound effect on both of us, and we see him as someone who helps us understand how "path one" on your chart here and "path two" do parallel each other. Remember, his starting point is the psychological side of the road—he's a medical doctor—rather than the churchy side, like Sanford and Kelsey, both Episcopal priests. And Dr. Edinger's work is directed primarily to those to whom the institutional religions no longer speak, as he says.[20]

Betsy:
Be that as it may, I know that when we last sat and listened to his psychological insights into the scripture stories, we felt moved, deeply. And we couldn't help but add our own faith perspective to what he was saying, of course, and that adds another shade.

I'd like to try to summarize how *we* hear Edinger's thought on the relationship between the two paths on our chart, and hope I do him justice, even though I'm abbreviating as I go. And for Dr. Edinger's own spelling out of all this, we refer you to *The Bible and the Psyche* on the Hebrew Bible, and *The Christian Archetype* on the events in the life of Jesus. So, would you take another look at the chart? You see that we've titled it "The Life of the Soul," because we've put it together for people who use words like "soul." If we were doing it for a strictly psychologically-oriented audience, it would be called "The Life of the Psyche."

Tom:
Maybe a better title would be "The (Possible) Life of the Soul," because we all start out at square one, but not everyone gets to the same place down the line.

Betsy:
That's right. We start out, grow—then often regress, or just stand still. The first point is that you see how we've used the paschal mystery as our "umbrella" for this stage theory. Well, we're not the ones who used it—it's the pattern built into creation and we're just re-

cording that. It's the pattern of the days of our lives, with the sun rising and setting and then rising again; it's the pattern of the year, of animal life—and of soul-life. And so, of course, the story of Jesus—birth, life, death and resurrection—mirrors this universal pattern too.

Tom:
As do the stories of many of the famous heroes of different times and places—you can find many of them in Joseph Campbell's book *The Hero with a Thousand Faces.*[21] And maybe we should throw in right here that we don't want to fall into the trap of saying that Jesus is *just one* of the many heroes with a thousand faces; for Christians, of course, he's more than that. That can be a pitfall when this sort of abstraction is carried to its logical conclusions, but that's an aside.

Betsy:
The individuation process, as Jung and his "orthodox" followers say (and "orthodox" is in quotes—maybe "classical" is a better word)[22] also has this pattern of life, death and rebirth. That means we can learn *about* it from other paradigmatic examples: the cycle of the year, whether that's seen through naturalist eyes or the symbolic language of the zodiac; the alchemical process, about which Edinger has also written at length;[23] the stories of the heroes—Ulysses and Gilgamesh, and heroines, too, like Dorothy going to Oz and then dying to that life and coming home to Kansas. You could just overlay any of these on top of the chart and it would fit.

For Christians and Jews, the story of Jesus is so much a part of their culture—and when we say, "for Jews," we mean that Jesus can be seen as an individual example of living out the pattern that was first set up in Judaic culture by the people of Israel as a whole—well, it's the Jesus-story that mirrors this pattern most fully for so many, many people in western civilization.

Tom:
And when they can come to know that story *in an inner way,* a psychospiritual way, if you will, they also learn about the individuation process in themselves. Jung can be quoted as saying that Jesus' story is the predominant story of western culture even for *non-believers*—because it's at the roots of western civilization; it's in our bones, so to speak.[24]

Sister:
And wouldn't he have used the word "myth"—the "Christian myth"—in the precise meaning of that word?

Tom:
Yes, that's right. The word has taken on overtones of falsehood, when actually it comes from the Greek *mythos*—legend, or telling of a story, with the implication that it was a true story that had become larger than life. We've done the word a great injustice, haven't we?

Betsy:
Now, all this isn't a new idea, of course—we've been urged to the "imitation of Christ" for centuries, called to the living out of our own paschal mystery. The thrust of Dr. Edinger's work—which we feel has so much application for believers as well as non-believers—is that the churches or institutional religions have carried the story of life, death and rebirth for most of us for well over three thousand years. We've lived the story *unconsciously*—and this just won't work anymore. It's not adequate today. It's gotten us as far as column two, "Normal Life," on the chart.

Minister of Christian education:
Wouldn't you say James Fowler's work bears this out too? He talks about how we grow in our use and grasp of symbols, for instance, so that they move from "out there" to "in here."[25]

Betsy:
Yes, many of our theorists have been giving us the message about these last two steps of the conversion process for a long time. Another way to say this is that the task of both religion and psychology is about calling people to the contemplative life, the life where they consciously experience the Christ story (or the story of the people of Israel, for those who can't connect as fully with Jesus) as happening now, within themselves, just the way we did yesterday with the scene of the annunciation.

Tom:
Jung's phrase is "the Christification of many."[26]

Youth minister:
I read somewhere recently that Jung's been called "the greatest religious educator of our time."[27]

Betsy:
And what we're talking about makes me think of Merton's good title, *Contemplation in a World of Action*—which is what we're talking about. Actually, that's a title given to some of his essays published after his death in 1968.[28]

Again, I don't want to suggest that we're seeing this as something new—because it's not. Our mystics have been urging us toward direct experience of our own living out of this life with God since the year one, but for most of us, we've let the churches contain the mystery for us, we've kept it at a safe distance. We've talked about uniting ourselves with Jesus, as *he* goes through the paschal mystery.

And the point I hear this particular teacher, Dr. Edinger, making so clearly is that when we let that happen, we avoid *going through it ourselves*. We let the collective—the Jewish people, the church—or the historical figure—Christ—go through it, and we sort of tag along for the ride. But if you remember what we were doing yesterday with step one of the whole incarnation cycle, the annunciation, we were seeing *all of that scene* as happening within ourselves, weren't we?—which, of course, isn't to say it didn't also happen historically.

Tom:
Here's a quote from Edinger: "The representation of the life of Christ—which we can see in a sequence of images—is a representation of the vicissitudes of the Self as it becomes manifest in an individual."[29] That's Self with a capital "s"—the image of God within us, in the psychological language.

And we can see the images of the life of Jesus—Dr. Edinger starts with the annunciation and goes through to the last judgment—as covering the entire chart sequence we have here, AND we can also see that the whole cycle really begins again with the last two columns of the chart, when we leave behind the unconscious way. What I mean is, Mary's hearing that she was going to be the Mother of Jesus meant dying to her old way—and, for us, when we *really* hear the message that God wants to incarnate within us, our old way has to go too.

Candy-shop owner:
But when you talk about "*really* hearing," you're not just talking about having someone tell you, are you?

Betsy:
Oh no—*really* hearing is having your socks knocked off by this bit of news.

Candy-shop owner:
Like, "Who—*me?*"

Betsy:
Yes, and "Where have you been all my life?" to the angel or whoever our messenger is.

Choir director:
Or, "Why didn't someone tell me about this sooner?"

Aerobics instructor:
Whoa. Wait a minute. I missed something as you rounded the bend back there. You're talking about the contemplative life—as in cloistered, *Agnes of God* contemplative life?

Betsy:
No, in a much broader sense. "Contemplative" as in "I know—through direct experience—that God lives within me, and that there is a love relationship between us." And this can be a way of being no matter what we're doing with our time—scrubbing floors, or chopping wood and carrying water, as the Buddhists say.

Tom:
Or teaching aerobic dancing.

Instructor:
O.K. I needed to get a handle on that word "contemplative."[25]

Carpenter:
I have to tell you, this sounds like loony-tunes time to me—not that it's not a great idea and all, but just that most people aren't interested in being contemplatives.

Tom:
Or, they've become arrested in their development at some midpoint on the chart, could you say?

Carpenter:
Yeah, but that's the norm—and if you're talking about meeting people where they are, then that's where they are—where I am.

Tom:
Definitely! But if we're *also* talking about where there is for each of us to—potentially—go, then we start asking questions about exposing ourselves to the idea that there's *more*.

Pastor's wife:
Which is where the dream comes in—because we don't *make* the dream happen. It's already happening, if we can just get hold of it and see it as religious experience, a connection with God, calling us to that "more."

Betsy:
I think the word "consciousness" is the key here. Nothing we're saying is new, but we're trying to head toward more conscious ways of living the lives we're already living. I have this mental image of Paul shaking some of the people he wrote to—shaking them by the shoulders when he met them in person—and saying "Don't you *know* who you are?"

Hang in with us just a little longer, O.K.? We certainly don't expect everyone to agree with us, but we really just want to let you know what works for us and where we're going. Basically, we believe that once people are touched by the presence of God, it creates a hunger that becomes the most important thing in their lives. And the dream, supremely so, touches in that way—and now I'm getting filled up because this is so moving to me and to the people I've seen it happen to. When those special dreams *do* come, and someone attends to them, lives change. My continual response—my only possible response—when I see this happening is awe. *(It's clear to see she really has chosen the right word here.)*

Tom:
Getting back to the chart. I feel as though we ought to stand up and sing that song from *The Muppet Movie*—you know, "Movin' Right Along." What this chart shows us is where there is to go, spiritually speaking.

And if the goal of the growth process is that conscious awareness of a love relationship with the living God within—whether you use the religious language, or the psychological language, or the scriptural images—then our uppermost question is, "How do we allow ourselves to be there?" And the whole thrust of this conference has been on the dream, and the channel that links consciousness and unconsciousness so the dream and other contents can get through—because we're in agreement with Freud's definition of the dream, so often quoted, which is that it is "the royal road to the unconscious."[30]

Nothing I know of has the power to make us more aware of the immediacy and incarnation of God in our lives and how we *too* are being continually created and re-created than the dream. Well, now, maybe you don't agree. What do you think?

Therapist:
Yes, it makes sense, once one agrees that the chart is a picture of what our life's about. I know we can move along this path *without* the dream showing us the way, but it certainly makes sense that it can be a tremendous aid, sort of the way the North Star is at sea.

Tom:
That's right. I guess we're feeling an urgency about the need for the kind of consciousness and intentional focus on the life of union with God that has just grown and grown.

I've got a quote here somewhere—just a minute *(as he thumbs through his papers)*. Yes, this is it: it's William Johnston, who's a favorite of mine, writing back in 1974. He says that between the mid-1960's and the mid-1970's, we had a "sudden evolutionary leap in consciousness" and that "we are faced with a new man" (excuse the exclusive language, please—that's his)—"a more mystical man, and it is on the mystical dimension of religion that we must fix our attention."[31]

Deacon:
As you're talking, I'm thinking that you're sounding a lot like Matthew Fox and his creation spirituality.

Tom:
Yes, he comes to the same sort of conclusions from his rootedness in the mystical tradition, especially that of women of long ago and all the Dominican mystics, his order.

In the appendices of *Original Blessing*,[32] Fox's book, there's an interesting "family tree" of western religious figures and others who have come from this point of view.

Betsy:
In the broadest historical context, we're touching on that old pendulum swing in all religious systems between the intellectual, abstract, objective approach and the subjective, process-oriented, mystical point of view; the current interest not just in the dream, but in psychology as a handmaid of religion, and in the incarnational, sacramental theologies belongs to the latter, the subjective. And the pendulum keeps swinging.

Tom:
So you could say that what Johnston sees happening is nothing new—I'm sure he would say that.

Seminary professor:
I like Matthew Fox's list that you're talking about, Tom, but it leaves off a lot of people that I would have added.

Tom:
Yes, including much of our present-day pop culture that has the whole contemplative strain—I'm thinking particularly of song writers—even some Beatles music—and our science fiction writers and TV programs and movies. Who else would you have included?

Professor:
Well, the Shakers for one, and C. S. Lewis for another, and I would have made it more ecumenical, completely inter-faith. But it's easy to criticize—Fox did a very good job.[33]

Betsy:
Please don't hear us saying that we *don't* think the collectives, the religious bodies, are not already doing this leading of people toward the contemplative life. Of course they are, and always have been. It's no accident, for instance, that the churches that have been most excited about the dream are the liturgical churches, the ones with the rich symbolic traditions. Kelsey and Sanford are both from the Anglican Church, and it's there and within, particularly, Roman Catholicism and the Lutheran churches that this interest in the language of the unconscious has particularly taken root in our time, because the symbols are already there, and the people haven't lost this language.

Sister:
It's the picture language of the child and the primitive.

Betsy:
Yes, the forgotten language.[34]

Private investigator:
I have a question. You said different stories, like Dorothy and so on, were the same pattern as the steps on this chart. And then, did I hear you say that astrology also pictured the same steps?

Tom:
Yes—and in a particularly elegant way, because we think of the zodiac in circular form rather than a straight line. It stresses how we really come back to the starting point, but at a more conscious level.

Private eye:
So, then, Aries would be comparable to the first column down?

Tom:
No, Pisces—the symbol of all the contents being under the water and swimming around together, which is what the infant's life is like. Then Aries is about the ego beginning to emerge, and Leo when it's really strong—the king of the jungle is a good symbol here. Then Scorpio standing for death to ego-centeredness . . . going back into the water, you see. And finally, establishing a new center, ending up with the sign of service to others that comes from inner abundance, Aquarius.

Private eye:
Hmmmmm. I need to think about that.

Betsy:
Yes—it's rich. We can ask, "Which of the zodiac signs tells me most about where I am in my own development?"

Can I shift a gear here? I have a short story I'd like to tell you before the morning's over. For many years I've been collecting stories and songs and poetry in which dreams figure, and I try to get to see movies that have dream sequences, just to see how the dream is handled. One of my favorite tales is Maeterlinck's *The Blue Bird*, which turns out to be a dream in the end—do you know it? *(Many people do.)* I had the book when I was very young, and it was my favorite story. Recently, I came across another one, a fairy tale from China, and I thought you'd appreciate it. Here's the story—it's very short, and I'm condensing it:

> Once upon a time there was the head of a clan with vast holdings. His servants worked from dawn till dark, especially one very old servant. This old man was just about exhausted, which made his master drive him even harder, till the old man groaned as he went about his work. At night he was so tired that he sank into deep sleep, and each night he dreamt that he was the king of the land.
>
> As king, he had wonderful food. His every wish was granted. He never had to work, but just enjoyed himself all day. In the morning after these dreams, the old man would awaken and have to go back to work.
>
> When his friends tried to console him about his life, the old man would say, "Half my life is lived at night, and half during the day. Even though my days are hard, at night I am the ruler of all. So, what have I to resent? All is even."
>
> Now, the ruler of the clan dreamt every night as well. And his dreams found him as a servant, rushing and running around to perform his tasks. When he was too slow, he got beaten with a stick and yelled at. He never had enough food in his dreams, and he would toss and turn all night, mumbling over his sad plight.
>
> Finally, in desperation, the master took his problem to a wise friend, who advised him in this way: "You have far more wealth and power than other men. How could it be otherwise than that your dreams would balance out your life of comfort with their hardship? How could you expect both your dream and your waking life to be the same? That is not how it is."
>
> And so the head of the clan mused over his friend's response, and decided to lessen the work load of his servants, especially that of the old man. He shared his possessions, so that he had less abundance, and they more—and his dreams became much more calm than before. However, never again at night did the old serving man dream of being a king.[35]

(Appreciation from the group.)

Betsy:
The fairy tale is a fine illustration of what we call the compensatory function of the dream, isn't it? One author says that the dream is the dance of different energy patterns—those we know dancing with the unknown, disowned parts of ourselves.[36]

Tom:
What a good fairy tale—it's new to me.

Betsy:
I like it too.

Before I forget, I want to tell you that in Japan, and probably elsewhere in the far east, there's a dream-changing goddess. Her name is Kannon, and you pray to her if you don't care for the dreams you're having. I have a married son who lives and teaches in Japan, and when I visited him and my daughter-in-law and her family, they gave our family a head of this goddess to take home. So, Kannon hangs on one of the walls in the Center where I work here in L.A., and reminds me of how universal the dream is. She has her eyes closed!

Thinking about her brings me back to our chart. I'd like to spend just a little more time with it, because the goddess idea is very pertinent to the whole developmental sequence.

Tom:
Can I interrupt for just a minute? I don't think we mentioned that the ideas from Erich Neumann we've used as the basis for the Jungian horizontal row, row two across, aren't the only Jung-rooted developmental theory. If you want to read up on current thought in that area, you might take a look at Andrew Samuels' book[37] here, where he contrasts Michael Fordham's approach with Neumann's and talks about this aspect of psychology as the Jungians have been exploring it. And, of course, we could have used several other developmental theorists; you can find good work on the life cycle as proposed by Erikson vis-à-vis religious development in the work of Evelyn and Jim Whitehead.[38]

Religious education director:
And both Kohlberg's and Maslow's schemas have been paralleled to the faith language a good deal.[39]

Betsy:
Yes. Ever since *Passages*[40] popularized work on the entire life span, not just childhood development, we've become aware of developmental psych as a topic covering the same turf that we've talked about as religious or spiritual stages of growth in times past. We chose Neumann's work for the chart, however, because we feel in our

bones that it's intrinsically valid, though people with special emphases will want to add their own embroidery to it.

Homemaker:
One question I'd ask is whether or not this map of growth is as valid for women as it is for men. I'm thinking of Lawrence Kohlberg's very linear, sequential outline of moral development, which he keeps revising,[41] and some of the women's work that says he's presenting as a universal model something drawn just from the world of men's experience.

Betsy:
Very important question. Carol Gilligan's work is important here, even though there's not been a lot of response to it yet.[42] Well, Neumann himself spoke to that question, and the reference is the 1959 issue of *Spring*.[43] But of course a lot has happened since 1959, and I was really excited when I picked up a book we highly recommend, Edward Whitmont's *Return of the Goddess*.[44] He speaks about the new archetypal feminine consciousness now being born that will complete Neumann's stage theory.

Tom:
Some other authors have tackled your question, especially as it applies to Jung's thought. You might check out Helen Thompson's *Journey Toward Wholeness;*[45] she quotes also the work of the Gelpis, which will be helpful.[46]

Betsy:
Remember now that Neumann was comparing personal growth stages in the individual to social, cultural growth, and so, even in the early 1970's, we hadn't seen anything we could call a "return of the goddess"—culturally. But since then, the surge of attentiveness to what the Jung-oriented people would call "the feminine energy" throughout the world really seems to indicate that the long-lost nurturing awareness and that global, all-inclusive perspective that goes with the feminine energy are on the increase, slowly. I'm thinking of examples like increased public awareness and action on behalf of the homeless and the hungry, and, certainly, all the women's issues.

Deacon:
So, if it's possible in the collective for the feminine to return, then it's also possible for the individual to have that energy rekindled.

Betsy:

Yes, not to replace the patriarchal consciousness, but to stand beside it. Think yin-yang. Actually, it's the shift in *individuals* in this way first that then makes the group shift possible.

Sister:

So, what that would mean in terms of a person's life is that he or she would become more androgynous, that the masculine and feminine energies within would live together in a complementary way?

Betsy:

Well, that's how I see it—and experience it too. You can use the alchemical word Jung used, the *coniunctio*—conjunction, that is; or you can use religious language like "mystical marriage" or "espousal"—we're not talking about anything new are we? The Song of Songs painted the picture for us centuries ago. The inner marriage may never have been described better.

Tom:

We have more thoughts on this topic in our book *Coming Home* and the manual for spiritual direction that goes with it, so that might be helpful too. Our thought there is that the chart is best used when it's pictured as a tube, so that the final vertical column can be seen as a return—or *homecoming*—to something that we once knew, but in a less conscious way. And that also keeps this step-by-step format from being a linear process. The little pictures at the top of the columns show you how we visualize it—so it's really a combination of feminine and masculine energies, and that makes it more appropriate for men and women alike. The idea of stages or steps is the journeying, masculine energy, and the concept of the inner home or perfected state or balance of opposites always having been there, waiting, is the feminine or receptive energy.

Homemaker:

I need to make sure I know what you're saying. Let me run it by you, O.K.?

Tom:

O.K.

Homemaker:

I'm looking at the second row across on the chart, where it says "The Individuation Process." So, early on—column one where the snake is, and probably part of column two, where you've started the individuation process—the person is very much at one with Mommy.

Betsy:
Yes.

Homemaker:
And, with any luck, the person becomes his own person—or her own person—and develops some sort of decent ego, which is what you've got here as the "patriarchal stage."

Betsy:
Yes, using that language because it's one of the qualities of the "masculine energy" in us to separate and discriminate. Or, the ego may not emerge well; Erich Fromm calls it the "escape from freedom" that takes one back to Mommy or finds a mother-substitute, like a safe group or organization.

Tom:
And if this "patriarchal consciousness" does take hold, the going from the extreme of matriarchy to the other represents a reaction.

Homemaker:
O.K.—I'm all right on that. But then, moving on to the "Death" column, it looks as though the extreme reaction doesn't work either—so now the extreme ego-attitude or patriarchal consciousness has to be balanced out by a return of the feminine.

Betsy:
Yes, we don't have to be at one extreme or the other. The psyche tends toward balance. There's a reclaiming of that which has been lost—which in this case was the feminine.

Tom:
Enantiodromia!

Homemaker:
And because it's now happening in individual people, like you and me, the same shift can happen in society.

Tom:
That's it! A perfect synthesis of this chart. Thank you!

Betsy:

And—can I go on?—if we go back to Dr. Edinger's Christian archetype thoughts, remember that he sees that cycle beginning with the
annunciation, just as the churches have always seen it. And very
near the end is an important event—this same return of the feminine
in a glorified form when we focus on the scenes of Mary's coronation.
It's the closest the Christian churches have come to allowing the old
"Great Mother" goddesses—stamped out by the early patriarchal religion in the cultural reaction—to return, and we have to ask ourselves about this incredible transformation of peasant woman from
Nazareth into Queen of Heaven. Surely, something in the collective
psyche hungered for that degree of honoring of the feminine, and has
for a long time. The old goddesses have been around all this time.[47]

Sister:

I want to recommend a book I've really been spending a lot of time
with—it's *The Cult of the Black Virgin* by Ean Begg.[48] It shows how
the black madonna Marian shrines are continuations of the early
worship of the goddesses.

Betsy:

So, then, maybe saying that we "return *to* the goddess" is more correct than saying that she is returning to us—she never left. And isn't
this what our ceremony last night was about? If the feminine part of
us that we pictured—the divine feminine part of us—is alive and
well, we then have that receptivity to the dream. They go together.

　　Here's a tip I've found helpful. You remember how we mentioned
animals yesterday morning, as being about both instinct and "oth-
erness"—or that which is different. We saw them as bridgers of that
split in us. Watch for animals—and plants too—in your dreams as
attributes of the divine feminine. Remember, she's Mother Earth,
Mother Nature, so they go with her. Or maybe it will be outer animals or plants that are sent to catch your attention. In Neumann's
book *The Great Mother*[49] he has two chapters I like on "The Lady of
the Plants" and "The Lady of the Beasts." The Marian version often
shows her in an enclosed garden—like the bride of the Canticles—
with flowers and animals.

Elderly minister:

I know the idea of God as male and female is still troublesome for
many people. How many years I walked around and even led a congregation, all the time with this too-small image of God.

Tom:
And with only the masculine side of God available to us, we were able only to have a rational approach to the dream, or none at all.

Betsy:
So, we could go on and on! What a huge topic. Someday we hope to get this dream workshop in book form, and then we'll be able to put in long footnotes about all the exciting things we've just brushed over. I'm not sure anyone will read them, but at least we'll feel less unfinished. *Remember*—we're talking major revolution here, folks!

Tom:
Well . . . whew! It's almost dinner time. Can I try to sum up this session? We've tried to present you with a picture of the ideal, of where there is to go—whether or not anyone takes the trip is another matter. And we're postulating that the dream is one of the primary ways of spiritual growth, the pointer along this journey of unfolding.

And knowing where there is to go makes it easier to get there. Otherwise you can have dreams of returning goddesses and masculine and feminine coming together—and think they're just nighttime versions of something from the Pussycat Theatre, when, actually, the dreams are leading us to some in-the-future version of man or woman fully alive—dreams are not pornographic, by the way.

Student:
And I just want to say that your talk about the times to come has been reminding me of the movie "2010"—there's something in there about the computer that's about to be shut down, but it wants to be like humans and it asks "But will I dream?" That's the mark of being human and alive for it.

Tom:
Well—that's a perfect way to end this whole morning. Thanks! And let's eat—all this heavy duty thinking has made me very, very hungry! (*And you are hungry too, and join the rest of the group in following the smells coming from the dining room. The closing day's dinner is chicken with fettucini and salad, with a fattening looking blueberry cobbler topped with ice cream for dessert. The conversations over the dinner tables are lively, ranging from discussion about the plusses and minuses of religious and psychological collectives, to the fine points of Kermit the Frog's rendition of "Movin' Right Along."*

After the meal, you stroll down to the lake one last time with some of the people you have met, checking out the gander and the hollow tree, then return to your room to pack your things. There's the bed, which for two nights was your special dream-reception spot, blessed and set apart for a sacred purpose by you. Will you be able to take home the same attitude of reverence you've brought to the sleep of the past two nights?)

The Afternoon Session

(The familiar music calls you back to the large room for the last time. Addresses are being exchanged, and you spot Tom in a corner talking to someone. He's wearing a blue T-shirt that says, on the front, "Jung at heart." Betsy is with some people talking over the pictures hanging on the walls of their channels to their deepest recesses.

Covering a long table in the front of the room are cards—like playing cards—with pictures on them. The retired teacher is telling others that she's been asked to invite them to look over the cards. Doing so, you see that they depict simple everyday objects and typical situations in nature: there's a candle, and a ring, a thunderstorm and a sunrise. The cards number almost a hundred.

Neil Diamond's voice calls out one last time, and the group gets settled for the final session.)

Tom:
A couple of nuts and bolts things to begin with, folks. First, please don't forget to take your picture with you if you put it up on the wall this morning. Second, after we finish in about an hour, please feel free to stay on the grounds for as long as you like. The sisters have told us that, as long as our rooms are cleared out, we're welcome to stay and picnic and just let the whole conference sink in through the evening.

Betsy:
Also, if anyone would like to spend any time with either of us, we'll be here, so please don't hesitate to let us know if that would be useful.

Tom:
I want you to know that my co-dreamer here was kind enough to eat my dessert as well as hers at lunchtime.

Betsy:
Well, it was a great sacrificial gesture, because I saw it would just go to waste—so I see that as an act of mortification and penance.

Tom:
Yes, truly beautiful. Now—we have a treat for you. I'll let Lucy and Bob tell you the story themselves.

Lucy (one of the pair of therapists):
Bob and I met each other when we were in school studying to become psychologists, and later on we discovered we had so much in common we thought we should get married.

Bob (her husband and partner):
That was three years ago.

Lucy:
While we were in school, we had one teacher who really cared about dreams, and he organized a dream group so we could share dreams and talk about them. It was very good, but we realized after a while that for some of the people—including me—we were getting into dream "oneupmanship." Do you know what that is?

Bob:
If you don't, it's the name we used when we felt we were trying to top each other's dreams with bigger and more sensational dreams—sort of "Anything you can dream, I can dream better!"

Lucy:
Well, it got to be sort of a joke, and we made up a song about what was going on—and the whole group adopted it as their theme song, just to remind us all of how easy it was to fall into that "Look at me, guys" position.

Bob:
Actually, the idea of poking fun at being off-base came from Albert Ellis, the Rational-Emotive Therapy founder in New York.[1] He has a whole book of songs about misdirected thinking. So, we thought you might like to hear our song. *To the tune of "Mary Had a Little Lamb," the couple sing:*

My dreams are the best of all, best of all, best of all,
My dreams are the best of all,
     Just thought I'd let you know.

Archetypal everyone, everyone, everyone,
Archetypal everyone,
     Each night there's quite a show.

Guess that means I'm far advanced, far advanced, far advanced,
Guess that means I'm far advanced,
     When asleep, I surely glow.

(Lucy and Bob are applauded roundly.)

Tom:
Oh, that's great. I thought I was the only one who played dream oneupmanship. Thank you both!

Moving right along, now, once again, I'll pass things back to Betsy.

Betsy:
Well, this really is wrap-up time now, folks. We'd like to explore a few ideas on where to go from here if you want to continue dream work in your own life. Why don't you make your suggestions, and I'll add some, and Tom will too, and I'll make a list on the board as we go.

Tom:
Well, number one, of course, is loyalty to your own dreams. Then we'd suggest a solid reading and grounding in the dream psychology we've sprung from here: C.G. Jung's writings and those of his followers—especially those combining the dream psychology with Christian and Jewish and other religious traditions.

We hope we've really stressed the point that working with the dream is *sacred* work, and that we need a religious attitude toward it—at least, that's our approach and certainly Jung's. Just remember that when you read about dreams in the popular press or even the psychology books, this isn't the *only* approach to the dream you'll find.

Therapist:
Could you give us a run-down quickly of other approaches? There are so many. I know I get confused about them all, and I'd like to be able to distinguish among them.

Tom:

Well, yes—let's do that. In fact, over here on the wall you'll see this chart which I brought in out of my car at lunchtime, just in case we needed to talk about this. *(Turning in the direction to which Tom points, you see a large chart of a strange-looking tree hanging on the wall. A copy of it is reproduced here in the book for you.)*

Professor:

It looks like an upside-down banyan tree or a mangrove.

Student:

Actually, it's like the monkey-puzzle tree—I just finished a course in forestry!

Housewife:

And out here in California you'll see the dragon tree—it's a desert kind of plant—but it looks very much like your tree there.

Tom:

And all the time I thought we had just made up the shape. Well, you can see what this chart's about.

We call it the "Tree of Life," with the addition of the word in parentheses, "Soul-"—so, it's the tree of the life of the soul, or what Jung calls the archetypal world.

Betsy:

And down through the centuries, two major ways of exploring it and trying to explain how to stay in touch with it have developed—the religions of the world and the psychologies of the world. We had to leave a lot off, just for space reasons. To really be complete, we could have added all the natural scientists who have explored the contents of the soul's life—the biologists and zoologists and paleontologists and so on, and the social scientists—the anthropologists, and the sociologists, et cetera.

Tom:

Basically, on the trunk there you see some of the major manifestations of our inner world: the images and dreams from the unconscious, all the created world, fine and folk art, the experience of loving and connectedness.

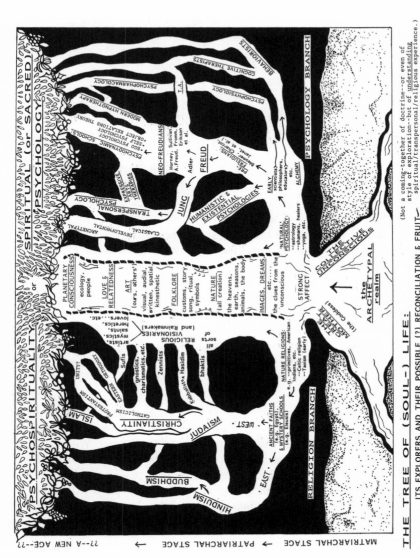

THE TREE OF (SOUL-) LIFE:

ITS EXPLORERS, AND THEIR POSSIBLE (?) RECONCILIATION & FRUIT

(Not a coming-together of doctrine--or even of
style of exploration--but of understanding
spiritual/transpersonal/religious experience.)

Young mother:
Could you not have added all emotions—I mean, couldn't hate be on there just as much as love?

Tom:
Yes, and those would come under "Strong affect" down at the bottom—love and relatedness got a special place because—well, why do you think?

Secretary:
Well, because they're the highest form of affect—and from the Judaeo-Christian point of view, they represent the nature of God.

Tom:
Yes—and also because you see that the tree starts below the ground with the religious side being represented by the early Great Mother and the psychological side being represented by the collective unconscious. Well, one of the hallmarks of both of these is relatedness or the linking up of disparate particles—and, yes, those of us from the western religious traditions often translate this idea into love.

Therapist:
So, another group you could add to the tree would be people like the modern physicists studying subatomic particles and their interconnectedness—the whole idea of the universe as a web.

Tom:
Absolutely. Fritjof Capra's work,[2] among several others', is about this.

Betsy:
The final fruit of that sort of thinking and perceiving is that we see the whole planet—and we could have put the whole galaxy or cosmos—as connected, and so we cannot help but be concerned about the ecology of the planet and the peoples of the world.

Tom:
Let's write in "galactic consciousness" at the top—that's certainly appropriate. Think what we've learned from the astrophysicists, and from the space flights. *(He writes this in above "Planetary Consciousness.")*

Betsy:
Just quickly, then, early-on—that is, in the most primitive times and societies—people were at the simplest root-level shown here. But then, with sophistication, they began to have an objectivity about their experience—they began to look at it. The two ways we've charted here are the ways of religion and of psychology, with their earliest antecedents, as you can see.

But even as these two branched out into all their sub-branches, there were always the people who stayed close to the trunk or core of the tree—we've mentioned the American Indians already, which would be one example. And then, as the world religions developed, in each were those who headed back toward the trunk—the mystics and contemplatives you see there for each faith tradition, the ones more interested in the *experience* of God than in dogma.

Sister:
Backing up, I think there should be another hypothesized branch, and that would be the philosophers. I see you've got the early ones down at the bottom, but that's an ongoing field of study.

Tom:
Yes, of course—actually, we had thought to build a three-D model of this tree with all the branches we've been talking about.

Betsy:
Or maybe we should grow a monkey puzzle tree in the yard and write on it in indelible ink.

Tom:
Then we could get everyone in. Where this all ends up—but *not yet;* we're not at the top or flowering or leafing-out point *yet*—is, we would hope, some common understanding about religious experience, or transpersonal or spiritual experience as we can call it.

Betsy:
And that's not saying that each of the branches will merge with the others and lose its identity—just that each will contribute its own special insights into how we can become conscious of the life of the soul, and the knowledge will begin to be pooled.

Pastor:
With people dipping in and choosing what's appropriate for themselves?

Betsy:

Yes. And, then, also being able to see other ways different people have described and accessed the same world. Mr. Spock would call it "unity in diversity."

Tom:

Staying with your question of the dream in different schools of psychology then, we find that each branch more or less has its own understanding of the dream. You're familiar with the Jungian one, which comes from Freud and his predecessors but goes way beyond it. All the depth psychologies are vitally interested in the unconscious—or the dynamics of the psyche between consciousness and the unconscious (which is why we can also call them psychodynamic schools of psychology). Remember, not all schools even acknowledge that there is the unconscious aspect of the soul or psyche.

Betsy:

Parenthetically, I recall Sanford's comment on different occasions that we have to be careful about how we speak of a "thing" that we title "the unconscious"—it's really not that clear-cut.

Tom:

Yes, that's true. We tend to try to give it boundaries when we deal with it. Well, depth psychologists have always been extremely interested in dreams, although they approach them differently. You'll find things in print that come from the straight Freudian or psychoanalytic approach, where the dream is assumed to have two characters: a *manifest* meaning of the symbols, or what they seem to be about, and a *latent* meaning of the symbols, which is what they're really about. In other words, the dream language is out to disguise the truth because we couldn't handle the latent meaning. There's something of an adversary position implied here on the part of the unconscious contents. And Freudian thought tends to be what we call "reductive"—that is, everything can usually be reduced to one of Freud's psychosexual stages, such as oral, anal, etc., or to sexual drive or the death wish. The spiritual ingredient is lacking—which is, as you probably know, the thing that led Jung to pull away from Freud, his early mentor.

On the other hand, several people like Bruno Bettelheim have reminded us that Freud—in translation, and in America, especially—has been reduced way beyond his original intentions. If I remember correctly he says, for example, that when Freud spoke of "the soul's activity" it came out in translation as "mental processes"—which is certainly very different.[3]

Betsy:
So, the dream is a large part of the work of all the psychodynamic people, even those who spin off into interpersonal and psychosocial directions, like many of the neo-Freudians and the T.A. pocket of people.

Temple school director:
T.A.?

Betsy:
Transactional Analysis—Eric Berne's life work. You know the little circles with Parent, Adult and Child in them? His writings are really valuable to me in his thoughts about life scripts, and also his very commonsensical approach to therapy.[4] Berne was a Canadian. He analyzed with Erik Erikson.

Religious education director:
Now, is he the hypnotherapist? I see you've got them coming off that branch too.

Betsy:
No, that would be Milton Erickson, with a "c"—he was centered in Arizona.

Tom:
And I would refer you to Ernest Rossi's book *Dreams and the Growth of Personality*—Rossi's a well-known Jungian right here in L.A. who has spent many years exploring the interface between Jungian thought and Milton Erickson's work in hypnotherapy.[5]

Betsy:
Now, it might be useful to point out that there's a continuum among these depth psychology people—the ones who honor the existence of the unconscious—from staying with what that part of us sends, in the form of the dream and other ways, to those who inject us with images arbitrarily. We already talked about this yesterday, when we went over "seeding" our dreams. Remember, that skill asked the psyche for a topic upon which to build a dream—but there are those psychologies which suggest that everyone focus on some sort of

transformative image (like a rose, or the mountain) whether or not their own unconscious has sent them that image. So, we're back to the subject of programming dreams.

Tom:
Which moves us further to the right-hand side of the chart. Behavioral psychology stems from learning theory—Pavlov, Watson, and those people. Its best known spokesperson in our country has been B.F. Skinner. The unconscious is *not* part of their work, although some have teamed up with the psychophysiology people to study rapid eye movements in sleepers—the R.E.M. studies—and the latter are interested in sleep research of all kinds.[6]

Betsy:
You might find some behaviorists interested in dream control though, as a way of learning while sleeping, they would say—or of relearning, reprogramming the brain-as-computer.

Aerobics instructor:
Well, from your standpoint, dream control looks like the ego thinking it knows more than the Self, doesn't it? Or the person trying to program the voice of God.

Betsy:
Exactly. Really, we personally run up a red flag about articles like "Get your dreams to do what you want them to do"—you see them all the time.

Tom:
Yes, it's a whole other way of treating the dream—not a sacred attitude at all. Let's see now. Oh yes, the spin-off branch from the behaviorists down there are the cognitive psychologists—people like Albert Ellis, whose songs you've already heard about, and Aaron Beck in Pennsylvania. And they would say, simply, it's our wrong cognitions or beliefs that cause psychological problems, by and large. And since cognitions don't usually come from the dream world, that's not part of their focus.

Homemaker:
Could you give us an example of a wrong cognition?

Tom:
Well, if I think everyone is supposed to approve of everything I do, and then someone doesn't approve of—say—my chart here, then I will think of myself as a failure. That's an example of an irrational belief—also known as screwed-up thinking—that could really rule my life. Their work is rooted in the ancient philosophers who taught about logic.

Pastor:
"It's not what happens to us, but our view of what happens": Epictetus, first century A.D.!

Mailwoman:
"The mind can make a heaven of hell, and a hell of heaven": John Milton?

Teacher:
Yes!

Tom:
Yes! Thank you—*that's* the viewpoint of the cognitive therapists.

Betsy:
I must say I like much of their work a lot, and I've found it very useful as an overlay to my basic stance. Martin Seligman, for instance, writes about "learned helplessness," which is something many women, especially, struggle with—never mind that! It's something *I* struggle with! It leads to a whole victim mentality. And, he would say, I—or others—*mis*learned and need to *re*learn correctly.[7]

Let's see now—did we get everyone on the chart?

Stockbroker:
No, there's the humanistic and existential psychologies and the transpersonal psychologists.

Betsy:
Oh yes. Well, that's a mixed bag too, because, as you may remember, Abraham Maslow spoke of the humanistic psychologists as a "third force" in that world, after psychoanalytic thought—or the Freudians—and behaviorism. So, these schools are really a reaction to the taking over of psychology, or the study of the soul, by depth analysts or learning theorists. Maslow and Carl Rogers are the grandfathers

here, and under the same broad umbrella you have people like Viktor Frankl and his logotherapy, and Rollo May, and Fritz Perls with his gestalt therapy, which is very involved with the dream, as you probably know. However, what's different is that the focus for all these is very much on the here and now, as they would say, not on what happened when someone was six months old, or how he or she is related to some deep collective substratum of the psyche that goes back ten million years, or to God.

So, the dream—for those in this group that do speak of it—is more often spoken of as something to give us insight about this minute, this time, today.

Tom:
Rather than that broader sense of the dream being part of a whole unfolding of our faith journey, with its roots going back to the beginning of time. It's a slight distinction, but an important one—and you'll find differing viewpoints under this umbrella, as Betsy says. Another feature might be more emphasis on the dream as giving us information about the outer world—less of an intrapsychic focus than we've presented here—which is not to say that we don't partially subscribe to that outlook too. Whenever I dream about a flat tire, for instance, I always check my car after the dream.

Telephone repairwoman:
And has the dream sometimes given you input about your tires?

Tom:
Yes, occasionally it has—I've gone out and found one low, and once found I had a flat I'd probably have just overlooked if not for the dream—overlooked until I started the car and got on the road, that is! I'll let Betsy go on with the transpersonal psychologists.

Betsy:
These are the first people I read that interested me in the whole subject of psychology, many years ago now—my work was religious education, and I found transpersonal educators spinning off the transpersonal psychologists and applying their work in public school settings, and I said, "But this is what we do in religious ed." So, I learned a lot from them, but then discovered that Jung had been using the word "transpersonal"—which just means "beyond the personal," or we could say "archetypal"—since the early part of this century.

In Maslow's last work,[8] he spilled over into what he called "a fourth force" in psychology, with self-transcendence becoming the new goal at the end of his hierarchy of needs, beyond his earlier described goal of self-actualization. Now, although the dream isn't focused on in transpersonal psych. as it is in Jung's work, what they are interested in is altered states of consciousness—and, of course, that's another way of describing the dream, as an "altered state." So, it is discussed in the transpersonal literature in the context of one of the *many* ways we become aware of "another world."

Teacher:
The name of my favorite soap opera!

Priest:
Well, what's interesting to me as you go on about these different schools of psychology is how Jung prefigured many of them, but maybe only now—or, maybe, not even yet—is his contribution being recognized, for many reasons.

Tom:
Yes, many reasons. Dr. von Franz was interviewed on the occasion of her seventieth birthday for *Psychological Perspectives,* and she said something about Jungians not wanting to be a big success. As I recall, she said something to the effect of: "See what happened to Christianity once it became a big success!"[9]

Priest:
But that's changing—I mean, look at all the books on Jung's thought that have come out in the past decade—both for psychologists and for the layperson.

Tom:
Right. So, maybe what we're saying is that we're heading toward the flowering part of the tree on our chart here, where this infant science (remember, modern psychology is only a century old) is outgrowing its earlier need to split into camps.
  I've certainly had a sense of détente in these past years, and of different schools in dialogue with each other.

Betsy:
Don't you think it's been the practical application of what's been learned that's making that difference? I mean, more and more ther-

apists and psychologists are eclectic in orientation, and we're learning that across the spectrum of human ailments, one sort of therapy works for one problem, and something completely different is most helpful for another. I'm thinking of all the biochemistry research on the brain, and how the neurotransmitters are involved in mental disorders of different kinds, and this is a complement to several other ways of viewing these disorders.

Tom:
Yes—and so many of Jung's contributions are just now being picked up on, such as his interest in the east, which is a major ingredient in transpersonal psychology. So, we're beginning to be able to use a common vocabulary about understanding the experience of the archetypal world.

On the other hand, you'll see that we've marked the time of a "new age" with lots of question marks—we're not there yet. We don't have any solid evidence at all that, say, behavioral scientists have any intention of dialoguing about a world they don't even recognize, by and large.

Betsy:
And on the other half of the chart—the religion branch—there's not much evidence yet that the Christian churches will ever be united. Of course, many would not see unity as a plus.

Aerobics instructor:
So, this is some sort of futurist hope or vision of yours, then?

Tom:
Just call it a dream!

Anyway, we're still in the stage of separating out of the embrace of the archetypal world in these two fields of study, as well as the others you've mentioned. And still to really flourish is the just-begun dialogue between religion in general and psychology in general.

Betsy:
But that's happening too.

Tom:
And if we had to choose one person most responsible for this dialogue, I think most of us would say it is Teilhard de Chardin.

Let's just look back for a minute. Many of us here can recall how paranoid most of our religious groups were about anything psychological in "the old days." When was that—about fifteen years ago, or a little more? Of course, there were outstanding exceptions from the time Freud first came into print, but by and large I think it's safe to say that the churches in general saw psychology as an enemy at first. Since psychology was equated with Freud, and he was into sex, and so many religious groups—Judaism being the outstanding exception—had this negativity about sexuality and the body and matter in general, well, psychology had to be something from the dark side.

Salesman:
And since the psychologists were the ones paying attention to dreams, the dreams got put in that basket too.

Tom:
Yes. And the study of psychology was often seen as a threat to faith.

Betsy:
But as people from the religious side of the abyss—here I'm back to Dr. Edinger's language—as they began to be aware of the value of psychology (think of Paul Tournier early on, and Ignace Lepp and Josef Goldbrunner—there are many examples), a bridge started to be built from that side of the chasm, so that there was not only the option of war but one of synthesis as well. Instead of this *(drawing on the board, see Diagram B):*

there became the possibility of this as well *(sketching a second picture, see Diagram C):*

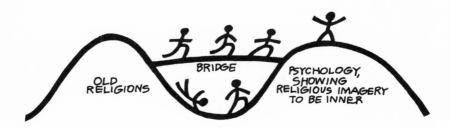

My own experience is that it's taken much longer for people from the scientific, empirical side of the gap—the world of the psychologists—to see what the ancient faiths have been doing to update, probably because the institutional heavy-handedness of traditional Christianity and other world religions, and also some of their rotten political involvements, have gotten in the way of their strengths.

Minister:
As though the religious bodies had discredited themselves to those outside them, and so the good things they still carried couldn't be appreciated for that reason.

Betsy:
Yes, that's it. I have a memory of going to transpersonal psychology and education conferences back in the early 1970's, and when I said that my work was religious education for a church, I would get these funny looks! Most of the people there were into the spiritual psychology they had discovered as a kind of "new dispensation"—it had become their new religion, actually, with its own priesthood in the therapists and analysts—and they couldn't fathom why anyone would want to stay hooked into the old way with all its abuses. They felt they had outgrown that, so that I must be terribly naive—all of which helped me really question what I was doing in a religious collective, so that was a plus in the end.

Priest:
And maybe all they had experienced of the religious collectives was their shadow side, and they didn't have any experience of the values the churches have held on to, by and large. The *Sister Mary Ignatius* syndrome, or Jim Jones, or TV preaching.

Tom:
Yes, again, I think you're right on target—this is an important point. So, for those of us who are the ones Jung calls "the happy possessors of faith,"[10] it's true—we can survive with *just* our traditional religious orientation. But I think we'd go much farther than Dr. Edinger, when he speaks of depth psychology as "an interesting addition to the more secure viewpoint they already possess."[11] For many of us still involved in traditional religion, depth psychology will be the primary source of the renewal that's absolutely essential if those institutions are to survive—so it's much more than an interesting addition. Those outside that world often don't know fully the tre-

mendous battles that are being fought within theological circles and religious structures for renewal.

Choir director:
A very obvious example would be the focus on the feminine we've learned from Jung, and how that has inspired so many to work for women's equality in the patriarchal religions.

Betsy:
Yes, certainly. That's the goddess returning *very, very slowly!* We learn from psychology and take that back to our traditional faiths to make them suitable for the new age that's upon us—all of which gets us back to the point that we made earlier, that one doesn't have to choose between "individuation" and "conversion." I really believe we can have "both/and" rather than "either/or."

Therapist:
Then you disagree with Dr. Edinger's viewpoint?

Betsy:
I wouldn't say that, as much as that we both come from our own experience—and mine is very different from his. He sees the institutional religions as dead, or at least dying in influence on those who are change-makers. And I've seen so much new life in the old faiths in the past twenty years that my own experience is quite different. Tom?

Tom:
Yes, we're coming from a different background. Dr. Edinger is very clear that he's speaking (as was Jung) for the people for whom the psychological understanding of religious truths has given hope where there was none before, because they had outgrown their childhood religion—if they'd had one—and they can't go back. And that's an enormous number of people, as you know.

And we usually speak to a different constituency, if you will—people deeply rooted in a religious tradition, often angry at the abuses in it, not giving it control over their lives in an unconscious way, but loving it too much to abandon all its plusses. Edinger himself has something valid to say[12] about the difference between unconscious containment in a collective and this sort of conscious participation in it.

Betsy:
So, from our point of view, the bridge and dialogue with the psychological viewpoint is the *hope* of the collective religious groups, because it will help their people take that next step in consciousness. Yet, it needn't replace the church or the synagogue or the temple. We stay, like so many of you here, because of the great strengths of the ancient faiths, which are . . . ?

Mailwoman:
The community life and support and fellowship.

Waitress:
The beauty of liturgy.

Nurse:
For Christians, the Eucharist and the other sacraments.

Religious school director:
The way an organized group can reach out to help the needy, and can make a difference.

Nurse's wife:
Some of the churches are good spokespersons on justice issues—and for the family.

Betsy:
All these. And, for me, one of the principal appreciations I have of institutional religion, with all its warts, is how it keeps God and the sacred mysteries alive for so many people who aren't ready yet—and may never be ready—to take the individual path. And many of these are my loved ones. Having worked in a parish I know what a difference that connection, unconscious as it may be, can make in people's lives. And Tom could tell us stories all night of the comfort that he as a priest has been able to give to those who are still very simple in their faith—and these are often the very poor as well.

Tom:
And from a strictly psychological viewpoint, you might say it's because those contained in the womb-like church project God onto the priest, but when someone's dying or has lost a much-loved one or whatever, the people are what matter, not the abstract psychological

principle. What helps is what's important, much more than why it helps.

Choir director:
Just that statement is a good example of the effect of the feminine principle in the church. You're talking *eros* rather than *logos*.

Stockbroker:
Could one or both of you spell out just a little the ways you *specifically* see depth psychology as helping with the renewal of the churches?

Tom:
Well, the first is in terms of training and the continuing development of those in the drivers' seats. If someone finishes the seminary and then stands still or only gets updated in theology for the next forty years, then you've got big trouble, especially if that person is getting more power. But as ideas like the ones we've been exploring together are dispersed and in the air, those with the power may continue their individuation process. Wouldn't you like to belong to an institutional religion where most of the leadership was getting more adult— maybe logging their dreams every night?

Sister:
And I've learned to walk on water too?

Tom:
Yes, well—it's begun to happen, on a very small scale to be sure, but I do think it's happening, and I hope I'm part of it. The other, even bigger and more important aspect of institutional renewal comes from what's made available and understandable to the people. I think both of us could go on for hours about people we've worked with—not to say ourselves—whose faith life has come alive and begun to make sense *only* through the psychological perspective. And their church or temple has presented that perspective to them.

Betsy:
Yes, we're talking about faith maturity again. And it's come to them—to us—because someone in their world, which is that organized world of institutional religion, offered them a way to understand their religious experience. And so people begin to move from their religion being an opiate—that's Marx—or the cause of their

neuroses—that's Freud—to an inner-directed conscious connection with it. Usually you could describe the transition as being from experiencing God "out there," to experiencing God "in here." It's happening. The grass-roots renewal going on—at least in the mainline religious bodies—isn't on TV but it's happening. And so, we have hope that that will continue and grow.

Candy-store owner's wife:
My husband told me once that I had a religious body!

Candy-store owner:
My dear, that's still true! *(This comment cracks up the serious group, and provides a welcome relief!)*

Pastor:
Well, what intrigues me—besides religious bodies—is that this tree chart of yours really parallels in a collective way the chart you gave us this morning, which is about how individuals develop. And we were saying then that very few people have reached the "new age" of feminine and masculine coming together—let's see, you call it a "new birth" on that chart.

Betsy:
Aha . . . you noticed that they're both about the same thing. So, if individuals, in general, are still in the patriarchal stage, then . . . ?

Pastor:
Naturally, the collectives made up of individuals are there too.

Betsy:
Yes—because groups change when people in the groups change.

Well, we've put your question about different ways of viewing the dream against a really broad backdrop—and we weren't sure when we began the other evening that we would do this. That is, some groups aren't interested in this sort of context for the dream, but others are—and we both think it's important, so I'm glad we had the chance to fly off into outer space like this.

And, very quickly, I'm just going to turn the tree over because on the other side we have another comparative psychologies chart that may throw a little more light on your question and some of the confusion at all the terms and methods. We don't have time to go into it at length, but I think it's pretty clear—basically, we've outlined here different views of what it is that causes healing.

Tom:
And since there's a continuum or scale with "needing healing" at one end—or, "not functioning as well as I'd like"—and spiritual growth at the other, we can look at the thinking of each of these schools from either a therapeutic viewpoint or a theological one.

Betsy:
There's always that twilight zone between "I need therapy" and "Things are O.K.—it's spiritual direction I'm seeking." Lots of times it's not quite so clear as these two poles on the scale, right?

Many voices:
Right!

Tom:
So, you can see that the dream would figure strongly in the healing and growth thinking of, particularly, the points of view under number four here—and these are the psychodynamic psychologies we were just talking about, the ones that recognize the presence of an unconscious part of the psyche.

Sister:
And want to be in communication with that part of us.

Tom:
Yes. Our sources here are both developmental and abnormal psych, as well as the religious input that you can see in several places—and we like to share with people we work with this much clarity about what we believe so they can participate intelligently in their own healing and growth. (*Here is a copy of the second chart for you.* →)

Now, where were we before we got into the monkey puzzle? Oh, we were listing suggested next steps for us as ongoing dreamers. Betsy, maybe you have some more things for the list there?

Betsy:
O.K. Some specific topics you might want to research or read up on are the things we didn't even mention in this brief time we've had

WHAT BRINGS ABOUT HEALING?

Different <u>expressive arts therapies</u>: music, art, poetry, dance/movement, writing, drama--used in a variety of ways, depending upon which theory provides rationale

IF DYSFUNCTION CAUSED BY:	THEN HEALING CAN COME THROUGH:	SOME EXAMPLES OF THIS STYLE:
1. Some foreign body (like a germ), or biochemical imbalance	removal of the intrusive object, or rebalancing of body chemistry, or activating body's/mind's self-healing	§ The medical model: therapy (from the Gk. = "to take care of") tied to body; drugs may be prescribed. § Various visualization methods
2. Incorrect learning, forming wrong habits or attitudes	tackling the problem: re-education, to learn ways that work better	§ Behaviorism, and its offshoot, cognitive therapy; some of T.A.
3. Lack of love, the force in the universe that both causes growth and promotes healing	experiencing a source of love--can be divine &/or human (may be called "unconditional positive regard").	§ Rogers' client-centered therapy § Religions that see God as love ("Love: nature's own therapy"--Berne)
4. Interference with the natural, inborn growth process, causing: a) FIXATION at some early level *[cartoon: I AM REALLY FIXATED -- MORRIS --]* or b) IMBALANCE in development, --dominant function exclusive --non-dominant function developed first (turn-type) --masculine or feminine energy develops exclusively --introversion gobbled up in extraverted world, etc.	going back & re-doing the growth process correctly, repeating, re-membering (via transference; healing of memories) or insight, understanding to help remove roadblocks to continuing development/ meet lower level needs so can move on to higher needs (e.g., meaning) encourage homeostasis within by provision of a free and protected space (a relationship, etc.) in which the psyche's natural tendency to wholeness & balance can manifest. Enable the person to witness & follow the clues sent by the deep stream of wisdom within, which help what is unconscious become conscious, thus redressing imbalance.	§ Psychoanalysis, other psychodynamic modes § Religious healings based on re-experiencing § many psychodynamic therapies § humanistic, existential, transpersonal ways § Jung's analytical psychology, & most of the "post-Jungians" § many ancient healing systems (e.g., yoga)
5. Sin: a) specific wrongdoing(s) b) fundamental option not for relationship with God	confession & propitiation (sacrifice, penance) shift in fundamental option, toward a basic choice for relationship with God	§ many religions, past & present § also a religious viewpoint, more theologically sophisticated
and, these 2 primitive approaches (included here for the sake of completeness): a) spirit intrusion (possession) b) sorcery, witchcraft	exorcism; extraction of spirit &/or trans-position into another (e.g., swine) countermagic	

here—things like: nightmares; dream clusters—which means a series of dreams around a theme; forming a dream group or having a dream partner; waking dreams or fantasy; e.s.p. dreams or unusual dreams—telepathic and precognitive dreams, like the one I told you the other night of my Mom's, about the zeppelin. What else did we not get to?

Candy-shop owner's wife:
Well, one thing we didn't mention much was the humor in dreams—I know I've had puns and funny, funny things come up in my own dreams, and I guess other people have had them too.

Betsy:
Oh, yes—that's a good one. And you're right—the dream director within has a weird sense of humor sometimes—just like the God of scripture.

Temple school director:
And there's that whole area of lucid dreaming[13]—knowing one is dreaming while it's happening.

Tom:
Yes, and special categories of dreams like flying dreams,[14] which deserve a whole session for themselves.

Betsy:
And there's a whole category we could call healing dreams.

Teacher:
And there's dream art. Think of all the famous artists who have painted scenes that could only have come from the dream world, like Dali.

Tom:
And Magritte.

Salesman:
And Rédon.

Homemaker:
And de Chirico, and Paul Klee.

Betsy:

All of these. So, we've just opened some doors a little wider in these three days, and for each of us there's so much more to keep on discovering about the dream—but the most important thing we can do is . . . ?

Several voices:

Keep on dreaming!

Betsy:

Yes! And keep these things in our hearts and ponder them—the interior life takes time.

Tom:

Another whole category we just want to touch on is the idea of using the dream in our work with others. Unless you're practicing therapy, you probably won't be involved in sharing specific dreams—although, within more and more towns, there are groups meeting just to share dreams and validate the dreaming process for the members of the group.[15]

How about you teachers among us? Do you incorporate the dream into your work in any way?

Nurse:

Maybe dream appreciation is what you're after in a classroom setting or wherever it is—not dream analysis. I've asked my C.C.D. kids to keep a book of their dreams, just as I do. I've told them we won't discuss them in class, but that this is a special way God speaks to them and they can learn to understand their dreams—but that's all I do.

Sister:

What grade level are they?

Nurse:

Fifth graders—and I only see them an hour a week, so even if I wanted to I wouldn't have time to do any more than that.

Sister:

You could suggest they draw pictures of their dreams or of the things in them.

Nurse:
Yes, some of them do that automatically.

Tom:
It's a natural next step that they've found on their own.

Teacher:
If you had any creative writing classes or art classes you could have the students use a dream image in a story or a poem or a picture.[16]

Student:
And in religious education we're always talking about symbols, so when something on that came up, it might be possible to hook in dreams.

Tom:
Give us an example, will you? What age students are you working with?

Student:
I have a high school Sunday school class at the Presbyterian church just the other side of the freeway—they're mostly freshmen and sophomores.

Tom:
O.K. How could you hook the dream into something about religious symbolism? Or am I putting you on the spot? I don't mean to do that.

Student:
Well, let's see now. O.K., we've been studying Old Testament history—not only in scripture but through historical sources too. You know, the kids always want to know if there really was a Noah's ark, and have they ever found splinters of the cross and all that. So, when we were going over the exodus last week and we got to the parting of the waters as the Hebrews leave Egypt,[17] if I had been paying attention to dreams and how getting into the waters or going through them has a personal meaning, I could have said something like, "Sometimes I have dreams of going into the water . . . and for me and a lot of people that's like going down into the parts of ourself we don't know much about." Is that what you have in mind?

Tom:

Great—I think that would be very natural and simple, and it would weave your own awareness of the power of the dream into something you're already doing. It hooks the dream and the biblical scene together. And you wouldn't have to do any more than that.

Betsy:

The problem is always the precocious boys and girls who launch into a let-me-tell-you-what-I-dreamt-last-night speech before you can stop them.

Parish secretary:

Well, at home, where I think most of the religious education takes place anyway, you can have a little more leeway, can't you? I mean, my children are still little—I have a three-year-old and a kindergartener—and I've always encouraged them to tell me their dreams. And from the time they were really little, we've put crayons and paper on the table so they could draw their dreams when they came to breakfast—it keeps them busy while I'm cleaning up the kitchen.

Tom:

So you've been listening and encouraging them for a long time, then.

Secretary:

Yes, and sometimes my husband or I will write down the story of a dream for them if it seems important, or if they've drawn a picture we'll write it on the back of the paper.

Young mother:

And what do you do with all these papers?

Secretary:

Oh, I save them—I have a big folder for each of the children's dreams and I've kept them all. So, someday, I'll have them for them.

Tom:

I think that's a terrific idea—is there anyone here who wouldn't like to have pictures and stories of their dreams as a child? *(General agreement that this would be a fine thing to have as part of our soul-story.)*

Betsy:
Could we talk a little about the cards on the table here?

Tom:
Yes—let's get to those. How many of you found a card that seemed to reach out to you or speak to you? *(About two-thirds of the group responds.)*

Tom:
Well, you noticed that these are pictures of very elemental, everyday kinds of objects and situations—they're archetypal images, and this collection is one I've put together over the years. Anyone could make it. I just got heavy cardboard and pasted pictures on it, and covered the parts that didn't have pictures (on some of them) with Contact paper—but that isn't even necessary. I keep my eyes out for pictures I really like or the ones I really dislike—like this one of people dying, or this one of an H-bomb exploding into a mushroom cloud. I keep adding to them.

Carpenter:
How do you use them?

Tom:
The point of having a collection like this—and you can make one as easily as I did—is to help people see and feel the power of these archetypal images, or images that express things from the collective unconscious, images that everyone shares and always has.

So, in a group—like this—or a class, I spread them out on the table or on a windowsill and ask people to look them over and see if any one picture really grabs them. Almost always, people will find something they go for; in fact, they usually ask, "Can I only pick one?"

Carpenter:
And what's the answer?

Tom:
It's simpler if everyone just picks one—and since the cards have a picture on both sides, you can often find a connection between the two anyway.

Then I ask a few people to talk about the image they've chosen. No more instructions than that. And always we could go on for an hour or more in a group of any size, because it's such a simple thing to do. But—the point is—once we start talking about an image that has plucked some chord inside us at that deep level, we find a lot of other things hooked onto it—especially strong feelings.

These are projective devices, in the language of psychology—and when as many people have spoken as we have time for, the one-liner summary is "See how powerful the language of symbols and images is." I don't have to go into the how-comes of that—I mean, I wouldn't be likely to go on about how symbols transcend words and unite consciousness and the unconscious and so on.[18] The point is: Pay attention to visual images.

Carpenter:
And when people get that message, they're better able to take the dream seriously, right?

Tom:
Exactly!

Betsy:
Something's popping into my head: I've noticed that the *most* familiar religious symbols—like a cross or the star of David—usually aren't picked as much as the less familiar. It's almost as though the very common ones that people know are too conscious—and the unconscious wants to speak to them in language that's different or "other" (as *it* is). I see Tom's got a Buddha here—is that selected by people who aren't Buddhists or from an eastern tradition?

Tom:
Yes, it is—and that reminds me of Frau Dora Kalff of Switzerland, the Sandplay expert. She notes that her Swiss and European and western clients who come to make sand trays will be drawn to the foreign and much less conscious objects on her shelves rather than the very familiar ones.[19] Yes—the unconscious is saying, "To get to know me, you have to go beyond what you already know."

Pastor:
Which helps us understand why some of our liturgy falls so flat!

Betsy:
Yes—the symbols can become trivialized or too much understood.

Tom:
Using a tool like the cards from time to time helps with the dream work in another way. It gives us a chance to say that there's no "one way" to understand any image, because you can make the point that Susie chose the card with the tree, and *for her* the tree is about X or Y or Z. But, then, Timmy might have chosen the tree too, and when he gets up to talk about it, he'll say something entirely different.

Professor:
Which might be just the opposite. I chose the tree card, for instance.

Tom:
What could you say about it for us?

Professor:
Well, it speaks to me because it reaches up and gets away from every-day life—but someone also could talk about how it goes down into the ground.

Tom:
And someone else could talk about how it *joins* heaven and earth, couldn't they? Did anyone else pick a tree card?

Grocery store clerk:
Yes—I did.

Tom:
And would you want to say anything about it?

Clerk:
Yes. I chose it because it looked like a place where there would be shade and a place to rest when someone was through working in the fields, or maybe if someone was walking along the road.

Tom:
So, you had a completely different association to the tree, didn't you? This helps us see how we have to work with our own symbols, and can't go to some dream book or another person to find out what a dream symbol means.[20]

Let's take about five minutes now to do a couple of things: First, I'll ask you to sketch your picture roughly in your notebook or journal, so you'll have a record of it. And when you've done that, we'd like you to gather in groups of two or three to show the others there your picture. If you want to talk about it, that's fine, but it's not necessary. There's something very valuable just about having part of our psyche *seen* or *visible* to another person or two. That makes it more real for us.

Then at home you can elaborate on your image and let it speak to you more if you want to. After a bit we'll pass the card box around and you can return them to us that way. *(Although you've not had a selection of images from which to choose, perhaps one or another picture has been inching its way into your awareness during this part of the conference. If so, it can be drawn in your notebook, and your thoughts about it recorded.)*

Betsy:
Now, let's see—we're tying up loose ends, aren't we? Is there anything else that's just floating around and needs to be pulled down to earth a little?

Youth minister:
Could we go back to using dreams in our work with other people? I've been sitting here trying to put together some kind of dream worship service in my head—it could be a special celebration, you know, not necessarily a Sunday service. Maybe on retreat, especially if we had worked dreaming into the things during the day, we could close with a service that highlights the dream.

Tom:
And what could you include in that?

Youth minister:
Well, the song we've been singing—*What You Hear in the Dark,* for one. And maybe we could pray for each other to be sent the dreams we need—it could be done in pairs or the whole group could do it. And the scripture readings could be about great dreamers.

Tom:
All right—that would work. Anything else that could go in?

Student:
The slides like yours could be a meditation—in fact, we could just steal *all* your ideas!

Betsy:
Well, there probably aren't very many brand new ideas left in this work, are there? You're very welcome to them—our licensing fee is only a few thousand! Seriously, though, just be sure to keep the publishers' credit lines on anything you reprint.

Tom:
A good time for doing something like your dream worship service would be an ecumenical gathering, wouldn't it? The dream is something that unites *all* religions. We have a Jewish-Christian Thanksgiving service in my area, and I wonder if the dream couldn't make us aware of our shared heritage—and, also, the dream *is* something to thank God for. The timing is appropriate too.

Youth minister:
You could ask the people to bring a symbol of something they've dreamed about.

Insurance agent:
Or have the cards out and ask them to find something they've had a dream about.

Sister:
We celebrate St. Joseph's feast day in my community, and since he was such a dreamer, we could have a dream prayer service in honor of him on March 19.

Betsy:
You'll find some carols about Joseph's dreams in the book we took the angel Gabriel carol from.

Counseling center director:
I find myself using dreams in the place where I work, and that grows as I use them in my own life, naturally. And we have spiritual guides there that look to people's dreams to show them the next step. We're always looking for more materials on dreams in spiritual direction.

Betsy:
We have some leaflets here from Pecos Abbey to give you on just this topic, and there are some other references we know of—you can catch us after we close the workshop.[21]

Therapist:
Can we back up for just a minute? How do dreams fit in—or do they fit in?—with all the expressive arts therapies, like music therapy and art therapy and movement and dance therapy and so on? We never talked about those.

Betsy:
Well, I think they have a very close fit, potentially, but, again, it depends on how much the therapist is in touch with his or her own dream life. For instance, I just finished doing a paper on dreams that surface in art therapy that might not surface till later in straight verbal therapy. Or they might not surface at all without the art—we don't know. And with all the expressive arts therapies, you have the two distinct emphases: one, on how the act of painting or sculpting or making music or listening to poetry or writing poetry, or whatever, is the source of healing, and the other on how the artistic, expressed product can give clues to the contents of the unconscious in a unique way. (The sandplay practitioners are experiencing this same two-way pull also, with some emphasizing the creating of the sand world, and others—calling themselves sand tray practitioners—focusing on the finished product and its meaning, and the dialogue about it with the therapist.)

But all these right-brain modalities activate the same part of the soul that gives us the dream, so they are incredibly fine adjuncts to our use of dreams in our own life and with anyone we serve. *(Smiling and laughing a little:)* Look how we've used "soul" and "psyche" interchangeably over these past few days. At one time, I remember having to stop and make a long explanation about how they were the same, but not really, but then again, and so on. Now, it's a non-issue—another sign of that science and spirit merger or fusion that we were talking about just a minute ago.

Candy store owner:
You know, as I keep looking back at the tree chart, I have a feeling it's about my prayer life too—but I'm not quite sure how.

Tom:
I'm glad you brought that up, because you're right—let's take a minute just to explore how that might work. One way to look at the tree is that the items mentioned on the trunk of the tree are some of the ways God's presence in the world—and in us—is revealed.

Betsy:
We use language like "God's ongoing revelation."

Tom:
And these, as you can see, have a direct connection to the feminine side of God—in fact, in Judaism they'd be seen as manifestations of the *shekinah,* or the (feminine) sparks of God unleashed on the earth. Let me check with our temple school director on that.

Temple school director:
Yes, that's what we'd say—and we'd see the world as filled with these sparks, which need re-collecting.

Tom:
When I read Jung and Edinger talking about the creation of consciousness, I hear it as the same thing—consciousness of the presence of God within us and all around us. Well, as we said earlier, the trunk is directly connected to the root or underground part of the tree, and the religious "ruler," if you will, of this is the feminine, the ancient goddess energy which has gone underground for a long, long time.

So, staying in touch with these everyday forms of revelation—soaking in them, really—is very much a right brain form of praying, a way of letting the feminine energy in us find its way to pray. Remember, the dream is that sort of revelation, the way we've been describing it at least—and we've been saying all along that it needs to be seen as part of our prayer life, a trigger to praying.

Candy store owner:
O.K.—and then, we also have the more formal way of praying that comes with our church or temple or whatever, if we belong to some organized religion.

Tom:
Yes, and these give the masculine energy in us a chance to pray—and notice how different these two styles are: "soaking in the sparks" all during the day and night, being aware of the presence of God—and also taking part in worship services with other people, usually conducted by some presider. We've got opportunities for both types of energy within us to pray—and when we use them both, we have a nice complementarity and balance in our prayer life. Does this answer your question?

Candy store owner:
Yes—I think so. I've done both kinds all my life, but I never thought of what you call "soaking in God" as prayer. Or, if I did, it was second-rate prayer.

His wife:
Mothers were told, in the old days, that getting up to feed a baby in the middle of the night was prayer—but it never seemed *as good* a prayer as going to Mass. So, you're saying that it's prayer from the feminine side of ourselves, and that we need that balance.

Betsy:
Uh-huh. Most of us are topheavy or lopsided with the more formal style, the masculine energy—but that's just a reflection of our churches and religious institutions, and our society too.

I think Tom has one final practical thought, and then we want to ask you to share a last reflection with us before we close our time together.

Tom:
Just a few words on possible pitfalls and problems in this weaving of dreams into ministry to others. I'm *not* talking about therapy now. My own feeling is that we're O.K. as long as we don't try to play analyst or expert. We can (1) share how important the dream is to *our* spiritual lives, and (2) encourage others to explore their dreams, and (3) affirm their attempts to do this. All without getting caught in the guru trap. That's the biggest pitfall.

Betsy:
The other one possible glitch we're often asked about is along the lines of, "Don't we need the skilled guide or analyst or therapist to be there once we begin opening up the channel to the unconscious? What might come out?—or go in? Is it safe to encourage someone to go inward in this way on their own?"

Tom:
Well, that's a very good question. Sometimes I get a little defensive when I hear it because my hunch is that the person is asking something like: "If God can communicate in this way, can't the devil get in too?"—and my own theology isn't very devil-focused, or not at all, I should say. So, since I don't sit around worrying about ways the devil can tempt someone, I'm not likely to think about that in con-

nection with the dream any more than I would about it happening when I drive to the bank or the post office. But, as you know very well, watching out for Satan is a high priority for many believers.

By the way, please don't hear me saying I don't think there's that objective evil in the world. There certainly is.

Choir director:
But how do you answer the question?

Betsy:
Well, I usually say two things. First, I always point back to the presence of the dream in scripture and how God used that way to speak to the, usually, simple souls of the biblical days—that gives our listening-to-dreams idea a firm base and makes it seem less extraordinary. And then, I say that, yes, the trained guide is an invaluable asset, but even when that person is not to be found—or can't be afforded—we're not alone when we explore our dreams prayerfully and as part of our spiritual life and when we're seeing them as sent from God. *God* is with us in the venture.

Tom:
Jung would say, trying to avoid the religious language to which his scientific colleagues objected, that the Self is wanting to be realized and that the psyche tends toward wholeness—if the ego can just get out of the way. It's something like Buber's "instinct of origination."[22]

Betsy:
And it's true that the dreams will so often show us parts of ourselves we haven't looked at before—and which may be unpleasant or very frightening to look at (and even "demonic" because they've been repressed)—but there's a kind of safety valve that's built into the process too. What I mean is that we're sent what we can handle, when we can handle it—and if something comes before we're ready for it, we tend to ignore it. Sort of the flip side of Paul's saying that we are sent the grace we need for whatever comes about.[23]

Tom:
And, just a P.S. here, it's important to note that in general we're talking about using these skills with people who are pretty well balanced, fairly "normal"—whatever that is! If you're dealing with populations with neuroses or personality disorders—as you might be in a counseling center, for example—then you're in a different ball-

park. And the dream is valuable there too, but the trained guide is very much more an essential part of the process.

Betsy:
I'd like to refer you to the introduction of Ann Faraday's 1972 book *Dream Power*.[24] She had been getting some heat from her fellow therapists for sharing dream skills with Mary Smith and John Doe, and she writes an eloquent defense of her own style of popularizing this knowledge. I remember reading that just after it came out and saying, "Good for her!"—and I think you'd appreciate it too.

Remember, the dream was, for centuries, among the common coin of spirituality—just like music, and prayer, and corporate worship—but it got lost. It started out as a gift to Everyman and Everywoman—then it vanished, and then it was reclaimed by a small group of people who had special knowledge, the psychologists. But that doesn't mean it has to stay there.

Tom:
Well, my friends, I'm sorry to say it, but the clock is telling us that this very special time together has to come to an end.

I don't know how we can properly say "thanks" for all your presence, and the gift of your beautiful dreams and imagery and contributions. I know Betsy and I had both been looking forward to spending this time with you—and, for me, it's been even richer and more blessed than I'd hoped. It's been a wonderful three days—and I thank you for your interest and, most of all, for being who you are. *(The group applauds him enthusiastically.)*

Tom:
And I give you my co-presenter and dream-worker, no, player.

Betsy:
You have been a delight to work and play and dream with—and I just want to say, "May God bless you all—and *many* sweet dreams!" *(She, too, is thanked with a hand from all.)*

Betsy:
And, now, please join us in this final experience. This is something for you to take home and digest, or maybe even stay with here for a while. We wanted to go back to the words of Scripture as a last gift to you about the dream, a gift from God to each of us. It's time for our workshop to come to an end. Will you just relax where you are once

more? *(One of the beautiful dream music selections begins to play in the background.)*

And see if you can put yourself back into neutral, after all these ideas have been bouncing around. No, we aren't going to ask you to sleep or dream, because this isn't the right setting for that. Instead, we'll ask if you'd follow along as a famous scriptural dream is read— and re-experience it for yourself.

Imagine it's you who is living this scene and dreaming. Let your eyes close, and fill out the scene with your own colors, and your own feelings, and your own pictures. There's no right way to do this. Just let it happen. *Your* way is the right way—for you. *(Over the music Tom's voice slowly reads the famous dream passage.)*

> Coming upon a certain shrine, as the sun had already set I stopped for the night. . . . Taking one of the stones at the shrine, I put it under my head and lay down to sleep at that spot. . . .
>
> Then I saw in a dream a stairway, which rested on the ground . . . and its top reached to the heavens . . . and God's messengers were going up . . . and coming down. . . .
>
> And there was the Lord standing beside me . . . and saying, "I, the Lord, am the God of your ancestors. . . . The land on which you are lying I will give to you and your descendants. . . . These shall be as plentiful as the dust of the earth. . . .
>
> And through them you shall spread out east . . . and west . . . and north . . . and south. In you and your descendants all the nations of the earth shall find blessing. . . . Know that I am with you wherever you go . . . and will bring you back to this land. . . . I will never leave you until I have done what I promised you. . . . "
>
> When I awoke from my sleep I said, "Truly, the Lord is in this spot, although I did not know it . . . " and in solemn wonder I cried out, "How awesome is this shrine. . . . This is nothing more than the abode of God, and that is the gateway to heaven. . . . "
>
> And early the next morning, I took the stone and set it up as a memorial . . . and poured oil on it . . . and said, "I will name this place 'House of God.' "[25]

Betsy:
(after a pause, still over the music) We're going to be outside in the garden, and we ask that you leave this room quietly, whenever you're ready. Perhaps you need to continue this experience for some time, even to write about it. Please take your time, and we'll say goodbye as you leave. *(Having allowed Jacob's dream to become your own in this abbreviated way, you give yourself whatever time is needed and leave quietly. Many in the group are still listening to the music,*

their eyes closed; others are recording whatever it touched in them. Those who have left ahead of you are saying goodbye to Tom and Betsy several yards from the door of the gathering room, in a garden by the orange trees.

There are hugs and a few more questions; more addresses are exchanged. Some take down their drawings; others copy book titles from those on display. What would you use this time for? Are there unanswered questions still needing to be explored? Or was your own experience something you would want to share with the group leaders?

You may decide to stay at the Center for a while, debriefing the entire three days and making notes on the conference. In your notebook or journal you can record your personal thoughts about dreaming.

And, finally, it is time to return to the busy world away from the Holy Spirit Center. The sun is setting. The blossoms on the orange trees reflect the pink spring sky of southern California. Their scent trails after you even as you drive away from the Center.

You have been

At a Dream Workshop.)

A Reflection on Jacob's Dream by a Dream Workshop Participant

I know you, Lord,
By your grace.
You found me
lying there,
on rock
stiffened.
How strong your call!
Do all your loved ones
hear this blessed song?
And now your voice in me—
it was time.
I was drawn and tired,
grumbling near the ground.
Is this your light?
falling like the morning's dawn
upon a tight and crumpled soul?
You move me.
I unfold
You hold me up.
Hosanna, Lord,
my one
my all
my home.

—Michele Clark,
February 1981

Notes

Acknowledgements:

1. From paragraph 14 of Vol. 12 of the *Collected Works of C.G. Jung* (Princeton: Princeton University Press, 1953).

Introduction:

1. From section 32 of "Song of Myself" in *Leaves of Grass,* first published in 1855 (New York: New American Library, 1955, p. 73).

2. See, among many books on this subject, Edward Whitmont's *Return of the Goddess* (New York: Crossroad Pub. Co., 1984).

3. Chapter 18 of Maslow's posthumously published final work, *The Farther Reaches of Human Nature* (New York: Viking Press, 1971), is titled "On Low Grumbles, High Grumbles and Metagrumbles." The first two types of grumbles, according to Maslow, are over our lack of basic or deficiency needs, and the metagrumbles issue forth from those who are close to—but not quite congruent with—the higher or "being needs" in their lives. However, Maslow says, if one can grumble about something, that indicates one's awareness of it—which is the necessary first step toward achieving it (see p. 241).

4. See Faraday's introduction to *Dream Power* (New York: Berkley Publishing Corp., 1972), especially page 17; also her second book *The Dream Game* (New York: Harper and Row, 1974).

5. The basic "starter" book we recommend to those looking for a way to integrate the dream into their spiritual life is Morton Kelsey's *Dreams: A Way to Listen to God* (Ramsey, N.J.: Paulist Press, 1978). Kelsey's other book centered on dreaming—a theme he picks up again and again in all his work—is *God, Dreams and Revelation: A Christian Interpretation of Dreams* (Minneapolis: Augsburg Publishing House, 1974 ed.). John Sanford's first work on dreams was *Dreams: God's Forgotten Language* (Philadelphia: J.B. Lippincott Co., 1968; reissued by Crossroad in 1984); this was followed in 1978 by *Dreams and Healing* (Ramsey, N.J.: Paulist Press), with the accurate subtitle "A Succinct and Lively Interpretation of Dreams." Many other authors could also be cited; we focus on these works because of their avail-

ability and also the ease with which they open up the world of the dream for the uninitiated. C.G. Jung's own description of the dream for lay persons will be found in his chapter of *Man and His Symbols* (London, Aldus Books, Ltd., 1964), particularly the section titled "The importance of dreams," on pp. 20ff. In addition, the heart of his writing on dreams has been excerpted from his *Collected Works* into a small volume titled *Dreams* (Princeton: Princeton University Press, 1974).

The First Evening:

1. Job 33:14–16, 29 (paraphrased).

2. See note 5, Introduction.

3. From Act II of Engelbert Humperdinck's opera, first performed two days before Christmas at Weimar, Germany in 1893.

4. Synesius, bishop of Cyrene, was one of the seminal thinkers in Greek Orthodoxy. His work on the dream, in 415 A.D., can be found in *The Essays and Hymns of Synesius of Cyrene,* by Augustine Fitzgerald (London: Oxford, 1930).

5. Genesis 28:10–22.

6. Genesis 37:5–11; 40; 41.

7. 1 Samuel 3:2–11.

8. Daniel 4:1–24. (This picture is the frontispiece for Jung on *Dreams* (see note 5 for Introduction, above).

9. The story of Joachim's dream comes from the *Prologue* of St. Jerome, quoted in the thirteenth century classic, *The Golden Legend* of Jacobus de Voragine (republished in 1941 by Longmans, Green and Co., Inc., New York); see pp. 521ff.

10. A picture referring to this apocryphal event can be found in *Dreams: Visions of the Night* by David Coxhead and Susan Hiller (New York: Avon Books, 1975); see plate no. 36.

11. Matthew 1:20–21.

12. Matthew 2:13–14.

13. Matthew 2:12.

14. Acts 10:9–16.

15. Revelation 1:1–2.

16. Several pictures of the dreaming Helena show her as youthful, even though she was supposedly seventy years old at the time—in the world of dreams, time stands still!

17. See *The Golden Legend,* pp. 271ff, for one version of the familiar story of Constantine. Also, Eusebius' *Church History,* c. 315.

18. Ambrose on the dream can be found in quotations in Kelsey's *God, Dreams and Revelation,* pp. 145ff.

19. *Dreams and Spiritual Growth* (see Acknowledgements) has a section on Jerome as a dreamer (see pp. 42ff).

20. References to Gregory Nazianzen on dreams (as well as many other early church fathers and doctors) are in Kelsey, *op. cit.*, p. 137. See also chapters 5 and 6.

21. St. Ursula's dream is recounted in *The Golden Legend,* pp. 627ff. The famous painting of the angel coming to her at night, by Carpaccio, shows Ursula's hand cupped to her ear as she sleeps, the better to catch the dream message.

22. Dominican lore has held this story dear; it is pictured in the altarpiece of S. Caterina, Pisa, Italy. The source of Jane's dream is Dominic's original hagiographer, Theodoric of Appoldia, writing c. 1290 (reproduced in the *Acta Sanctorum*).

23. Also pictured in Pisa, and painted by Fra Angelico as well (now in the Louvre).

24 and 25. Both scenes are pictured in the famous frescoes of the life of Saint Francis by Giotto in the Basilica of San Francesco in Assisi, c. 1300.

26. Source (in French) *Roman de l'Estoire dou Graal,* ed. by W.A. Nitze (Paris: Champion, 1927).

27–29. Pictures of these three dream scenes can be found in Coxhead and Hiller, *op. cit.* (plates 41, 37 and 33 respectively).

30. *Journal of Dreams* by Emmanuel Swedenborg contains 286 dreams he recorded in 1743–44. First published in Swedish in 1859, an English edition was reissued in 1977, ed. by W.R. Woofenden (New York: Swedenborg Foundation, Inc.).

31. See the Knox translation of Thérèse's *Autobiography* (New York: P.J. Kenedy & Sons, 1957), pp. 230–231, for this moving dream of the French saint just before her death in 1897.

32. Don Bosco's recorded dreams guided him all through his life in his work with the street boys of Turin and his founding of the Salesians. See *The Biographical Memoirs of Saint John Bosco,* ed. by Giovanni Battista Lemoyne, S.D.B. (New Rochelle, N.Y.: Salesiana Publishers, Inc., 1965). Also, *Dreams, Visions and Prophecies of Don Bosco,* with an introduction by Morton Kelsey from the same publisher (1986).

33. See *Hecker Studies: Essays on the Thought of Isaac Hecker,* ed. by John Farina (Mahwah, N.J.: Paulist Press, 1983).

34. The Siena Cathedral altarpiece, the famous *Maestà,* painted by Duccio at the end of the thirteenth century, had on its reverse side, originally, forty-four scenes from the life of Christ. The one we use here represented the calling of Peter and Andrew, but it also illustrates perfectly the idea of the haul of (inner) fishes. A print of this masterpiece is available from the National Gallery of Art, Publications Service, Washington D.C. 20565. The original is in the permanent collection at the Gallery.

35. As noted in the Acknowledgements, this meditation is adapted from the work of Strephon Williams of the Jungian-Senoi Institute and Journey Press (P.O. Box 9036, Berkeley, CA 94709).

The Second Day—Morning

1. Psalm 127:2.
2. Psalm 63:2–9.
3. "What You Hear in the Dark," by Dan Schutte, on the St. Louis Jesuits' album *Earthen Vessels* (Phoenix, AZ: North American Liturgy Resources, 1975).
4. Matthew 10:27.
5. The Egyptian Nile goose was called the "Great Chatterer," and was thought to be the creator of the world, laying the cosmic egg which gave birth to their sun god; in India, the "Great Cackler" goose was the vehicle of Brahma; Aphrodite of ancient Greece rode on her goose, and Rome was once saved from a Gallic invasion by the alert geese of the temple of Juno, ever afterward making them the sacred symbol of watchfulness.
6. From the sound track album of the film *Jonathan Livingston Seagull*, music and vocals by Neil Diamond, 1973 (Columbia Record #KS 32550).
7. As one example of this, *New Age Journal* for November 1985 had a bold cover blurb: "DREAM CONTROL: Can learning to change the content of your dreams improve your life? . . . " as a lead-in to an article based on Stephen LeBerge's book *Lucid Dreaming* (Los Angeles: J.P. Tarcher, Inc., 1985). The authors of the article and LeBerge take the term "lucid dreaming" beyond its original meaning of knowing that one is dreaming while in the dream, to a new definition of controlling the contents of the dream, a very different attitude than that of incubation—or inviting God's guidance into our lives. See also *Omni*, April 1987.
8. *Ancient Incubation and Modern Psychotherapy,* C.A. Meier (Evanston: Northwestern University Press, 1967); *The Sacred Pipe,* Black Elk, ed. by Joseph E. Brown (New York: Penguin Books, 1971); *Seven Arrows,* Hyemeyohsts Storm (New York: Ballantine Books, 1972); *Collected Works of C.G. Jung*—Vol. 8, par. 549; Vol. 12, par. 171; Vol. 5, par. 571 (Princeton: Princeton University Press); *The Understanding of Dreams and Their Influence on the History of Man,* Raymond de Becker (Bell Publisher, 1968), and *The Dream and Human Societies,* G.E. von Grunebaum and Roger Caillois, eds. (Berkeley: University of California Press, 1966).
9. Genesis 1:2.
10. *Ruah* translates variably as "Spirit of God," "breath of God," and "mighty wind." From the Hebrew, it corresponds to the Greek *pneuma*.
11. For example, see Romans 9:20–21.
12. See Matthew 23:37.
13. See Exodus 13:21.
14. Tom is referring to a liturgical celebration held at Mount St. Mary's College, November 2, 1985, with Matthew Fox, O.P. as celebrant.
15. See note 5, Introduction.
16. *New Catholic World,* March/April 1984, Vol. 227, #1358.

17. Jung spoke of this inborn tendency toward wholeness as "the religious instinct." See *Memories, Dreams, Reflections,* Jung's autobiography (New York: Random House, 1969), p. 196, for one of many places in C.G. Jung's writings where he speaks of the autonomous desire of the psyche for wholeness.

18. The reference is to Jung's essay on "Flying Saucers: A Modern Myth," first published in 1958, and found in Volume 10 of his *Collected Works* (Princeton: Princeton University Press, 1964).

19. *C.G. Jung: Word and Image,* Aniela Jaffé, ed. (Princeton: Princeton University Press, 1979), pp. 66ff.

20. *The Story of C.G. Jung* is the van der Post film. It is replete with scenes of Jung's living environments, from childhood through old age, providing an excellent immersion into the life and times of the psychologist. However, van der Post comes close to canonizing Jung through his 1959 film presentation, somewhat obscuring the humanness of his subject.

21. *Matter of Heart,* revised version of 1984. Conceived and written by Suzanne Wagner, directed by Mark Whitney, executive producer George Wagner.

22. Betsy is referring to lectures by Frau Helene Hoerni-Jung, lecturing on iconography and icons, Küsnacht-Zürich, 1985–86.

23. See Numbers 21:6–9.

24. Grimm's fairy tale #161 (to be distinguished from "Snow White and the Seven Dwarfs," #53).

25. A good source at present writing for these journals, in hard and soft covers, is Publishers Central Bureau, Dept. 378, 1 Champion Avenue, Avenel, N.J. 07001-9987.

26. Still in use by Jung's family, the tower-house at Bollingen is not easily seen by the public. We have access to it through photographs, however, both in the films mentioned above and in *Word and Image,* pp. 188ff.

27. Matthew 7:13.

28. Although there are exceptions to the silver/moon pairing in folklore (as in the tales of the Toba people of Argentina), this is a very common association; gold and the sun are most often seen as complements. See the Appendix of symbols in *The Woman Sealed in the Tower,* Betsy Caprio (Ramsey, N.J.: Paulist Press, 1983).

29. The Jungian approach to the sand tray (and there are others) is best described in the work of its originator, Dora Kalff. See her *Sandplay: A Psychotherapeutic Approach to the Psyche* (Santa Monica, CA: Sigo Press, 1980).

30. See note 4, Introduction.

31. Credence Cassettes, National Catholic Reporter Publishing Co., Kansas City, Missouri 64141. This set of tapes was produced in 1986. Sanford is echoing Jung, who writes throughout his *Collected Works* cautions such as this one (from Vol. 13, para. 199): "Of course, we all have an understandable desire for crystal clarity, but . . . in psychic matters we are dealing with processes of experience . . . which should never be given hard and fast

names if their living movement is not to petrify into something static . . . the shimmering symbol express(es) the processes of the psyche far more trenchantly and . . . far more clearly than the clearest concept."

32. This is thought number 81 from the *Tao Te Ching,* as translated by Gia-Fu Feng and Jane English (New York: Random House, 1972). It is the idea that ends this 2,500-year old collection of aphorisms, which form the basis of Taoist spirituality.

33. "The Seven Sleepers" is recorded in *The Golden Legend* (see note 9 for the first evening). The time setting for it is the reign of the Roman emperor Decius, 252 A.D., which was still the time of persecutions of the Christians. At the end of the story, the medieval hagiographer confesses that his historicity may be askew, and that the seven sleepers may only have slept 196 years, which makes no difference to the tale in terms of its didactic value.

In Anna Jameson's famous work of the last century, *Sacred and Legendary Art,* Vol. 2 (Boston: Houghton Mifflin & Co., 1985 ed.), she writes of how carvings and painted representations of the seven holy sleepers are found in churches all over Europe, reflecting the widespreadness of this legend. In many places, she writes, one finds the seven men all in a row (suggesting a precedent for the seven dwarfs in the "Snow White" tales). Gibbon tells us that Mohammed introduced this legend into the *Koran* as part of divine revelation.

The Second Day—Afternoon:

1. It should not be hard to find your own picture of this famous and often-reproduced scene; try bibles, Christmas greeting cards, art books, or send to one of the sources listed in note 44, below.

2. The association between wingedness and heaven pre-dates the idea of heaven being within us. To the ancients, heaven was "up there"—where only the birds with their wings could fly. See *Coming Home* by your authors (Mahwah, N.J.: Paulist Press, 1986), pp. 226ff.

3. Any of the translations of Ignatius' exercises will illustrate this point. See, for example, the Louis J. Puhl 1951 translation, reissued by Loyola University Press of Chicago.

4. Published from 1968 on by Word, Inc. of Waco, Texas in a series of workbooks that are still a landmark in religious education.

5. The intrapsychic approach being described, for both a scriptural event and the dream, is not the only possibility. This point will be developed in the third day afternoon session.

6. The motif of transpersonal annunciation shows up cross-culturally. To cite just two examples, there is the dew that comes down from heaven in the story of Gideon and the fleece (Judges 6:36–40); the dew is often seen to be a prefiguring of the Spirit impregnating Mary by Christian iconogra-

phers. Farther from our culture is the story of the Kirghiz of Siberia in which the young maiden is made pregnant by the sun or the eye of God beaming down on her (see *The Golden Bough* by J.G. Frazer, originally published in 1922; pages 602–03 of the 1944 one-volume abridged edition from Macmillan, N.Y.). Conception from sunlight is a motif found in many cultures, and in India there is the tale of impregnation by shooting stars.

In the basic reference on folklore motifs, Stith Thompson's *Motif-Index of Folk-Literature* (Bloomington, IN: Indiana University Press, 1955), the blanket category for such tales is his T510: "Miraculous Conception," which he differentiates from V.312: "Belief in Immaculate Conception."

7. The left side and its symbolism is detailed fully in one of the standard reference works on symbolism, *A Dictionary of Symbols* by J.E. Cirlot (New York: Philosophical Library, 1962; see pp. 287–89 esp.). The original connection with left and the unknown is presumed by many authors to have come from the predominant righthandedness of humans; the left, therefore, would be not normally the hand (or side) with which one reaches out into the material world, but its opposite (i.e., the side with which one goes within to the spiritual or non-material world). In the west, this took on overtones of left as inferior and even evil (*sinister* is the Latin for left), leading to sheep on the right and goats on the left hand of God at the final judgment (Matthew 25:33) and, at the crucifixion, the good thief on the right and the bad thief on the left (Matthew 27:38). In ancient China, however, the left or weaker side is honored because it is the right or stronger side that tends to violence and, therefore, self-destruction.

8. An example of the reversed positions can be found in a Fra Angelico missal illumination (c. 1340) still in the Dominican museum of San Marco in Florence. The artist was illuminating the letter "R" and used the space between the "legs" of the letter to contain the seated virgin, since she had to be closest to the ground; God the Father leans over from the circle at the top of the letter, and the angel is put in the only possible space, to the right of the letter. Here, the exigencies of the art form are responsible for the changed positions. This painting is reproduced in *Angelico,* by John Pope-Hennessy (San Francisco: Harper and Row, 1983), one of the series of beautiful yet inexpensive Scala Books available in many museum bookshops.

9. A complete listing of this sort of bridging image can be found in the companion volume to *Coming Home,* titled *A Manual for Spiritual Direction* (Mahwah, N.J.: Paulist Press, 1986); see p. 16, under images of the sacred marriage.

10. See the beautiful *Angels* by Peter Lamborn Wilson (New York: Pantheon Books, 1980), especially pp. 178ff.

11. One such representation is found in the famous Siena Cathedral altarpiece (see note 34 for the first evening, above). The staff also has classical and earlier roots, being found in the healing (and snake-entwined) staff of Hermes and Asclepius of Greece, and the lily scepter, Cretan symbol of the goddess and queen. If we trace the images in Marian art back to their

pre-Christian roots, we see Mary as the latest of many incarnations of the ancient divine feminine, a thread referred to elsewhere in this book—but beyond our present scope.

There are also paintings and frescoes of the annunciation where Mary is spinning, which links her to the early great goddesses as spinner of fate. (See, for example, *The Great Mother* by Erich Neumann [Princeton: Princeton University Press, 1955], pp. 232ff. and plate 96.)

12. The picture referred to is from an anonymous altarpiece of the fifteenth century, now in the Kunsthistorisches Museum, Vienna.

13. The more elaborate annunciations are predominantly Flemish Renaissance versions of this scene. The speaker refers to one by Rogier van der Weyden, c. 1464, now in the Louvre.

14. The distinction used here is between Revelation, considered by most Christian churches to have been concluded with the end of the apostolic era, and God's ongoing revelation in everyday life to all peoples. *The National Catechetical Directory for Catholics of the United States* (Washington, D.C.: U.S. Catholic Conference, 1979) calls this second sort of revelation "manifestation" or "communication."

15. Jung reminds us that "Ever since the *Timaeus* (of Plato) it has been repeatedly stated that the soul is a sphere." (Vol. 9ii of the *Collected Works,* Princeton: Princeton University Press, 1959), par. 212.

16. We are still in a time when these two words—*psychology* and *spirituality*—are viewed by many as referring to two separate forms of human experience, since much of psychology doesn't acknowledge the spiritual, and much of spirituality doesn't acknowledge the psychological. The authors postulate (in the third morning and afternoon sessions) a time when this division will not be so marked, at least in terms of the experiential side of life if not the doctrinal.

17. Danaë's tale is found in Ovid's *Metamorphoses.*

18. This is a much later, alchemical version of the Zeus-Danaë myth, and can be found (with a picture of the agonizing virgin) in *Alchemy: The Medieval Alchemists and Their Royal Art* by Johannes Fabricius (Copenhagen: Rosenkilde and Bagger, 1976), pp. 42ff.

19. In Chaldean.

20. Again, the viewer of this multitude of pictures of the annunciation will see that it is the Flemish masters, using oils, that have turned the wings of their angels into rainbows; the earlier Italian painters, many working in fresco, often had less variety and intensity of color available to them.

21. One of the most famous of the several Fra Angelico annunciations, this one is often reproduced and can be found in *Angelico* (see note 8, above), p. 16. Formerly from the altarpiece of San Domenico in Cortona, Italy (c. 1422–23), it now hangs in the diocesan museum there, and is considered Angelico's first masterpiece.

22. Tom is referring to Betsy's book mentioned in note 28, above, *The Woman Sealed in the Tower.*

23. Best exemplified by the circle or enclosed space.

24. An important point made by Dr. Edinger in his talk on "The Christian Archetype," Claremont, California, January 19, 1985.

25. In his commentary on the Canticles, Bernard of Clairvaux, initiator of the Cistercian reform in the twelfth century, describes the prefiguring of Mary in the Hebrew scriptures.

26. From his talk on "The Christian Archetype" at St. Simon's Island, Georgia, May 11, 1982.

27. Angelus Silesius ("the angel of Silesia") was the pen name of Johann Scheffler (1624–1677), who wrote *The Cherubinic Wanderer* in four days of his Lutheran youth. He became court physician to a Lutheran duke, then converted to Catholicism and was ordained to the priesthood. The verse cited is #120, which is rendered in the J.E. Crawford Flitch translation (London: George Allen & Unwin, Ltd., 1932) as: "Into this little drop, this I, how can it be / That there should flow the whole Sea of the Deity?"

28. In *Jung and the Post-Jungians,* Andrew Samuels writes: "Jung saw psychosis as a movement into the collective unconscious from which a 'normal' person is separated and protected by ego-consciousness" and " . . . for some psychotics, (in the Jungian view) breakdown may be a psychological breakthrough" (p. 204). Here we see how Jung's thought anticipated that of later psychologists like R.D. Laing and Thomas Szasz about the nature of psychosis. (Samuels' book: London: Routledge and Kegan Paul, 1985.)

29. *Woman's Mysteries: Ancient and Modern* by M. Esther Harding (New York: Harper and Row, 1971). See also *Virgin: Images of the Untouched,* Joanne Stroud and Gail Thomas, eds. (Dallas: Spring Pub., 1982).

30. *Goddesses in Everywoman: A New Psychology of Women* by Jean Shinoda Bolen (San Francisco: Harper and Row, 1984). Bolen revisions Jung's thought about "masculine energy," finding it better represented for modern women by the virgin goddesses.

31. See note 2, above.

32. One of the best cat-echetical references is *The Archetypal Cat* by Patricia Dale-Green (New York: Houghton Mifflin, 1963), a reissue of her *Cult of the Cat.* It has several pictures of Bastet, cat goddess of fertility and joy in ancient Egypt; priests bow before her and her kittens.

33. God as cloud appears in the desert, then over the ark and the temple; sometimes it is called "the glory" or "the radiance," the shiny cloud or *shekinah.*

34. From Edinger's Georgia talk (see note 26): " . . . the idea, then, is that . . . at the beginning of the incarnation cycle comes a willingness to allow the cloud, the transpersonal reality, to rest on one and incarnate and come into manifestation in one's own life . . . and this is as likely to be a dark experience as a bright one."

35. Canticles 2:1.

36. While the great majority of annunciation pictures have the lily, some of the Sienese artists substituted the olive branch for the lily—not for

aesthetic or theological reasons, but because the lily was also the emblem of their rival city, Florence. We can interpret it as a sign of peace also.

37. 2 Corinthians 3:6.

38. The painting referred to is by Jan van Eyck (c. 1425–30), and now hangs in the National Gallery of Art in Washington, D.C., one of its greatest treasures. Also on the marbled floor can be seen the astrological signs of Scorpio and Sagittarius—the darkest time of the year in the northern hemisphere; Mary standing on them shows the artist's view of *the source* of the new light (at the winter solstice, in Sagittarius).

39. See "The Stages of Life" in Vol. 8 of Jung's *Collected Works* (Princeton: Princeton University Press, 1960; originally, 1931). Here Jung discusses his concept of individuation as the turning-around and going-within process of the second half of life (in contrast to other psychodynamic theorists who use "individuation" to mean the growth process from birth on, such as Michael Fordham in *Children as Individuals* (London: Hodder and Stoughton, 1969). This essay contains the often-quoted sentence of Jung,

> " . . . we cannot live the afternoon of life according to the programme of life's morning; for what was great in the morning will be little at evening, and what in the morning was true will at evening have become a lie" (par. 784).

40. See note 21, above, for one of the Fra Angelicos; the second is from twenty years later (c. 1445), and now hangs in the Prado in Madrid. The later work lacks some of the naive charm of the earlier.

41. From the collection of the National Gallery of Art in Washington, D.C., this annunciation is by Giovanni di Paolo of Siena (c. 1460); in it, he shows off his mastery of the new science of perspective drawing, and he places an aging (and doubting?) Joseph off to the side in front of a hearth, out of earshot of Mary and her heavenly visitor. Above the chimney soars a stork, associated with new babies for centuries and also with the coming of spring (i.e., new life). The other bird found occasionally in these pictures is the swallow, a symbol of the incarnation, for it was thought to hibernate in nests under eaves and holes in walls, returning to activity in the springtime. (The dove, of course, symbolizes the Holy Spirit. In *The Woman's Encyclopedia of Myths and Secrets* [San Francisco: Harper and Row, 1983], Barbara Walker reminds us that the dove was also the totem animal of Venus in ancient Greece and Rome, standing for sexual union and life. [See pp. 252ff.])

42. Edinger's comments on this dual image: " . . . my suggestion is that the expulsion from the Garden of Eden and the annunciation of the conception of Christ are two different expressions for the same thing." He is referring to the autonomic tendency of the psyche to show both faces when its deeper realms are activated (*op. cit.*). See also, on Eve, John Sanford's treatment of the Genesis story in his book on the Hebrew scriptures, *The Man Who Wrestled with God* (King of Prussia, Pa.: Religious Publishing Co., 1974; reissued by Paulist Press in 1981). See pp. 111ff.

43. Jung defines enantiodromia in par. 708 of "Psychological Types," Vol. 6 of Jung's *Collected Works* (Princeton: Princeton University Press, 1971. Originally published 1921).

44. Three of the best sources of art prints are:
• Philadelphia Museum of Art, Box 7646, Philadelphia, PA 19101
• The Metropolitan Museum of Art, Middle Village, N.Y. 11381
• National Gallery of Art, Washington, D.C. 20565

45. See "The Container or Enclosure," pp. 31ff. in *Coming Home: A Manual for Spiritual Direction* (Mahwah, N.J.: Paulist Press, 1986). Usually Mary is in her house in the pictures; if not, she is still in enclosed space: on a porch or (in the icons) on a throne, often with a canopy above it.

46. Described in *The Gnostic Gospels* by Elaine Pagels (New York: Random House, 1979), a fascinating true story, winner of the National Book Critics Circle Award. The Nag Hammadi texts were discovered in 1945.

47. The apocryphal *Protevangelion* can be found in *The Lost Books of the Bible* (New York: Bell Publishing Co., 1926; reissued 1979 by Crown Publishers, Inc.); Chap. 9:7–17 is the annunciation story. The original translation on which this work is based is that of William Hone, published in 1820. The story is sometimes called the "Pre-Annunciation." The *Protevangelion* (second century) is also known as *The Revelation of James*, and was valued as authentic by the early church fathers, but eventually dropped from the canon. For paintings or representations of this scene, look to icon series of the life of the mother of God; it is rare.

48. The story from Catherine-lore is that her father, in punishment for her refusal to marry, took away her little prayer spot under the stairs of the family home in Siena. To compensate for the loss, Catherine created a "little cell" in her heart where she could pray always in union with God—an early example of centering prayer.

49. From *Contemplation in a World of Action,* essays of Thomas Merton (Garden City, N.Y.: Image Books, 1973). These essays were published after Merton's bizarre death in Bangkok in December of 1968.

50. Edinger, *op. cit.*

51. Jung, in dream seminars given in Zurich from March 23 to July 6, 1925, speaks of the purpose of analysis: to lead the person to an original experience of the autonomous psyche. His words are, "If I had to choose an image of this (original experience), I would choose the annunciation."

The Second Day—Evening:

1. From *The Gospel in Art by the Peasants of Solentiname,* Philip and Sally Scharper, eds. (Maryknoll, N.Y.: Orbis Books, 1984).

2. *The 'I' and the 'Not-I': A Study in the Development of Consciousness* by M. Esther Harding (Princeton: Princeton University Press, 1965) is one of the early books that made Jung's thought accessible to English-speaking readers.

3. These basic Jungian terms are defined throughout the literature. See, for example, the book mentioned above, pp. 76ff and 101ff. See also *Man and His Symbols.*

4. See C.G. Jung's caution against "believing that the unconscious always knows best" in "On the Nature of Dreams" in Vol. 8 of the *Collected Works* (Princeton: Princeton University Press, 1960; originally published, 1945), par. 568.

5. *The Oxford Book of Carols,* collected and annotated by Percy Dearmer, Ralph Vaughan Williams and Martin Shaw (London: Oxford University Press, 1928; new edition, 1964).

6. The first mention of "the feast of the Incarnation" is in the Sacramentary of Pope Gelasius, 496 A.D. The first visual image we have of the annunciation, however, is earlier, being found in the catacomb of Priscilla in Rome, dating from the second century. The angel in this rock painting is wingless.

7. *The Oxford Book of Carols* contains introductory material on the history of the traditional carols. There are 197 in this definitive book, many of them being secular folk tunes that were given didactic religious texts by clerics. The "age of the carol" is the Renaissance and the century following it (c. 1450ff).

8. Genesis 12:1–6.

9. See the manual for *Coming Home* for examples of the so-called "masculine energy," pp. 15ff, under the title "Symbols of Change and Transformation."

10. *Man and His Symbols* explores the contrasexual energy in several places; see also *The Invisible Partners* by John Sanford (Ramsey, N.J.: Paulist Press, 1980).

11. See note 27, above, for the source. This verse (#172 in the Flitch translation, to which #117 has been added) is also quoted by Jung in *Mysterium Coniunctionis,* Vol. 14 of his *Collected Works* (Princeton: Princeton University Press, 1963), par. 444, in a different translation. Jung places the annunciation image within the context of alchemy in this work . . . inner alchemy.

The translation Jung is using contains this line which explicitly refers to the overpowering of the soul by God: "God, make me pregnant and His Spirit shadow me. . . . "

12. This old favorite has music by J.S. Bach and words by Edwin Hatch (1886).

13. The annunciation described is attributed to Hans Memling, c. 1470. The floor of Mary's room, as in so many of these pictures, is a collection of mandalic tile squares.

14. Luke 1:26–38.

15. Gabriel is called the "Salutation Angel" in French.

16. From *The Zohar* of thirteenth century Spain comes Gabriel's title of "supervisor of dreams." In Jewish lore, Gabriel is also guardian of the

celestial treasury. Milton says that Gabriel is chief of the guardians of paradise (in *Paradise Regained,* 1671). By tradition, this archangel speaks in a low voice.

17. The Islamic name for Gabriel is Jibra'il, the angel who brought the words of *The Koran* to Mohammed. In addition to the details cited in the prayer here, all of which come from the Muslim tradition, Gabriel is also supposed to have hair of saffron, and when he enters the ocean of light each new day one million drops fall from each of his wings (it is said) to become new Islamic angels!

18. This final slide is an expectant virgin carved of limestone from the fourteenth century, now in the collection of the Metropolitan Museum of Art in New York City. It is French, 16 3/4″ tall.

The Third Day—Morning:

1. The icon described is now in St. Catherine's Monastery at Mount Sinai, the Greek Orthodox treasury of icons which escaped the iconoclasts' destruction of works of art during the sixth through the ninth centuries. It is presumed to be from the end of the twelfth century, painted in the Byzantine capital of Constantinople. The icon can be found on the cover of Kurt Weitzmann's collection titled *The Icon: Holy Images—Sixth to Fourteenth Century* (New York: George Braziller, 1978) and as color plate #27, and in black and white in a book still being sold as a "coffee table art book," titled *Icons,* by Weitzmann and his colleagues Manolis Chatzidakis and Svetozar Radojcic (New York: Alpine Fine Arts Collection, 1980), plate #54.

In the icon, Mary is spinning (see note 11, above). The angel is clad in very agitated drapery, which (comments Weitzmann) underscores the scene's high emotional pitch. Barely visible on the virgin's upper body is a seated Christ in a mandorla, as in the icons of the sign; the imprint of her son is already present, even as the angel greets Mary. She is dressed in deep blues and purples, and looks distressed by the visitation. The icon, considered one of the unique masterpieces of Comnenian art, measures 16 1/2″ wide by 22 1/2″ in height; it is well worth a picture search to see this charged and most beautiful representation of the Annunciation.

2. Archbishop Romero's words are quoted in *The Church Is All of You: The Thoughts of Archbishop Oscar Romero,* James R. Brockman, S.J., translator (Minneapolis: Winston Press, 1984), p. 48.

3. Augustine's famous phrase of union with God is from the opening paragraph of his *Confessions,* late fourth century A.D.

4. *Icons* (see note 1, above) has a complete description of the iconostasis (see p. 7).

5. See Luke 1:19 and Judges 13:3.

6. More specifically, this gesture of the eastern rite deacon imitates the traditional painted pose of the angel in iconography, in which one wing

is higher off the ground than the other, indicating that the angel has just landed. The pose states, to the viewer, that the angel has come from above.

7. *Kataphatic* is from the Greek, and means "with images"; *apophatic* means "without images." See Morton Kelsey's *Companions on the Inner Way* (New York: Crossroad, 1983), p. 7, on the distinction between these two prayer ways and, more completely, *Spiritual Friend* by Tilden Edwards (New York: Paulist Press, 1980), pp. 18ff.

8. Basil the Great, founder of Eastern monasticism, compares "the enigma in dreams" to scripture for obscurity, saying the additional time each takes to understand helps their meaning stay with us longer. See Kelsey's comments on Basil in *God, Dreams and Revelation,* pp. 136ff.

9. "Synchronicity: An Acausal Connecting Principle" was a monograph first published in German in 1952, then in a revised edition in 1969. The separate edition in English traces, in its introduction by Michael Fordham, Jung's interest in the idea of synchronicity back to his acquaintance with Albert Einstein, who had been a professor in Zurich between 1909 and 1913 (Princeton: Princeton University Press, 1973).

10. *The Tao of Psychology,* Jean Shinoda Bolen (San Francisco: Harper and Row, 1979).

11. See, for example, par. 320 in Vol. 5 of Jung's *Collected Works* (Princeton: Princeton University Press, 1956).

12. Some authors would use the word "complex" for what we are calling a "pocket of energy"; however, that word has gathered around it negative connotations which have diminished its usefulness and skewed its original meaning. "Constellation of energy" is another non-pejorative phrase, implying consciousness of the complex.

13. One of the best descriptions of active imagination will be found in June Singer's *Boundaries of the Soul* (Garden City, N.Y.: Doubleday, 1972), chapter 12. Almost all the basic Jungian books, however, will have ideas on dreaming the dream onward. See also chapter 5 of *Coming Home.*

14. Jung, the last person one would label anti-intellectual because of the richness of his own scholarship, nevertheless makes a resounding case for the helping professional to be firmly rooted *first* in his or her own lived experience: " . . . between what science calls psychology and what the practical needs of daily life demand from psychology there is a great gulf fixed." From "New Paths in Psychology," first published in 1912 and reprinted in the appendix of Vol. 7 of the *Collected Works* (Princeton: Princeton University Press, 1953); see par. 409.

15. Neumann's developmental scheme comes from his book *The Child* (New York: Harper and Row, 1976).

16. Throughout his all-too-short life's work, Maslow grumbled about those who would make his suggested stage theory—the hierarchy of needs—into a lock-step game of snakes and ladders. Erik Erikson, also, is another famous stage theorist whose developmental ladder has been cast into cement

by some of his readers and apologists, and he too has spent many years asking them to use his format as a guide, not a rigid, pigeonholing map.

17. From a keynote address by Jean Houston to the transpersonal education conference of May 1978, "Children of the New Age" (California State University, Fullerton).

18. See note 12, second day, afternoon session. Edinger's later books are: *Melville's Moby Dick: A Jungian Commentary* (New York: New Directions Publishing Corp., 1978), *The Creation of Consciousness: Jung's Myth for Modern Man* (Toronto: Inner City Books, 1984), *Anatomy of the Psyche: Alchemical Symbolism in Psychotherapy* (La Salle, Ill: Open Court Publishing Co., 1985), *Encounter with the Self: A Jungian Commentary on William Blake's "Illustrations of the Book of Job"* (Toronto: Inner City Books, 1986), and *The Bible and the Psyche: Individuation Symbolism in the Old Testament* (Toronto: Inner City Books, 1986).

19. The book based on the Christian archetype material referred to throughout the present work is *The Christian Archetype: A Jungian Commentary on the Life of Christ* (Toronto: Inner City Books, 1987).

20. In this, Dr. Edinger is rooted in Jung's often-quoted statement that "I am not . . . addressing myself to the happy possessors of faith . . . " found in "Psychology and Religion" in Vol. 11 of the *Collected Works* (Princeton: Princeton University Press, 1958), par. 148 (originally from a 1938 address in English).

21. *The Hero with a Thousand Faces,* Joseph Campbell (Princeton: Princeton University Press, 1949).

22. See note 28, above.

23. See note 18, above.

24. From the same source as note 20, above, "That is to say, what happens in the life of Christ happens always and everywhere. In the Christian archetype all lives . . . are prefigured and are expressed over and over again . . . " (par. 146).

25. See *Becoming Adult, Becoming Christian* by James Fowler (San Francisco: Harper and Row, 1984).

26. Jung, *op. cit.,* par. 758 (in the 1952 essay "Answer to Job").

27. The youth minister is quoting Elsom Eldridge, who with Chandler Brown pioneered the Centerpoint study programs in St. Louis.

28. From Merton's book (see note 49, above): "Real Christian living is stunted and frustrated if it remains content with the bare externals of worship, with 'saying prayers' and 'going to church,' with fulfilling one's external duties and merely being respectable" (p. 178).

29. Another way to say this: The sequence of events in the life of Jesus parallels the individuation process, although one might not go through them in the same order, nor through all of them. Also, an event like the annunciation can keep on unfolding: we might have an initial happening that corresponds to the annunciation in our own soul-life, which then becomes the nucleus around which further similar (inner and outer) experiences cluster.

This way, we build up our own inner legendry about that event in our lives, just as the annunciation event in Mary's life has built up its own lore through centuries of accretions of legend, art, music, etc. Concurrently, one might also be experiencing the initial or core happening of inner nativity, with its own energy cluster developing, and also any of the subsequent events in the Christian archetype. (See Edinger's explanation of the developmental process of the alchemical stages in *Anatomy of the Psyche* [see note 18, above], especially pp. 14–15; alchemy describes the individuation process in yet another language to that of the Christian story.)

30. Freud on the dream is presumed background for those who would understand Jung on the dream, although the former's standpoint is far more narrow. Freud's dream writings are found primarily in Volumes IV and V of *The Standard Edition of the Complete Psychological Works of Sigmund Freud,* James Strachey, ed. (London: Hogarth Press, 1953–74). See especially Freud's seminal 1913 work *The Interpretation of Dreams* (New York: Avon Books, 1965, included in the standard edition of Freud, above).

31. *Silent Music,* William Johnston (New York: Harper and Row, 1976), p. 21.

32. *Original Blessing,* Matthew Fox (Santa Fe: Bear and Co., 1983).

33. Another branch that might well be on the "creation spirituality" family tree is the German romantic movement at the turn of the nineteenth century (centered in Munich and the Tübingen school) which reached down to Tillich and Heidegger. See *Romantic Idealism and Roman Catholicism: Schelling and the Theologians* by Thomas F. O'Meara (Notre Dame: University of Notre Dame Press, 1982), especially pp. 188ff.

34. The famous work of this title is Erich Fromm's *The Forgotten Language: An Introduction to the Understanding of Dreams, Fairytales and Myths* (New York: Holt, Rinehart and Winston, 1951).

35. The unabridged version of this Chinese fairy tale, attributed to Lieh Tzu of the Chin dynasty (late third-early fourth century A.D.) is titled "Dreams," and can be found in *Chinese Fairy Tales and Fantasies,* translator and editor, Moss Roberts (New York: Pantheon Books, 1979). Fairy tale lovers will appreciate the tales of the Orient, particularly the Chinese tales which come from, usually, Taoist sources—a contrast to the Confucian philosophy which dominated the state and external life. Roberts writes: "According to the Taoists, the artifices of civilization only lead people away from the original and benign state of nature . . . (which is in contrast to) the fundamental premise of the Confucian order: the social hierarchy founded on hereditary right" (Introduction, p. xviii).

36. Unidentified analyst quoted in doctoral dissertation of Richard Guy Dunn for International College, Los Angeles, April 1985, titled "Animal Imagery in Dreams," p. 247.

37. See note 28, second day's afternoon.

38. *Christian Life Patterns: The Psychological Challenges and Reli-*

gious Invitations of Adult Life, by Evelyn Eaton Whitehead and James D. Whitehead (Garden City, N.Y.: Doubleday and Co., Inc., 1982).

39. See "Inner Passages," by Betsy Caprio, in the *St. Anthony Messenger* for February 1978; the chart included in this article is based on Maslow's hierarchy of needs, including his final need of self-transcendence, and parallels Kohlberg's stages of moral development as well.

40. *Passages: Predictable Crises of Adult Life,* by Gail Sheehy (New York: E.P. Dutton and Co., 1976); Sheehy retains Erik Erikson's word "crises," by which he means turning points or watersheds, not necessarily with the negative connotation "crisis" usually suggests. See also her follow-up book, *Pathfinders* (New York: Wm. Morrow and Co., 1981), which continued the focus on adult growth begun in *Passages,* and which was also aimed at the general reader.

41. See *Philosophy of Moral Development,* Lawrence Kohlberg (New York: Harper and Row, 1981).

42. See *In a Different Voice: Psychological Theory and Women's Development* by Carol Gilligan (Cambridge, Mass.: Harvard University Press, 1982).

43. See Erich Neumann's "The Psychological Stages of Feminine Development," translated by Rebecca Jacobson in *Spring,* 1959 (New York: Analytical Psychology Club of New York, Inc.).

44. See note 2 for the Introduction, above.

45. *Journey Toward Wholeness* by Helen Thompson (Ramsey, N.J.: Paulist Press, 1982); see especially pp. 46ff.

46. See *Experiencing God* by Donald Gelpi (New York: Paulist Press, 1978), especially pp. 36 and 327; also "The Androgyne" by Barbara C. Gelpi in *Women and Analysis,* Jean Strouse, ed. (New York: Dell Publishing Co., Inc., 1974).

The masculine/feminine questions are only being raised here; we see them argued on all sides in analytical psychology at this writing, thrown out by those who reject Jung's early twentieth century Hegelian style of thesis-antithesis-synthesis, revised by others (e.g., James Hillman's archetypal psychology). Your authors stress again the importance of thinking of these terms as universal types of energy, *not* as typical of "men" or "women." A work that will be helpful in clarifying some of the argued facets of Jung's thought is *A Critical Dictionary of Jungian Analysis,* by Andrew Samuels, Bani Shorter and Fred Plaut (London: Routledge & Kegan Paul, 1986).

47. The 1980's have seen an outpouring of research and books on the ancient goddesses, too numerous to list here. Outstanding among the many are two by Merlin Stone, her *When God Was a Woman* (San Diego and New York: Harcourt Brace Jovanovich, 1976) and *Ancient Mirrors of Womanhood: A Treasury of Goddess and Heroine Lore from Around the World* (Boston: Beacon Press, 1984), Marija Gimbutas' *The Goddesses and Gods of Old Europe: 6500–3500 B.C.* (Berkeley and Los Angeles: University of California Press, 1982 ed.), Pamela Berger's *The Goddess Obscured: Transformation of*

the Grain Protectress from Goddess to Saint (Boston: Beacon Press, 1985), and a more personal art book, *The Mother's Songs: Images of God the Mother* by Meinrad Craighead (Mahwah, N.J.: Paulist Press, 1986).

These books and other historical, archaeologically-based works are a complementary body of work to that of the religious feminists (e.g., Ruether, Schüssler-Fiorenza, Daly, *et al.*), and provide both men and women with a feel for the former prominence of the divine feminine, its submergence—and, possibly, its re-emergence.

48. *The Cult of the Black Virgin* by Ean Begg (London: Routledge & Kegan Paul, 1985).

49. See note 11, second day's afternoon, above.

The Third Day—Afternoon:

1. Information on Rational-Emotive Therapy and Ellis' books can be obtained from the Institute for Rational-Emotive Therapy, 45 East 65 St., New York, N.Y. 10021.

2. Capra's ground-breaking book of 1975 overlaying physics with consciousness research is *The Tao of Physics* (Berkeley: Shambhala). Since then he has authored *The Turning Point: Science, Society and the Rising Culture* (Austin, Texas: S&S, 1982). See also *The Dancing Wu-Li Masters: An Overview of the New Physics* by Gary Zukav (New York: William Morrow, 1979).

3. See the lengthy treatment of Freud's skewing by his American interpreters presented by Bruno Bettelheim in *Freud and Man's Soul* (New York: Alfred A. Knopf, 1983).

4. Berne's work, if we can get beyond his language, is really a reaction against the exclusiveness of the psychoanalytic community of mid-twentieth century America. A very good introduction to it is the anthology of selections from his major writings, edited by Claude Steiner and Carmen Kerr, *Beyond Games and Scripts* (New York: Ballantine Books, 1976).

5. *Dreams and the Growth of Personality: Expanding Awareness in Psychotherapy* by Ernest L. Rossi (New York: Brunner/Mazel, 1985, 2nd edition).

6. Still the most comprehensive book on the sleeping state (for the layperson) is Shirley Motter Linde's and Louis M. Savary's *The Sleep Book* (New York: Harper and Row, 1974). Earlier, but still valuable, is Gay Gaer Luce's and Julius Segal's *Sleep* (New York: Coward-McCann, Inc., 1966). More recently, we have writing like that of Christopher Evans of Great Britain on the brain-as-computer (see his *Landscapes of the Night: How and Why We Dream*. New York: Viking Press, 1984). Dreams in this mechanistic view are programs that come on-line by accident during the reprogramming of the brain-computer that goes on during our sleep.

7. See *Helplessness: On Depression, Development and Death* (San Francisco: Freeman, 1975). At this writing, controversy rages in the psy-

chological community whether there should be a disorder titled "the self-defeating personality," which would describe someone with "learned helplessness." Some writers/psychologists have redefined the word "masochistic" to describe such a person; our allegiance in this matter is with the feminist therapists who would see any such designation—especially with the latter, perjorative label—as detrimental, especially for abused women and children. The 1987 revision of the *DSM–III (Diagnostic and Statistical Manual of Mental Disorders)* includes such a disorder.

8. See note #3 of Introduction, above.

9. "Conversations with Marie-Louise von Franz at 70," Ernest L. Rossi, interviewer, in *Psychological Perspectives,* Vol. 17, No. 2 (Los Angeles: C.G. Jung Institute of Los Angeles, Fall, 1986).

10. See note #20, above.

11. Edward F. Edinger, speaking at the Harvest Conference sponsored by the Centerpoint Foundation, Nashua, New Hampshire on "The Sacred Psyche," Fall, 1985. Also in *The Bible and the Psyche,* p. 11.

12. In *The Creation of Consciousness,* p. 62, Dr. Edinger implies that one can remain a conscious participant within a religious collective while proceeding with the individual unfolding, a point of view also suggested by Whitehead's "philosophy of organism." The philosopher says, for example, that religion must "face change in the same spirit as does science. Its principles may be eternal, but the expression of those principles requires continual development" (*Science and the Modern World.* New York: The Macmillan Co., 1925, p. 188). His implication is that the institutional religions are capable of change, and that their credibility can be re-established if they are open to this. The history of world religions certainly gives witness to that capacity for change—the problem has always been that it happens *so slowly* that generations can fall away from them as they are waking up to the need for continuing development.

Your authors, obviously, believe that this sort of development is not only possible, but essential, if the organized religions are to survive. The ancient faiths may find that it is their American constituents who will play a major part in that development, for "at the heart of the American culture is a permanent hope for transformation. . . . [It is] the key to an American spirituality" (Anthony Padovano, speaking to the 26th annual convention of the Catholic Theological Society of America, June 1971).

13. See *The Dream Game,* note #4 for the Introduction, above (pp. 334ff); also an older, but seminal work, *Lucid Dreams* by Celia Green (Oxford: Institute of Psychophysical Research, 1968), and some skepticism about this state in James A. Hall's *Jungian Dream Interpretation: A Handbook of Theory and Practice* (Toronto: Inner City Books, 1983), p. 91. See also *Dream Work,* by Jeremy Taylor (Ramsey, N.J.: Paulist Press, 1983), chap. 16.

14. Faraday, *op. cit.,* p. 71.

15. Dream groups have plusses and minuses—Taylor (see note 13, above) gives twenty-one basics for such a group in chapter 8 of his book. The

one-to-one tradition is so much a part of Jungian style that a dream group may seem a contradiction in terms; however your authors have found that, with good structure and leadership, a dream group can be helpful for two sorts of dreamers: *the beginner,* who can learn the skills of working with dreams more quickly when exposed to several others' approaches and commitment, and *the more experienced dreamer* who has no one with whom to work individually.

Some of the guidelines we use are:

- all material is kept in confidence by group members;
- a dream should be shared with the group only after the dreamer has done some initial work on it, and after the dream is no longer fresh and new;
- the role of the group members is not to add their personal associations to the dream images, but to help with amplification (the universal associations), and to express their feelings about the dream rather than to try to analyze it;
- the goal of such a group is, primarily, dream appreciation rather than interpretation; it is an adjunct to the individual work the dream calls each of us to do.

16. An important aside: any visual or written work about the dream needs to be treated with the same reverence and confidentiality as the dream itself.

17. Exodus 14.

18. Cards with images of typical symbols and scenes can be made, as the text suggests. Another very useful set of 96 pictures can be purchased, and the visual side only used. These are titled the *Star + Gate Symbolic System* (from Cloud Enterprises, Box 1006, Orinda, CA 94563, and also for sale in many bookstores). The cards come with a spread sheet on which to lay them out and complex directions; we use them just for the pictures, as described in the text. Another source of very unusual picture cards is a now out-of-print book with serrated cards built into it, *Seed* by Ram Dass (New York: Crown Publishers, 1973), which may still be found in used book stores. The cards need editing, depending upon what sort of persons one works with.

19. From statements by Frau Kalff in her teaching seminars in Zollikon, Switzerland and the United States. See also her book *Sandplay,* esp. chapter 8 (see note 29, second day morning, above).

20. See Jung on symbols in dreams, for example, par. 339ff of "The Practical Use of Dream-Analysis" in Vol. 16 of the *Collected Works* (Princeton: Princeton University Press, 1954; originally, 1934); this essay is also included in the small volume on *Dreams* (see note 5 for the Introduction, above). "It is far wiser," Jung writes, " . . . not to regard dream symbols . . . as signs or symptoms of a fixed character. . . . "

One of the most exciting exposures to the dream in recent years has been the twenty half-hour films made by Windrose Films of Toronto with Fraser Boa interviewing Marie-Louise von Franz, titled "The Way of the Dream." In these films, Dr. von Franz comments on dreams told by dreamers, as well as historical, scriptural dreams; she refused to offer any interpretation of personal symbols, confining herself to amplification, since these were not her clients and she had only a small amount of personal history for each dreamer.

21. The leaflets referred to are from Dove Publications, Pecos, NM 87552; at this writing, two specific titles (#95 and #96) deal with dreams in spiritual direction. Ask for their complete list, which is being added to regularly. See also Kelsey's book on spiritual direction (see note 7, third day morning, above), esp. pp. 139ff.

Background reading on Jung and Christianity, in addition to other books mentioned throughout the notes, will be found in Kelsey's *Christianity as Psychology* (Minneapolis: Augsburg Publishing House, 1986); John Dourley's work, especially *The Illness That We Are: A Jungian Critique of Christianity* (Toronto: Inner City Books, 1984); and Murray Stein's *Jung's Treatment of Christianity: The Psychotherapy of a Religious Tradition* (Wilmette, IL: Chiron Publications, 1985), as well as earlier works that are now standard, like that of Victor White and the Ulanovs. And, more specifically on dreams, with the same sort of spiritual context, are *Symbols of Transformation in Dreams* by Jean and Wallace B. Clift (New York: Crossroad, 1986) and Robert Johnson's *Inner Work* (San Francisco: Harper and Row, 1986), a book that summarizes this special teacher's approach to the inner life. A broader perspective, with much that is useful, is taken by the quarterly *Newsletter* of the Association for the Study of Dreams (Box 3121, Falls Church, VA 22043).

22. See Martin Buber's essay "On Education" in *Between Man and Man* (Boston: Beacon Press, 1955), pp. 85ff.

23. 2 Corinthians 12:9.

24. See note 4 for Introduction, above.

25. Genesis 28:11–22.

Appendix: Questions Often Asked About Dreams

Dream Recall:

Q: Does everyone dream every night?

A: Yes—we all dream several times every night (as the Rapid Eye Movement or R.E.M. studies show).

Q: Why don't I remember my dreams?

A: Primarily, because you have not been aware of their importance. We live in a society that hasn't valued the dream for many centuries, so we haven't learned to recall our dreams.

Q: Are there things I can do to help me remember my dreams?

A: Certainly! Here are some recommendations:

- Keep a pad and pencil or pen by your bed at night, so that you can record any dreams on awakening.
- Make recalling dreams a prayer intention as you fall asleep.
- Avoid alcoholic beverages or sedatives in the evening.
- Read about dreams and dreaming: this stimulates the unconscious to the recall of dreams, as if you were saying to it, "I really care about this subject."
- On waking, try not to move around. Lying in the same position in which you awakened, allow any dream that might be present to "replay," like a movie or TV show you might be recalling.
- See if you can program yourself to awaken without an alarm.
- There is some evidence that B-vitamins help with dream recall; this might be an avenue to explore.

Q: Should I record dream fragments?

A: Yes, definitely. We recommend that the bedside dream log be waiting with the next morning's date and the next dream number, as if to say, "Here I am, expecting something to be entered into me." Then, whatever you recall on waking can go at this date and number—even if it's only one image, or even if it's just a color, or a feeling, or a sound. After it, you'd write the next number, and the next day's date.

       Now, even though you won't work with all these dream fragments, nor do they necessarily fit clearly into the broader picture of your ongoing dream life, still this procedure shows that you've honored what has been sent to you via the dream. That approach or attitude, in turn, stimulates further dream recall.

Q: I find I can be compulsive about recalling my dreams, and very upset if I miss one or feel that something got away during the night. Is this normal?

A: We would say it's not unusual for beginning dreamers to feel this way, once they've gotten an idea of just how valuable the dream is and can be to them. However, it's really helpful to remember that if the soul is supposed to have some guidance on any subject, and if God is in charge of the process, that guidance will come—provided we're in a listening attitude. It may come through another dream, or through some event in waking life; God speaks in many ways. To agonize over the "one that got away" is somewhat like the old scrupulous attitude of "did I say enough prayers or do them all right?"—and, if you think about it, it's an attitude of the ego that thinks it has to make things happen and be in charge of the process.

Q: Does dream recall get easier?

A: Yes, it does. It becomes a habit, a learned skill, just like riding a bike, or remembering to brush your teeth in the morning, or driving a car.

The Source of Dreams:

Q: Where do dreams come from?

A: The answer to this question is as varied as the many schools of psychology and the various world religions. In this book, we have taken the position that the ultimate source of dreams is God—that is, that God is the Creator of our humanness, has designed us to "tend toward wholeness," and sends the dream as one of the many ways we can learn about heading toward that wholeness.

The model of dreaming that sees them as the day-residue left in the brain-as-computer is 180 degrees away from this viewpoint, and there are many shades of answers to this question in between our religious answer and the mechanistic one.

Q: Do daydreams come from the same place as night dreams?

A: Yes, they do. Both come from that part of ourselves of which we are unconscious. Daydreams, of course, are more likely to have our consciousness involved in their creation, but they still give us information in the same way that the night dream gives it to us.

Q: If one is as open to the unconscious as you are suggesting, is there not the danger that the forces of evil will also become the author of dreams?

A: This is really a question about one's fundamental option: this is one's basic choice and orientation in life and whether it is for relationship with God or against such relationship. If one's life—of which the dream is just one part—is basically oriented toward God, the strength of that position, we believe, is far stronger than other powers.

Q: Where do nightmares come from?

A: The nightmare is a very powerful dream, pointing toward something that won't or can't be ignored. The nightmarish image assumes its potent form so that we'll be sure to notice it and attend to it. The source is the same as any other dream, and one of the things faithful dream-workers find is that when they work with their dreams on a regular basis, the nightmares diminish in number. For example, if you attend to the tiger cub in a dream, it may not have to keep growing and getting more fierce to get your notice; it may not have to turn into a raging animal of the jungle.

Selecting the Dreams To Explore:

Q: Can we possibly understand all our dreams?

A: No, not unless we give up all the rest of our life and do nothing but focus on our dreams.

Q: Then how do we know which ones to spend time on?

A: The rule of thumb is this: spend time with the dreams that have the most powerful affect or feeling for you. You might, for instance, have a dream that has very unusual content, but little feeling; it would be even more important to spend time on a dream with a strong feeling tone to it (pleasant or not), even if this latter dream has only garden-variety subject matter. The strong feeling says something important that is not-yet-conscious has been touched.

Q: If I have a recurring dream image, does this make any dream with that image more important—and, therefore, one on which I might well spend time?

A: Yes, that's right. If, for example, houses have been a repetitive symbol for you in your dreams, then each subsequent house dream has added importance *for you.*

Dream Images:

Q: Can I go to a dream book to find the meaning of a particular dream image?

A: Please avoid books that say certain images always mean certain things. There are excellent reference books on symbols (like Cirlot's *A Dictionary of Symbols* and Cooper's *An Illustrated Encyclopedia of Traditional Symbols*) that will give you many associations and amplifications for various images. These authors have researched the lore of symbols in many cultures, and sometimes reading about a dream image in one of these books or one of the fine folklore dictionaries will give you a "hit" on what that image means to you. Any dream image must always be looked at within the context of the dreamer's life and his or her associations for it.

Q: Are animal dreams common?

A: Yes, they are. Animals are usually thought to be about those parts of ourselves which are instinctual, and yet, since the animals are non-human, we can also view them as possibly being about the *other* non-human reality—that is, the spiritual world.

Q: What about dreams of dying?

A: Very often dreams about dying point to some part of us that is dying, or needs to die. Or they might indicate that a phase of our life is dying or needs to die. Within our religious context, we would see death as leading to rebirth, so a dream about death is hopeful—it points to the potentiality for some new life to emerge.

Q: How about dreams of people who have died?

A: There are two major ways you might look at such a dream. The first, and more common, would be to ask if the person stands for some part of yourself, if you act in some way like the person in the dream—and whether or not that way within you either has died, or needs to die.

The second way you might look at such a dream would be to ask yourself if the earthly relationship you had with the person in the dream is still unfinished. If, for example, the person died before you had a chance to say goodbye, or to say how much you loved him or her, the dream may be a reminder that you can still do that. People report dreams of loved ones who have died and let them know, in the dream, that they are happy and at peace; these are not uncommon—and are most comforting.

Dreams and Spirituality:

Q: How can I integrate my dreams into my spiritual life?

A: A good question—it shows you want your inner life to be of a whole, rather than having the dreams be over here and your prayer life over there—and this, of course, is the ideal. Here are a few suggestions:

- Use the dream images that are important to you to "seed" your prayer time. For example, if you dreamt about a river, that might lead you to prayer about flowing in harmony with God's will; it could also lead to scriptural passages about rivers and water; it might send you to some local spot near a river that could become a prayer spot for you, and so on.

- Make the acts of asking for dreams, recording them and spending time on them forms of prayer. These can be offered as such, just as recalling a dream during the day can be a natural way of turning toward the One who sent it.

- Anyone who has had what's known as a Big Dream—one of the special ones—and who sees his or her dreams as a gift from God will naturally be led to prayer of thanksgiving when such a dream comes.

- Carrying dream learnings into daily life helps ground their content, and makes the dream a contributor to the quality of everyday living. In this way, we have an ongoing dialogue between our waking and sleeping hours; this incarnates the dream.

Old Dreams:

Q: I remember some special dreams from my childhood. Is it ever helpful to go over them again—or to spend time on old dreams I never understood?

A: Writing down childhood dreams (as an adult) is a way to honor them, and to celebrate the fact that the dream life has been part of your life for many years, even if it wasn't appreciated until now.

The general rule of thumb about old dreams is that if they still have strong feeling attached to them, they can shed light on our present situation. The strong feeling indicates that they tap into some still-unconscious cluster of energy in the psyche that is "tender." So, by all means, take a look at any old dreams that are still capturing your attention.

Q: I've had some incredibly special dreams in the past. At the time, I worked with them, and now they're sitting in old journals—"unloved." I feel as if I've abandoned them, and they were too precious for me to do that. Is there anything I can do about this now?

A: Yes, there is. Some people keep a "life dream log" containing their most special dreams. They illustrate it as best they are able, record the Big Dreams in it, often using colored inks or pencils. Some people even take up calligraphy so they can write down the dreams as beautifully as possible, a la illuminated manuscripts. Such a log becomes a life-record of God's goodness to them—and, think of it, a treasured gift to pass on to succeeding generations.

Children and Dreams:

Q: What can I do to help my children pay attention to their dreams?

A: Children seem to enjoy sharing their dreams, and usually it's the adults in their lives that hush them up, saying things like "it's only a dream." You can ask your children if they dream, affirm them when they report that they do, provide drawing materials so they can illustrate their dreams, and save the pictures they draw so they can see that you treasure the dream. Also, you can tell them how important dreams are in your own life, and let them see you recording and illustrating your dreams.

Q: Should I try to interpret my children's dreams?

A: No—the goal might better be to *appreciate* their dreams with them now, and lead them to that sort of appreciation, so that when they are ready they'll do their own interpreting of their dreams. In addition to making dreaming an intellectual activity (and thereby reducing it to "schoolwork"), interpreting your children's dreams could very well lead them to think they can't do this for themselves, thereby giving up their own power to you (and, later, perhaps to others) inappropriately.

Sharing Our Dreams:

Q: Is it helpful to share dreams with others?

A: Yes, with some guidelines. Usually it is very helpful to share one's important dreams with a trusted companion on the inner journey—this might be one's spouse, or spiritual director or guide, or a prayer partner, or a therapist or analyst. Children will find themselves naturally wanting to share their dreams with their parents, if the parents encourage them to do so. Any relationship in which a dream is shared, however, should be one of confidentiality.

Q: What's wrong with sharing the dreams more widely?

A: Our viewpoint is that the dream is sacred, just as all the contents of a person's soul are sacred. "Splashing" one's dream life all around is not the way one treats sacred material. Jung spoke of the psyche as being like the vessel used in alchemy, in which it was important for the top to be tightly stoppered so that the ingredients within wouldn't evaporate during the "cooking" process. In just the same way, the contents of the psyche need to be contained by the person and perhaps another trusted companion, not diffused far and near. Our psyches can "evaporate" too; the boundaries we mention here are very important.

Q: How about dream groups? Are these a good place to share dreams?

A: Yes—*if* the members of the group share a common understanding about the sacredness of the dream and its value to the soul of each. When such a group gathers together, in an attitude of reverence for the dream and each other, a shared dream can be enlightening to all—and the dreamer can get helpful insight into the dream. We suggest that no one offer interpretations, but ask questions, suggest directions for further research and amplification, explore the dream feelings, view each other's art work, and just appreciate the dreams presented.

A dream group is a place where one can witness to the goodness of God about the gift of the dream. Dream groups can also share information, good books, pictures of great dreamers, movies that are dream-like (e.g., *The Wizard of Oz,* any Fellini film), speakers, and so forth.

Dream Control or Programming:

Q: I've seen books and magazine articles on learning how to program my dreams. Is that a good idea?

A: Our feeling is that this is a form of ego-control which defeats the purpose of dreaming. After all, we spend most of our waking hours trying to program things the way we think they should be (the ego in charge); if we believe that, at bottom, God is the author of our dreams, why would we want to interfere with this very precious communication that we receive during the nighttime?

Q: How does dream incubation or invocation differ from dream control?

A: The former (as described in this book) is an attempt to ask for guidance through the dream, usually by a question. Dream control is usually associated with efforts to force out the dream we want to have, or to get the answer we desire. The latter seems, to us, more like dream manipulation—there's really a world of difference between the two. We should point out that dream incubation is a practice found throughout the religions of the world since ancient times, one considered to be harmonious with a sacred attitude. Dream control or programming has no such roots.

Next Steps:

Q: What's the best thing to do after I get started on attending to my dreams?

A: Keep on with it! You've embarked on a fascinating, life-changing adventure, and if you are faithful to this most special practice, your life will never be the same again. We wish you many Sweet Dreams—and a peaceful soul when the Bittersweet ones appear.

Other work by the authors

Co-authors of
Coming Home: A Handbook for Exploring the Sanctuary Within
Coming Home: A Manual for Spiritual Direction (companion volume)
Animals Within Us (in preparation)

Thomas M. Hedberg:
"Cats and Catholicism" in *Catholicism and Jungian Psychology* (Marvin Spiegelman, ed.)

Betsy Caprio:
Experiments in Prayer
Experiments in Growth
Star Trek: Good News in Modern Images
The Woman Sealed in the Tower
First Steps (in preparation)